THE *THINKING CLEARLY*
Series editor:

The *Thinking Clearly* series sets out the main issues in a variety of important subjects. Written from a mainstream Christian standpoint, the series combines clear biblical teaching with up-to-date scholarship. Each of the contributors is an authority in his or her field. The series is written in straightforward everyday language, and each volume includes a range of practical applications and guidance for further reading.

The series has two main aims:
1. To help Christians understand their faith better.
2. To show how Christian truths can illuminate matters of crucial importance in our society.

Also in the *Thinking Clearly* series:

THE *THINKING CLEARLY* SERIES

Series editor: Clive Calver

The Bible

DEREK TIDBALL

MONARCH
BOOKS

Mill Hill, London & Grand Rapids, Michigan

First published by Monarch Books in the UK 2003,
Concorde House, Grenville Place,
Mill Hill, London, NW7 3SA.

Published in the USA by Monarch Books 2003.

Distributed by:
UK: STL, PO Box 300, Kingstown Broadway, Carlisle,
Cumbria CA3 0QS;
USA: Kregel Publications, PO Box 2607
Grand Rapids, Michigan 49501.

ISBN 1 85424 608 9 (UK)
ISBN 0 8254 6219 3 (USA)

British Library Cataloguing Data
A catalogue record for this book is available
from the British Library.

Book design and production for the publishers by
Bookprint Creative Services
P.O. Box 827, BN21 3YJ, England.
Printed in Great Britain.

Contents

Acknowledgements

The writing of any book is a team exercise. The team behind this book goes back a long way to parents and Sunday School teachers who initially taught me the Bible and gave me a taste for it as God's special word to us. I am thankful for godly teachers who taught me in a more formal way at school and for lecturers who deepened my thirst for it. Thanks are due to congregations I have pastored and to which I have preached, who have taught me much about what matters and how to teach the Bible for myself. A request from Spring Harvest to teach an overview of the Bible in four sessions was a special delight and challenge. I also owe my thanks to Tony Collins of Monarch Books who has waited patiently for this one and been an unfailing encouragement.

I would like to thank two former students and good friends in particular for their help with this book. I am grateful to Simon Johnston for reading the first part of the manuscript and commenting on it at a time when he was writing his own first book. And I am very grateful indeed to James Bemrose who worked through the whole manuscript, checked all the references and saved me from many mistakes. Those that remain are, of course, my responsibilities, not his. Having just completed 30 years in Christian ministry, I pray that both Simon and James may still be teaching the Bible in 30 years' time with the same passion and enthusiasm which is mine but with greater clarity and persuasiveness in the power of the Holy Spirit.

Derek Tidball,
London Bible College,
March 2003

Introduction

I was deeply shocked. I was attending a conference of pastors, biblical scholars and practical theologians. The subject was the Bible. It had been disappointing enough to learn from one research project that virtually no one ever preached on the Old Testament; this meant that more than half the Bible which the church claimed to be its sacred Scripture was ignored. But worse was to come. Several participants dogmatically announced that they could not use the Bible at all in their ministries. It was a book, they claimed, that justified, even advocated, violence against women, child abuse, cruelty to animals, repressive attitudes towards law and order, holy war, patriarchy and male chauvinism. To them the Bible was an obstacle to making Christ's love known and should be ditched along with the sacrifices of Israel.

This was not the Bible I knew. The Sunday School I attended began each week with the singing of the simple chorus:

> Jesus loves me! this I know,
> for the Bible tells me so . . .

I was taught that "the best book to read is the Bible". And I had no reason to doubt it. There were the wonderful stories of heroism – stories of Moses, Gideon and David. There was the majestic poetry of the Psalms. There were the pithy sayings of Proverbs which oozed wisdom about life. There were the

9

thundering denunciations of the prophets against injustice.

Above all, there were "the stories of Jesus" which I loved to hear – stories of his healings, miracles, encounters with people, of his teaching and of his death and resurrection. True, there were the more puzzling bits of Paul and the other letters, like Hebrews, which seemed obscure. But I suppose I assumed even they would make sense at some stage. Revelation, of course, was read as if it were tomorrow's newspaper and spoke of all the issues our post-war world was confronting. It was exhilarating, assuring and totally scary, all at the same time.

Never did I doubt, nor have I since had cause to doubt, the claim of the verse which was often quoted and applied to the Bible from Psalm 119:105: "Your word is a lamp to my feet and a light for my path."

Of course, my understanding of the Bible has developed greatly since then. In school I was introduced to studying it in a more formal way and encouraged to read it less devotionally. At university I encountered those who attacked it both from an historical and a philosophical (usually Marxist) viewpoint. At Bible college I entered into the world of biblical scholarship and discovered the views of many who sought to undermine its sacredness and authority. But I also found my reading of it enriched beyond measure by wise and discerning teachers who had a living faith in the Christ who was central to its message and who were more than a match academically for the sceptics.

Since then, in ministry and in the world of the university, I have constantly been aware of the developments which have undermined the relevance, value and trustworthiness of the Bible in the eyes of many – developments which have led to the sort of reactions with which this introduction began. The very idea that such a book can be "true" today, and "true" for everyone, is called into question.

The critical voices are not to be dismissed lightly. Many of them are challenging, even disturbing. A naive literalism provides no adequate defence.

But there are answers. The antagonists can be sensibly

silenced. My excitement about, and commitment to, the Bible remains undiminished. I believe it to be the fully trustworthy, written revelation of God to his creation. I know its message still has life-giving and transforming power. We ignore it, as is all too obvious in our Western world, at our peril. We study it and live by it to our profit.

It is common to speak of the Bible in crisis. But the Bible is not in crisis. By and large, churches that build their common life around it are vibrant and thriving. It is those which marginalise it that are dying. Christians who read and study it often have a secure faith. Those who do not are often the ones who are struggling and insecure in their relationship with God. The crisis occurs where the Bible is not read, or where, if it is, it is not read both with informed minds and with submissive hearts. The blend is essential.

This book is a very basic introduction. We start by focusing on where the Bible came from, that is, how it came to be written and reach the form in which we have it today. Then we look at what it says. This is by far the most important part of the book, for it is what is in the Bible that is of paramount value for our Christian lives. We may know a lot about the Bible, just as we might know a lot about a person, but that is no substitute for knowing the Bible or the person directly. Then the camera, as it were, draws back a bit and we introduce questions of the Bible's inspiration and authority – words which Christians have traditionally used to explain it. Finally, we try to be practical. Here we look at the major issue of how to read the Bible sensibly. It is in these chapters that some of the assaults mounted against it will be addressed.

Although it seemed to me to make sense to lay the book out as I have done, it would be possible to begin reading at the start of any of the sections. You do not have to start at the beginning!

The Bible is a book for everyone, not just for preachers or scholars. Pope Gregory the Great said, "The Bible is water where lambs may safely walk and great elephants swim." I hope this book will help some to begin paddling and others to venture out a little further into the waters with confidence. It is not written for the cross-channel swimmers, nor for the Olympic competitors. There are plenty of books to which they can turn for instruction.

Before the journey begins, we need to issue a health warning. Jesus lamented that the lawyers of his day diligently searched the Scriptures "because you think that by them you possess eternal life". They were right in their thinking. Yet he bemoaned, "These are the Scriptures that testify about me, yet you refuse to come to me to have eternal life" (John 5:39–40). Unless the written Word of God leads us to the living word of God, our reading of it is futile.

1

The Origin of the Bible

The Bible which we read comes to us as a finished package. But, before it reached that stage, a long process was involved of its books being written and edited, and then collected together. Two collections are housed in one Bible: the Old Testament gathered together by the Jews and then owned as Christian Scripture, and the New Testament brought together by the early Christians. Each Testament contains a number of smaller collections of works that can be grouped together, like the prophets or the gospels. This long process was all overseen by the Holy Spirit, who guarantees that the books of the Bible which we have, although shaped and selected by human authors, are the very words of God to us.

The Origin of the Bible

When my son started to read the Bible, he insisted on reading from the beginning, from Genesis chapter 1. I tried to dissuade him (foolish man that I am!) and suggested that there might be easier starting places, more exciting entry points. "No," he insisted. That was where he had started with every other book. So why not the Bible?

The answer is that the Bible is a very unusual book. It is a single book made up of a whole library of books, 66 in all, divided into two main groups called the Old and the New Testaments. The story which it tells stretches from before the beginning of time to after the end of time, from before the creation of an ordered and inhabited world to after the re-creation of the heavens and the earth and the introduction of eternity. Most of it, though, relates to the story of human beings. It records God's dealings with people from the earliest days of history through to the first century of the Christian era, with the dividing line falling between the Testaments at the birth of Jesus Christ. That is a long time. It is also a long time ago.

So how did these 66 books get written in an age before the printing press, let alone before the computer? And how did they get collected together to form one coherent story? And how did Christians come to recognise them as the sacred book of their religious tradition and the foundation authority of their faith? Was the process of bringing the Bible to birth as we now know it anything like the process of publishing a book today? Or did it just drop from heaven ready-made, like the golden tablets supposedly discovered by Joseph Smith, the founder of Mormonism?

The God who speaks

The God of the Bible is a God who communicates. The tone is set in the opening chapter. In Genesis 1 the claim, "God said . . ." occurs nine times. He is not usually a silent God but one who longs to enter into a relationship with his creatures. Relationships are formed by communication. There are many different ways we communicate, using gestures, facial expressions, actions, art, music and mime. The ultimate way in which God spoke to us was in a person, through his Son, Jesus (Hebrews 1:2). But the clearest way we humans normally communicate is through words, even though they can prove very difficult at times. So why should it surprise us that God speaks to the people he has made, and loves, through words?

Throughout the Bible, we encounter a God who speaks face to face with his friends, talks with his people through priests and prophets, makes himself known through the sayings of the sages, reveals himself through the poetry of the songwriters and announces his good news through his apostles. His words, unlike ours, always achieve what they set out to do. When he speaks, worlds come into being (Psalm 33:6) and miracles occur (Psalm 107:20). His words are never wasted and never impotent (Isaiah 55:11).

But which words are we talking about? Christians believe that God's words are found recorded in the Bible. It has been a fundamental article of the Christian faith that the Bible is a book given to us by God which makes known his character, his truth, his laws, his salvation and his ways to his creation. It is a communication stamped with his own divine nature and authority. Only in very recent history would anyone claiming to be a Christian have questioned that.

What is more, the Bible is believed not merely to *contain* the words of God but to *be* the word of God. The Bible is different from a box of chocolates. A box of chocolates contains chocolates which you can find and enjoy if you first remove all the layers of packaging. The Bible is more than a book which contains a few truths from God if only you can uncover them and set aside the bits that they are wrapped up in. It is, from beginning to end, God's word: a coherent whole.

This presumes, of course, that we read it intelligently. The Bible contains the words, "There is no God" (Psalm 14:1). But God did not say that. The Psalm makes clear that it was a fool who said that. Other parts of the Bible might seem to imply that God believes in a flat earth and a three-decker universe. But as its Creator, he knows more about our cosmos, and knows it more accurately, than our scientists have yet discovered. The Bible contains quite a bit of "picture" or metaphorical language.

Nonetheless, we can claim that the Bible as a whole *is* the word of God. That is how it self-consciously views itself with its claim, made over 3,000 times, to be recording God's words. Look at some of the individual pieces of evidence which go to make up the total picture:

- Exodus 20:1 declares, "And God spoke all these words . . ."
- the prophets preface their own preaching more than 100 times with the words, "Thus says the Lord . . ."
- Paul speaks of the Old Testament as "the very words of God" (Romans 3:2)
- the gospels report the words of Jesus
- the apostles claim that their words were given to them by the Lord (2 Peter 3:2)
- Peter recognises Paul's writings as Scripture alongside other parts of Scripture (2 Peter 3:16)
- it frequently says, in one place, that a saying was spoken by

God, and, in another place, that the same saying was said by a man, and *vice versa*. Look, for example, at Genesis 12:1–3 and Galatians 3:8; Exodus 9:16 and Romans 9:17; Isaiah 29:13 and Mark 7:6; and Psalm 95:7, 8 and Hebrews 3:7. There seems to be a complete identification between the words of God and the words of Scripture.

These and similar claims are so woven into the fabric of the Bible that people came to understand that they were not limited to the specific words they introduced, but that they applied to the Bible as a whole.

As well as this, it seems obvious that if the Bible is a communication of God, then it will be marked by God's own character. Any book betrays something of the character of its author. In most cases it betrays his or her biases, idiosyncrasies, tortuous use of language or ignorance! But a book which came from God will surely be marked by reliability and truthfulness, for he is a God who cannot lie (Numbers 23:19, Titus 1:2, Hebrews 6:18). It is impossible that God should deceive, mislead or disseminate disinformation. It is not within his nature to do so, any more than it is in the nature of steam to be frozen or rain to be dry. Therefore, we can conclude that his word is truthful (John 17:17) and without a flaw (Psalm 18:30, Proverbs 30:5–6).

As James Packer puts it, summing up a long-held view: "What Scripture says, God says", and what God says is to be the rule of faith and life in his church (*Scripture and Truth*, ed. D. A. Carson and John D. Woodbridge, IVP, 1983, pp. 335 and 326).

The authors who wrote

All this would seem to suggest that the Bible was beamed down from heaven as a finished product, simply to be received and read by men and women. But evidently that is not so, for the Bible is every bit as much a human book as it is a divine one. We will look at how those two views can be held together when we look at its inspiration in chapter 11. For the moment, I am only concerned that we be realistic and acknowledge the human dimensions involved. The human side of the Bible is apparent in a number of ways.

First, each book of the Bible reflects the time and culture in which it is set. So most of the books assume a way of life and arrangements within society with which they are familiar. They are able to critique certain practices, such as dishonesty in business, or racial prejudice in the community, or corruption of power by the state, from a moral and spiritual viewpoint. But there is much about the shape of family life, the role of the father, the political system, the existence of slaves or the procedures for adoption (to give just a few examples) that they just take for granted. While some are able to prophesy the future, none parade anachronisms. We never read of computers, nor of aeroplanes, because they had not been invented before the Bible was finalised and such references would have made no sense until our own time. No writer gives an introduction to nuclear physics. The books reflect the scientific understanding of the world in which they were written. Each book of the Bible is rooted in a particular cultural soil. That does not prevent it from speaking timeless truths. It does, however, make the important point that the Bible is anything but a clinical, systematic theological textbook which has been written in a sanitised spiritual laboratory and a cultural vacuum.

Second, the human side of the Bible is very evident in the variety of styles of writing. Those who contributed to its writing obviously brought their individual talents and personalities to bear. Some were great poets; others wrote as if they were writing a civil service memo, recording issues in laborious detail. Illustrations pour out of some, the metaphors and pictures stumbling over each other and lying like wrecked vehicles in a pile-up on the page. Others simply tell it as it is. Some are visionaries; others keep their feet firmly on the ground. Some write in elegant, cultured Greek, while most writers in the New

Testament use a more common style. Some write with purpose and pace, while others write reflectively, refusing to be hurried and never quite seeming able to reach a conclusion. Some are passionate activists; others diffident philosophers. There is clearly no single divine Author, dictating a manuscript from on high. There is rather a God who created a world of infinite variety, channelling the services of his infinitely varied messengers to his own ends.

Third, the humanity of the Bible is evident in the perspectives which the authors adopt. Take the gospels, as one clear example. The first three accounts of Jesus have much in common. They share the same basic framework of his story, tell several of the same stories, overlap in much of his teaching and give similar accounts of his death and resurrection. It is because they are so similar that they became known as the "synoptic" (that is, sharing the same synopsis) gospels. Yet even they differ from one another. Matthew writes like a rabbi to help Jewish Christians understand all that took place. Mark writes like a popular journalist, giving a breathtaking account of Jesus's life which concentrates on his actions. It seems that the other gospels built on his. Luke writes much more as a historian who has researched Christ's life and set it out in a very orderly fashion. He mentions stories and people which the others omit. While there is no reason to doubt the truthfulness of any of the gospels, the writers are plainly writing to their own agendas. When it comes to John's gospel, we enter a different world. Written some decades later and in a reflective fashion, John gives us an account which is different from any of the others. Once again, the experience of the human authors is apparent.

The Bible, then, is both a divine revelation and a human composition. Both aspects of its nature need to be held in tension. If the problem of an earlier generation was that they played up the divine nature of the Bible and played down its human dimensions, the problem today is the reverse. Both one-sided emphases are equally wrong. The former puts the Bible out of reach for many people and removes it from the real world. It discourages research and any intelligent interpretation of the text. But today, many Christians have become so dazzled by the way in which the Bible was put together, by its similarities to other ancient books and by the multitude of interpretations that can be given to it (whether reasonable or not) that they have forgotten it is a revelation from God. They stand in judgement over it, rather than in humility before it. They determine what it is credible to still believe in the Bible, rather than letting the Bible determine what it is right for them to do in their lives. To approach the Bible with such an attitude is to ensure that you cannot unlock its message. It will not yield even its plain message to the arrogant.

The role of editors

How were the books written? People used to give a very simple reply to this question. The first five books, known as the Pentateuch, were written by Moses. David wrote the Psalms, or most of them. Solomon wrote Proverbs. Isaiah wrote Isaiah – the whole of it. Luke wrote Luke. Paul wrote the letters which carry his name, including the letters to Timothy and Titus. John wrote Revelation.

The reason it seemed so simple was that these appear to be the claims made by the text itself. Exodus 24:4, Numbers 33:2 and Deuteronomy 31:9, 22 all tell us that Moses recorded what we are reading. And while the Psalms themselves often do not indicate who the composer was, the titles of them often do, attributing many of them to David. It is self-evident that Paul wrote the letters that carry his name in the opening verse. Why? Because they say he did. Only Hebrews, which does not give an author, is a problem. It's simple, isn't it?

The issue is not, in fact, quite as straightforward as it looks. Moses records his own death in Deuteronomy 34. Unless he did so in anticipation, someone else must have at least wrapped up his writing assignment for him. There are many different styles of writing in these five books, which may suggest more than one author. Some strands constantly use the name Yahweh, the personal name for God, and others Elohim, the more general name. One strand shows great interest in the covenant, and another strand shows great interest in the work of the priest and the tabernacle. Some biblical scholars say these strands were woven together much later. Even within these books there are hints, such as that in Exodus 38:21, of other people recording things under the instruction of Moses. Other historical works in the Old Testament give indications that they may have been composed over a period of time and written by several generations of historians.

The headings of the Psalms appear to have been added later and may not be such a reliable guide as they seem. Clearly, a careful process of editing and arrangement has gone on to shape the book as we now have it. Jeremiah's words were recorded by his servant Baruch (Jeremiah 36:17–18). He may have dictated it all (Jeremiah 36:32), but it begs the question as to whether Baruch took down accurately every word Jeremiah spoke or whether he put the authentic thoughts of Jeremiah into his own words. We know that earlier there had been a "company of prophets" (2 Kings 6:1) who appear to have gathered around a well-known prophet. Did they record some of their master's words and deeds?

Mark's gospel has two endings, a longer and a shorter one. Did Mark write them both or has someone tried to tidy up an abrupt ending by adding a little more? Was John 7:53 – 8:11, which is not included in the earliest manuscripts, from John's pen or the pen of a later editor? Did Paul dictate his letters, rather than write them himself (see Galatians 6:11, where he seems to have taken over to write the conclusion in his own hand) and, if so, how much latitude did he give his scribes? Does that account for the different ways of expressing himself and the different range of vocabulary some have found in Colossians, Ephesians and the later letters that carry his name? Or did others write some letters even after he had died, and insert his name at the beginning because they were members of his "school" and were carrying on his work? Some argue that it was an acceptable practice to do this in the ancient world and that it would not have been thought deceitful.

Scholars believe that many of the books of the Bible went through a number of stages of composition, like a number of editions, before ending up in the form in which we have them today. They come to these conclusions on the basis of the flow of the book, the variations in vocabulary, style and even subject and mood within it, and, sometimes, on the basis of what the book itself seems to suggest. This has led them to suggest, for example, that Isaiah was written by two or three people, rather than one individual, since it addresses such a sweep of Israel's history. That, of course, is not a problem if you believe in the ability of a prophet to foretell the future, but many people do not – hence the suggestion that there was more than one Isaiah. As another example, some scholars suggest that 2 Corinthians 10 – 13 was originally part of another letter which got stuck onto the earlier chapters, perhaps more by accident than design.

It would seem that the Bible is the product not only of authors but of editors too. Does that matter? The area, at best, is one of informed guesswork. We have some very early manuscripts of Bible books. Some manuscripts known as the Dead Sea Scrolls, which cover most of the Old Testament, go back to 250 BC. An early fragment of John's gospel, kept in the John Rylands Library in Manchester, is dated at 130 AD and we have copies of all the gospels dating back to 200 AD. But we have no "originals" or autographed proofs. So we cannot be sure.

Two things seem to me significant in the debate.

On the one hand, as we shall see, the books in the New Testament were credited with authority and included in the canon of the Bible on the basis of their apostolic authorship. It was the fact that they came from the pen of an apostle (or, at least, the tongue and mind of an apostle) that led to their recognition. If that proves to be untrue, then the authority of these books is called into question. To say that it was customary in the ancient world for disciples of a great leader to write books after his death, using his name, as is often claimed, is not agreed beyond dispute. And it would leave a shadow of suspicion falling over the New Testament. Is it as reliable as it appears? So, yes, the issue is important.

On the other hand, if we believe that God is capable of inspiring individual authors and guaranteeing the trustworthiness of what they wrote, why cannot we equally believe that God is more than capable of watching over the process of editing and transmission? Can that process not equally be inspired? If so, then what we read today remains the trustworthy word of God.

A baby may be conceived in a moment and delivered at a particular point of time. But a baby is not really the product of a moment. Ideally, the baby develops for the nine months between conception and birth and even then might take some time to be delivered. Similarly, the various documents of the Bible may have taken some time to come to birth in the form we possess. That is not a problem, especially since we know the Bible is a living book, quite able to address us in our contemporary world today.

The composition of the Bible

This process may account for how the individual books came into being, but how was the Bible as a whole agreed upon? Who decided what to include and what not to include? When was it decided that the cut-off date was reached and no more entries were to be considered?

These questions concern what is called the canon of Scripture. The word "canon" comes from the Greek word for "measure" or "rule". It is the correct standard by which things are judged. Here we must separate the Old Testament from the New, but the canon of both testaments emerged through a long period of discussion and debate.

Jewish understanding divides the Old Testament into three

great blocks. Ezra was a significant figure in causing "the Law", that is the first five books of Moses, to be given recognition as authoritative documents concerning the constitution of Israel (Nehemiah 8:11).

The next section is composed of "the Prophets", by which the Jews mean not just the major prophets, like Isaiah, Jeremiah and Ezekiel, nor just the twelve minor prophets, but the historical works from Joshua to 2 Kings as well. These history books are included among the Prophets because they are not "neutral" history but history written from a prophetic perspective. These books were called "the early Prophets". When the New Testament speaks of "the Law and the Prophets" (e.g. Matthew 5:17 or Romans 3:21), it is these two sections of the Old Testament combined that it has in mind.

The list of books to be included in the Prophets seems to have been agreed by Jewish authorities by the second century BC. Prophecy was believed to have ceased after the time of Ezra and so, although there were some interesting and spiritually instructive books written subsequently, they were not considered sufficiently "inspired" to be included within the Prophets. They can be found in the Apocrypha, which is usually printed in non-Protestant versions of the Bible. But the writings of the Law and the Prophets seem to have been fixed as we have them today before New Testament times, since that is how they appear in the Dead Sea Scrolls and in the important Greek translation of the Hebrew Scriptures known as the Septuagint. The Dead Sea Scrolls are an early collection of manuscripts found preserved in caves by the Dead Sea between 1947 and 1956. They cover the whole Old Testament except the book of Esther. The Septuagint was translated by Jewish scholars in Alexandria in about 200 BC.

"The Writings" – the remainder of the Old Testament – are the ragbag of documents which are left, including Ruth, Chronicles, Ezra, Nehemiah, Esther, Job, Psalms, Proverbs, Ecclesiastes, Song of Songs, Lamentations and Daniel. Agreement about these books came much later. After the fall of

Jerusalem agreement was reached at a Jewish "council" (though it probably was not a formal event) as to which books were to be included and which were either too recent or risky and so were excluded. By about 90 AD, then, the canon of the Old Testament, as we know it today, was accepted as definitive Scripture.

The order of the canon has changed a little in the Christian Bible, not least in that the minor prophets come last, rather than before the Writings, as in the Jewish canon. The reason is so that Malachi, with its pregnant expectation of the coming Messiah, can prepare the way for Jesus.

The early Christians took over the Old Testament canon ready-made. But how was the canon of the New Testament agreed upon? It was also formed through a gradual process of discussion and discernment. Paul's letters were probably the first to be put together in a recognised collection. We have evidence of them being referred to as such by 140 AD, although the pastoral letters of Timothy and Titus were only included subsequently. Around the same time, we know that Christians were reading in their worship from the gospels, which they called the "memoirs of the apostles". John's gospel, however, appears to have taken a little longer to be accepted. Some other "gospels" failed to gain recognition because they were tainted in one way or another. Shortly after 300 AD, Eusebius, the earliest historian of the post-New Testament church, referred to a collection of seven "catholic (by which he meant general or universal) letters", which included the letters of Peter and John. Acts came to be recognised as a particularly valuable document by about 200 AD. Revelation was accepted earlier in some parts of the church than others but universal recognition was given to it by the fourth century.

The need to define which documents were authoritative and which were not gained impetus because of the heretical teaching of Marcion in the second century. He believed the God of the Old Testament and the God of the New to be very different. He wanted to ditch the Old Testament and anything which smacked of it in the New. He therefore proposed a "canon" which was very restricted but which suited his purposes. Other writings began to circulate which advocated Gnostic teaching and contained secret revelations given by Jesus after his resurrection. These pressures, together with that of persecution, meant it was important for Christians to know what they stood for and what documents were authoritative for their faith.

Although the major outlines of the canon were agreed long before, the discussion went on about some books until about 350 AD. In spite of fairly widespread consensus, Hebrews, James, 2 Peter, 2 and 3 John and Jude were particularly disputed. Other documents, such as *The Didache* and *The Shepherd of Hermas*, hovered on the margins of the canon. Eventually, they were excluded and agreement was reached. It was an agreement which took into consideration a number of factors. Was the document written by an apostle or by someone very closely associated with an apostle (like Mark and Luke)? Was it orthodox in theology? Did it have a widespread appeal or was it just addressed to a small exclusive group within the church? Also, had it stood the test of time? Was it evident that Christian believers found it beneficial in generating faith and encouraging spiritual maturity?

While the recognition of the canon has not silenced all discussion – Martin Luther famously wondered whether James should be included, describing it as "an epistle of straw" – the canon has really settled the issue as to which are the "official" documents for Christians. Later in the book we will argue that, as they are read today, they still carry the authenticity of God and inspiration of the Spirit with them. God spoke through human authors, supervised the development of the documents through the hands of scribes, editors, collectors and copyists, and then oversaw the formation of the canon.

2

The Story of the Bible

The books of the Bible were originally written in Hebrew or Greek. From earliest times they have been translated into other languages so that their message might be available to those who could not read them in the original. Here we trace the story of the Bible's translation into English. William Tyndale's magnificent early efforts in translation met with much opposition from the church and cost him his life. But he left his mark on all that followed, especially on the Authorised Version, one of the most significant translations there has ever been. Since the late 19th century there have been a multitude of others. We survey the main translations, explain the principles behind them and look at their strengths and weaknesses.

The Story of the Bible

The person who wants to read the Bible today is immediately confronted with a problem. Which version should he or she use? There seem to be so many variations. To ask which one is best may be to ask which is the most reliable translation or which is most suitable for the reader. The answer to the one question could be different from the answer to the other.

Different versions excite strong opinions in the church, opinions which are not always very well founded. As a pastor in the 1980s I encountered people who campaigned for me to use the King James Version (KJV) of 1611, virtually on the basis that "It was good enough for St Paul, so it is good enough for me". Such a position is naive. It reveals an ignorance about the way the Bible has been translated down the centuries and the way in which the language we speak is dynamic and constantly developing. Words change their meaning. In the KJV the word "let" means the exact opposite of what it does today. There it meant to "prevent" or "hinder" rather than "permit" or "allow". Uninstructed readers could therefore find themselves in serious trouble if they took the ancient translation at face value.

This chapter briefly tells the story of the Bible as it relates to English translations so that readers can get something of a guide to where the various versions fit in and can begin to understand contemporary translations. As it does so, the picture to bear in mind is that of a tree. The main trunk is formed by the KJV, since no other translation has exercised such an influence. But the trunk feeds on a variety of roots and shoots out into numerous branches. Today's Bible tree is flourishing.

Translations before the Reformation

The earliest Old Testament manuscripts were written in Hebrew. But by the third century BC, many Jews lived in Greek-speaking cities and were struggling to understand their native tongue. So 72 elders in Antioch, representing the twelve tribes of Israel, obtained an accurate Hebrew manuscript from Jerusalem and translated it into Greek. The Septuagint, as this translation became known – the title (which is Greek for "seventy") comes from rounding the 72 down – exercised significant influence on subsequent translations. Sometime earlier, the Jews living in Palestine also translated most of the Hebrew manuscripts into Aramaic, the local language. They adopted a fairly free approach and often went beyond the strict act of translating and strayed into paraphrasing and questions of interpretation as well. Their works, known as the Targums, find their origins in the work of Ezra who, according to Nehemiah 8:8, led the Levites in not only reading from "the Book of the Law of God" but also in "making it clear and giving the meaning so that the people could understand what was being read". The Targums were the Old Testament versions in use at the time of Jesus.

The earliest New Testament manuscripts were written in Greek but they were quickly translated into a number of other languages so that those who could not understand Greek could read the message. Among the earliest versions were translations into Latin, Syriac and Coptic, an Egyptian language. By the tenth century the New Testament, or parts of it, had been translated into Gothic, Ethiopic, Armenian, Georgian, Arabic and Slavonic as well.

One Latin translation, however, stands head and shoulders above others because of its subsequent influence. Jerome (c.331–420), a learned scholar, translated the whole of the Bible, going back to the original Hebrew for the Old Testament books, rather than using the Septuagint. Called the Vulgate, his version became the standard work for the church and shaped the doctrine of the Latin (Catholic) church for centuries. Unfortunately, Jerome had introduced a number of inaccuracies into his translation (though he may have been working on the best evidence available at the time) and some of these became sources of conflict at the time of the Reformation.

English was not completely bereft of its own translations, but almost so. Various free translations of the Psalms and the gospels were undertaken, such as the Lindisfarne Gospels in around 950. But not until the end of the fourteenth century was the entire Bible translated into English, a task traditionally associated with John Wycliffe (1329–1384). Wycliffe, known as "the morning star of the Reformation", was passionate about the reform of the church and to that end initiated a translation of the Vulgate Bible. He attacked various practices and doctrines of the Roman Church. Wycliffe died of a stroke, otherwise he would undoubtedly have been persecuted as a heretic. His followers, who were called Lollards, were certainly persecuted. In 1407 the Archbishop of Canterbury issued a decree forbidding the private translation of the Scriptures into English and specifically forbidding anyone to use Wycliffe's translation. In 1428 the authorities who opposed the Reformation exhumed Wycliffe's body, burned it and threw the ashes into the river Swift: a just punishment, so they thought, for a heretic.

The Reformation and its heirs

Separate from the Reformation, but greatly helping its cause, was the work of the Dutch Christian humanist, Erasmus (1469–1536). He broke with the philosophical tradition of the

Middle Ages and provided the world with a new edition of the Greek New Testament and a revised Latin version to challenge the supremacy of the Vulgate. His more objective translations, his insistence on a more straightforward interpretation of the text and his work on Paul went hand in hand with the reforming work of Martin Luther (1483–1546), but Erasmus did not go all the way with Luther. He differed on the doctrine of justification, that is, of how people can be put in a right relationship with God, and he had no desire to split the church. It is often said that "he laid the egg which Luther hatched".

The Reformation, which took place in the 16th century and led to the division of the church between Catholics and Protestants, is a complex phenomenon. There were wide cultural and political currents at work which directed the reforming stream on the course it took. In England the desire of Henry VIII to secure his succession by fathering a son was the major precipitating factor which caused the split with Rome. But, whatever the wider causes, the role played by the Bible was also momentous.

In the story of the English Bible one name stands above all others. William Tyndale (1494–1536), a graduate of both Oxford and Cambridge, believed that people's ignorance of the faith and acceptance of misguided practices in the church would be overcome only if the Bible was translated plainly into their mother tongue. Early in his career, when arguing with a senior official of the church, Tyndale uttered the memorable words, "If God spares my life, ere many years I will take care that a ploughboy shall know more of the Scriptures than you do." So he discovered his life's great project.

Encountering strong discouragement from church authorities in England, he fled to the continent, and there, in 1525, began to translate the New Testament. Before long, England was closed to him. He was a fugitive for much of his life, translating the Bible on the run. That makes the extent and the quality of his output all the more astonishing. After the New Testament was published and revised, he set to work on the Pentateuch and other parts of the Old Testament. He wrote other books, engaged in theological controversies and translated a number of Lutheran works as well. Those who bought and sold his New Testament in England were soon persecuted and pursued with venom by Sir Thomas More, the Lord Chancellor and unrepentant Catholic. At one point, Tyndale himself offered to return to England, give up writing and face whatever consequences there might be, if only his Bible might be published; such was his passion.

Tyndale was protected by the English merchants of Antwerp, and so for many years he evaded the grip of those who would have captured him. But eventually he fell into a trap, probably set by Sir Thomas More, who ironically had himself fallen foul of the king's marriage plans, been judged a traitor for refusing to back Henry and was himself to be executed. The trap having been sprung, Tyndale was soon found guilty of heresy and sentenced to death. So, in October 1536, at Vilvorde, just north of Brussels, he was publicly strangled and his body burned. As he died he prayed that the Lord would open the eyes of the king of England.

Tyndale may have paid the ultimate price for translating the Bible and many in England may well have wanted his work suppressed, but the seed had been sown and had been scattered over England. Changing political fortunes soon nurtured its tender shoots in a healthier spiritual soil. Others took up the cause. Even before Tyndale died, Miles Coverdale edited a complete English Bible and dedicated it to the king. The Matthew Bible followed in 1539 and was the first actually to be printed in England. The Great Bible, known as such because of its size, followed. Some 20 years later, after the interruption of Queen Mary's reign, came the Geneva Bible, dedicated to Queen Elizabeth. It is named after the place where it was translated and was the first Bible to include verse numbers. It was the Bible of Shakespeare, John Bunyan and the Pilgrim Fathers. It proved a popular version with the common people. All of these translations owed an immense debt to the work of

Tyndale. A Bishops' Bible, which was less Protestant in tone than the Geneva Bible, was also translated and became the "authorised" version placed in cathedrals from 1570 onwards.

When James I came to the throne, it was proposed that a new "authorised version" be translated to sweep away the confusion of the others. Fifty-four scholars set to work in teams of six and worked away at it in Oxford, Cambridge and Westminster Abbey. Officially, it was a revision of the Bishops' Bible but it drew on all its predecessors and follows Tyndale's wording very closely in many places. It was published in 1611 and for nearly three centuries was unrivalled. The rhythm of its language, whether in the poetic or prose sections, meant it was admirably suited for reading aloud and exercised a profound influence over the English language, well beyond any impact it had spiritually. Even today, some of our popular sayings and ways of speaking owe their origins to the King James Version (KJV).

Modern English translations

Three major streams of Bible translation began to emerge from the late 19th century onwards. One stream flows directly from the KJV and aims at providing the most "literal" translation; the second stream provides us with entirely new translations; the third provides freer translations and paraphrases which are often the work of single authors. In what follows we can only mention the principal translations in each stream. But first we must ask why these streams eventually sprang from the KJV, causing it to recede into the background. Several factors gave rise to this new phase of Bible translation.

First, there was the availability of earlier manuscripts of the Bible than were accessible in the days of Tyndale and the KJV. A wealth of early manuscripts from the fourth and fifth centuries gave Bible translators a great deal of help and allowed them a much greater degree of confidence in the accuracy of their work than the translators of earlier days could ever have had. Such a manuscript is often referred to as a "codex". Among the most important is the Codex Sinaiticus, which is a complete version of the New Testament dating from the fourth century; it is kept in the British Library, London. From the same time, but not quite as complete, is the Codex Vaticanus, housed in the Vatican Library, Rome. Comparing the different manuscripts helps greatly in the task of securing a trustworthy translation.

Second, there was a great deal of growth in the understanding of ancient languages.

Third, as has already been mentioned, there is the fact that our own language is constantly developing and changing.

"Literal" translations

The first break (other than some private ventures) from the KJV came when the Church of England asked for a revision to be prepared in 1870. Fifty scholars worked on it and eventually the complete Revised Version was published in 1885. They approached their work cautiously, only changing what they considered essential, and still, in the Old Testament, basing their work on the solitary Masoretic Text which the KJV had used. Even so, 30,000 changes were made in the New Testament, 5,000 of which were made on the basis of using the wider variety of manuscripts. In 1901 the Americans published their own variant of this, known as the American Standard Version. It lacked the Apocrypha, which the English edition included.

The Revised Standard Version (RSV) followed in 1952. Translated in the same tradition as Tyndale and the KJV, it was the work of American and Canadian translators and aimed for the same quality of English as they had achieved. In its day, it commended itself very widely and achieved as much recognition and authority as any translation since the KJV. A New Revised Standard Version (NRSV) came out in 1990 which removed some archaic language and used inclusive language. It was a great improvement on the RSV but its continuing desire to be as near-literal a translation as possible, while laudable, made the style somewhat stilted.

Many evangelical Christians favour the New International Version (NIV) which was first produced in the early 1970s and has gone through a number of editions since. Inclusive language editions were published in the United Kingdom but not, sadly, in the United States. The latest edition is called Today's New International Version, but currently only the New Testament is available; the complete Bible is not due until 2005. A team of 100 interdenominational biblical scholars, sponsored by the independent Committee on Bible Translation but supported by the International Bible Society, worked on the NIV. They were committed to the belief that the Bible was the infallible, that is, totally reliable, word of God. They aimed to be faithful in their translation of the original Scriptures while using clear, modern language which could be used both in private reading and public worship. Although, as the translators themselves confess, no translation is ever perfect, it achieves a very high standard of accuracy and readability.

New translations

The New English Bible was much trumpeted when it was published in 1970. It was an entirely fresh translation which broke away from the tradition of Tyndale and the KJV. Undertaken by British scholars who represented all the major denominations, it received something akin to "official" approval. But it suffered greatly from being very formal in its style, highbrow in its vocabulary and often somewhat novel in its translation. It never established itself as a popular translation. It was followed by a Revised English Bible in 1989 which altered some of the earlier translation in a more conservative direction, while making it more readable and, in part, introducing inclusive language.

While the Roman Catholic Church brought out its own editions of the RSV, it was The Jerusalem Bible, published in 1966, which made an impact. It has proved to be a popular translation well beyond Catholic congregations. It is known for the freshness and elegance of its translation. A revision appeared in 1985 which adopted inclusive language but retained some older expressions, for example, using "Yahweh" as the name for God in the Old Testament.

Freer translations and paraphrases

While the above translations seek to stick closely to the original manuscripts and provide a "literal" translation, others translate the original with a much greater degree of freedom. Such works fall into two groups. There are those which base their translation on the principle of "dynamic equivalence" and those which do not claim to be other than a paraphrase – a free rendering of the original – and which are often a personal reworking of the text.

Among the former, the two chief examples would be the Good News Bible, now mostly known as Today's English Version (TEV), and the Contemporary English Version (CEV). The idea of a "dynamically equivalent" translation is this: a literal translation will translate the words into their exact equivalent in another language, but a dynamically equivalent version will go further and translate some of the concepts or meanings as well. An obvious example occurs in the measurements found in the Old Testament. Most people do not know how long a *cubit* is, nor how much an *ephah* weighs. So why not translate them into contemporary terms and use metres and kilograms? To a great extent this is a helpful, even unobjectionable, step. The problem comes in deciding where to draw the line. Do you translate a "sheep" into something else for urban populations who have no experience of sheep? And, if so, what do you make of expressions like "the Lamb of God who takes away the sin of the world"? Careful judgements have to be made.

Both the TEV and CEV have succeeded in producing translations which use very simple English and so make the Bible very readable for those whose knowledge of the English language is not highly refined and who cannot cope with a huge range of vocabulary. The cost, of course, is that some of the finer nuances of the text are lost. Also, it does not always make for such good reading in a public service. Nonetheless, from my membership of a church which used the TEV shortly after it was produced in 1966, I know it opened up the Bible to many who had struggled with it before.

Personal paraphrases and translations of the Bibles, especially the New Testament, abound. Many of them are known by the name of their authors. Those by Weymouth, Moffatt, Goodspeed and Knox, to name just a few, and even that by the much respected William Barclay, have now receded into history. One paraphrase which has lasted longer than others and still has good mileage in it is J. B. Phillips' *New Testament in Modern English*. Written by a Church of England parson, who struggled throughout his life with depression, Phillips was aiming to put the New Testament into language that his youth club members would understand. His skill as a translator was such that there are many crystal clear passages and memorable phrases which still speak with persuasive power today. He later wrote a little book in which he testified that working so closely with the Bible as he had done over the years had convinced him it had *The Ring of Truth* about it.

The most recent work in this category is *The Message*. Eugene Peterson is a wonderful craftsman with words and has now put the whole Bible into contemporary language. Whole passages in *The Message* can be brilliantly insightful. To my mind, his paraphrase of Colossians, for example, is unsurpassed. But readers will soon be aware that there are times when Peterson expands freely on what the text actually says and times when he resorts to North American colloquialisms which mystify the British.

One paraphrase/translation stands, somewhat confusingly, in the middle of these two groups. Kenneth Taylor published *The Living Bible* in 1971. It was a very free paraphrase, as could be seen by its length. It was not based on any original translation of the original manuscripts but on the KJV and its successors.

Taylor's aim was to connect with his children and their ilk. In the hippy generation it was a wonderful evangelistic tool and connected with a lot of other people in addition to his own kids. Most recently, however, a New Living Translation (NLT) has been published. Released in 1996 by Tyndale, the same publishers as the original *Living Bible*, it owes nothing to Taylor's work. It is rather a serious translation of the original texts, using the dynamic-equivalent approach. It is wonderfully readable without trading on accuracy. This version was further enhanced when a British edition was published in 2000, smoothing out any American phrasing that might jar on British ears. It is profitable both for private and public use and deserves widespread recognition since it scores highly on the twin dimensions of faithfulness and accessibility.

Problems for Bible translators

The above story has hinted at some of the difficulties which face any Bible translator. They relate both to the original text and to the intended readership. Nothing of any importance in Christian belief hinges on it, but what does the translator do when the various manuscripts and ancient texts disagree with each other? How can the translator choose the right meaning when a word has more than one meaning? The Hebrew word *ruach*, for example, may mean breath, wind or spirit, and the spirit may be either a human spirit or the Spirit of God. Similarly, what do you do when several words are all translated by one English word. Does it matter? Are we missing anything when we translate, for example, the four different Greek words *philia, storge, agape* and *eros* by our one word "love" or when we fail to distinguish between "you" referring to a single person and "you" referring to a group, as the Greek does? When not handled properly, this could have quite an influence in encouraging a distorted, individualistic approach to the Christian faith. Then there are the problems which arise because not all languages function in the same way. Different sentence structures and different rules regarding punctuation can lead to complications. It is thought, for example, that in 1 Corinthians, Paul is sometimes first quoting his readers (10:23, where the NIV inserts quotation marks) and then answering them. But Greek did not use quotation marks, so careful judgements have to be made when translating those passages.

On the other side there are the problems associated with the readers. We have already been introduced to the fundamental issues here. The language of the readers is not static, so allowances must be made for the changes of meaning which occur over time. Also, do translators translate the words literally or do they try to express the thought forms in contemporary ways? Which is, in reality, "more accurate"?

A simple but profoundly important area where these matters have come to a head in recent years is the use of exclusive and inclusive language. When Psalm 1:1 says, "Blessed is the man . . .", does it mean than no women are to be blessed in the way it envisages by God? When Paul addresses his readers as "brothers", is he intending only to address the men? Here is an example where, like it or not, the English language has undergone quite a revolution in recent days. Thirty years ago it may well have been accepted that words like "men" and "brothers" included women and sisters, depending on the context. But that is no longer acceptable, nor easily understood. Consequently, it is right to include the female gender explicitly in any references where they are clearly embraced in the original. Inclusive language versions of the NIV and NLT have done that sensitively. But even if the principle is clear, the translator will face any number of specific verses where a judgement has to be made as to whether the language should become inclusive or remain exclusive. In Ephesians 6:4, to give just one example, the NIV and the NLT have both left in the word "Fathers" rather than changing it to "Parents", as might have been expected. The NRSV, which usually opts for more inclusive language, does the same. Here the translators have decided, again quite rightly in my view, that, given the historical circumstances, it is proper to retain the exclusive language because in Paul's day it clearly was fathers, not mothers, who would have been in the role Paul is addressing. History is not, then, being rewritten.

The crunch, of course, comes in the language we use about God. God is revealed as the "Father" and traditionally referred to as "he". Not all the images of God, nor the terms used for him in the Bible, are masculine. Isaiah 49:15, Matthew 23:37 and the idea of God as "Lady Wisdom" (Proverbs 8) are just a few of the places where feminine imagery is used of God. The essential thing in this debate is to remember that God is neither male nor female. He is not a human being and therefore is not to be reduced to either one gender or the other. Any language we use about God is inadequate. We stretch human language to express what is inexpressible. We do so because we have to speak somehow, however deficiently. The weight of the biblical evidence comes down on the side of referring to God as male, since the preponderance of revelation about God uses masculine imagery. Given this, it seems preferable to maintain the masculine gender for God, but respect and sensitivity are due to those for whom that is a stumbling block in their faith.

Putting it in perspective

It is salutary to remember that while the problem in the Western world is to decide which Bible we are going to use, given our embarrassment of riches, the issue looks very different elsewhere. Of the almost 7,000 languages which have been identified in the world, only about 5% of them have a full translation of the Bible, while a further 13% have a complete New *or* Old Testament. Another 14% have at least one Bible book translated. This means that, while the vast majority of the world can read the Bible in a language which they know, 68% of the world's population still have no part of the Bible in their native tongue. It is estimated that 380 million of the world's population do not have any portions of Scripture translated into a language they understand.

Since this is so, three things should perhaps follow.

First, we should never take the ease with which we can obtain a Bible for granted. It is to be greatly regretted that we can buy a Bible so easily, in any number of versions suitable for our needs, and yet we read it so little and live by its message even less.

Second, we should redouble our efforts to see that the Bible is translated into more and more languages so that its message is available to that 68% who are denied access to it in their own native tongue. Agencies such as the International Bible Society and the Wycliffe Bible Translators deserve our full support.

Third, we should thank God for people like Tyndale who paid in blood for a banned book to be available in plain English. We are heirs of a rich, and costly, heritage.

3

The Foundation Documents:
Genesis to Deuteronomy

The first five books of the Bible are known as the Pentateuch. While many regard them as full of irrelevant material because they belong to such a past age, they lay essential foundations for our understanding of how God relates to his creation and to the men and women he has made, whose relationship with him was disrupted through sin. Here we find the story of creation and the stories of Abraham, Isaac, Jacob, Joseph and Moses – all rooted in history. Exodus speaks of the deliverance of the children of Israel from Egypt and of the laws God gave them. Leviticus teaches them how to live holy lives. Numbers records their journeys in the wilderness. Deuteronomy explains the covenant they entered into with God. Each of these books has continuing significance for Christians.

The Foundation Documents:

Genesis to Deuteronomy

Most people read the Bible like they use the London Underground. They pop up at various points without having a clue what lies just around the corner or how it all connects up. When I occasionally walk around central London and resist the temptation of going to the tube station nearest my appointment, I am always amazed how close things are to each other. I am fooled too often by the fact that nearby places are on different underground lines, so I think they are miles apart when they are not.

In reading the Bible or listening to it preached, we often pop up into the story of David, or Isaiah, or Abraham, or John, or Jesus, without having much of a clue as to how it all fits together. If you don't believe me, try this exercise.

An Old Testament sort-out

Place the following people and events in the correct biblical order:

Elijah
The flood
Joash

44

The exodus
Ishmael
Samson
Hosea
Joshua
Ezekiel
Ezra
Solomon
Hezekiah

How did you do?

(Answers can be found at the end of the chapter.)

These next eight chapters will hopefully give you the big picture and unfold the story of the Bible as a whole. We will obviously not be able to enter into too much detail. That would defeat the point. We are drawing a map of the major roads of the Bible, rather than presenting a detailed street atlas.

We begin with the first five books: Genesis, Exodus, Leviticus, Numbers and Deuteronomy – the foundation volumes on which all the rest of the Bible is built. Although they seem to relate to a very distant age and some parts seem very obscure, believe me, without them we would not make much sense of the rest. They are fundamental.

It looks as if they were written by Moses, the great prophet whom God used to deliver Israel from slavery in Egypt and to mould the twelve restless tribes into a nation. But there are some bits, like those concerning his own death, which he clearly could not have written. Scholars used to argue they could detect different strands within them which later editors had skilfully woven together. Some strands seem to take a special interest in the concerns of the priest, and others in the perspective of the law. Other scholars believe the books are not nearly as old as they look and that some of them were written at a much later date. Their authors, it is said, made them look as if they were actual history from an earlier time, but in fact they were written later, to be used in a debate about how Israel's faith should be practised. Ancient precedents carry authority. But all these ideas are speculation, none of them proven. There is no convincing reason why, after recognising that the documents went through a process of formation, they are not much closer to what they claim to be than many modern theories suggest.

In any case, our concern is not with the composition of these books but with their content as we have received it.

Genesis

The story of creation (1–11)

The opening chapters of the Bible introduce several key principles and spell out assumptions which the rest of the Bible will often take for granted.

Creation is no accident but the result of the activity of a personal, powerful and orderly God (1:1 – 2:1). The climax of his creation came when he made human beings "in his own image", with the remit of both relating to him and being caretakers over the earth (1:27–30). All that God made was good, except that man was lonely. Consequently, God created a female companion as a partner in the management of creation and the quest for sexual fulfilment (2:4–25). From the start, God's intention for men and women to relate in marriage is signalled (2:24). Sadly, the wonderfully open relationship they enjoyed with each other and with God was soon spoiled as they chose to disregard his instructions in a desire to become gods themselves. Terrible consequences followed, not just for Adam and Eve, but for the whole human race which succeeded them. From that time, people have broken relationships with God, with each other and with creation itself. We are all now condemned to live life "east of Eden" (3:1–24). But, even at the darkest moment, God indicated that he had a rescue plan in mind which would lead one day to the restoration of his relationship with men and women (3:15).

The evidence of this "fall" soon became apparent in Adam and Eve's family. Cain, their eldest son, killed his brother in a fit of jealousy (4:1–16), unleashing a murderous streak from which we still suffer. Yet God's purposes continued to unfold in the emergence of culture. Cities, music, technology and art arose (4:17–22), witnessing simultaneously to the wonder of humanity's creative potential and, when used for destructive purposes, to our fallen natures. The population increased rapidly but, within ten generations, the world God had made was in such a state of disorder that he chose to wipe it out, by means of a flood, and begin again. God chose Noah and his family as the slender thread which would connect the old pre-flood world with the new (6:1 – 9:29). Things were never quite going to be the same, but God entered into a "covenant" – an agreement – with Noah, promising that he would never destroy the earth in that way again.

After the flood, Noah's family became prolific, and clans and nations began to emerge (10:1–32). But the warning bells soon began to ring again. The same desire within humans to reach above themselves reared its head, as it had done in Eden. This time they built a tower to "reach the heavens". God soon put a stop to it, however, by scrambling their languages so that they could no longer easily communicate with each other (11:1–9).

Important themes, then, emerge from these chapters: God's grace and judgement, creation, the nature and responsibility of humanity, sexuality, sin and "the fall", the rise of culture and nationhood, and the unity and diversity of tribes and tongues. So, too, does the idea of the "covenant", which becomes increasingly important as the story unfolds.

The story of Abraham and his sons, 12 – 36

God's desire to bless his creation remained undimmed, despite the setbacks. So, once more, he chose an individual so that the people of the world might enjoy his favour rather than his curse. Abraham left his home and began a journey with God

(12:1–9). His calling was spelled out in another covenant and confirmed in a binding ceremony (15:1 – 17:27), during which male circumcision was introduced as the sign of the covenant. A far from perfect individual (12:10–20), Abraham learned to trust God through the school of hard knocks and built a wonderful friendship with God (18:1–33).

Abraham had to learn to trust God chiefly when God promised him a son. How, indeed, could he become the father of "a great nation" unless he had at least one heir? God kept Abraham and Sarah waiting until it was clearly impossible for them to expect a child by the normal means of procreation. Yet Isaac was born to them, patently demonstrating that he was a child of "promise" rather than a child by rights (21:1–7).

Isaac's story is more briefly told (24:1 – 26:35) and seems mainly included to prepare the way for Jacob to move centre-stage. The flaws in Isaac's family resulted in his younger son Jacob, rather than his older son Esau, becoming his heir. But Jacob sensibly deemed it wise to make himself scarce for a time and, as he fled, God promised him that what he had pledged to Abraham would be fulfilled through him (28:10–22). Again, it was all part of God's mysterious plan to demonstrate that people's relationship with him has always depended on his grace and promise and not on human rights or works.

Jacob was the original "Mr Fix-it". So it took some time for God to mould him and get him to a point of trust. When Jacob was somewhat nervously bringing his fugitive years to an end and returning home to Esau, a significant showdown occurred when he wrestled with God. Jacob was given a new name, Israel, but was left with a limp (32:22–32) – a powerful and permanent reminder that God, not he, would have his way.

The story of Joseph (37 – 50)

Jacob settled in Canaan and had twelve sons (46:8–25) who became the leaders of the twelve tribes of Israel. His last-but-one son, Joseph, was marked out to play a special role in the story. He was the favourite son and, perhaps as a result, a precocious kid. So his brothers decided to sell him into slavery and cruelly tell their father that he had been killed (37:1–36). On the surface, Joseph's story seemed to lurch from bad to worse. In Egypt as a slave, he was falsely accused of seducing his master's wife and imprisoned. He lay forgotten in prison for a good time (39:1–23). Yet Genesis makes it clear that when others had forgotten him, the Lord had not. It was in the divine plan. Pharaoh had a dream which disturbed him greatly. Joseph had the God-given gift of interpreting dreams, so he was taken out of prison to advise Pharaoh (41:1–40). The dream warned of a food crisis which was about to descend on Egypt. As a result, Joseph became a senior civil servant and remained in a position of power for years, managing the crisis (41:41–57).

The crisis affected people well beyond Egypt; Jacob's family, away in Canaan, were caught up in it. Jacob sent his sons down to Egypt in search of food. To cut a long story short, it led to the reconciliation of Joseph with his brothers, to old Jacob seeing his precious son again, and to them all moving to Egypt (42:1 – 49:28). Jacob died there but was buried back in Canaan – a symbol that his descendants would one day possess that land. This was how the children of Israel settled in Egypt.

Genesis ends on a fitting note. The human story has been full of ups and downs but, over it all, God has been working out his plan and purposes. Joseph's brothers had meant to harm him, but Joseph tells them he held no grudge against them "for God intended it for good to accomplish what is now being done . . ." (50:20).

Exodus

The deliverance from Egypt (1 – 12)

The people of Israel prospered in Egypt and became numerous. A new king came to power who knew nothing about Joseph and subjected the Israelites to tyrannical oppression (1:1–22). But God's plans to bless the world through them were not to be thwarted. In spite of a policy of infanticide towards the Hebrews (as they had become known), God arranged for one of their infants, Moses, to be saved and, ironically, brought up in none other than Pharaoh's own household (2:1–10). When Moses became aware of his own identity he sought to do something about the plight of his people (2:11–25), but his strategy was typically human rather than divine. So, like Abraham and Jacob before him, God took many years to prepare Moses, in a desert, for his calling as the great liberator of Israel (3:1 – 6:27).

Confrontation with Pharaoh followed confrontation (6:28 – 11:10). Plague after plague was inflicted on Egypt to persuade Pharaoh to release the Israelites from bondage. When God could not countenance his defiance any more, the angel of death visited the Egyptians, killing all their firstborn. That night, following a special celebratory meal, the children of Israel escaped from bondage (12:1–51). The exodus, as it is called, became the defining moment for Israel, and the Passover meal became their most regular act of celebration. They quickly ran into what looked like an insuperable obstacle to their escape. With a sea they could not cross in front of them, and an army they could not escape behind them, it appeared as if their flight had been in vain. But not so. God stepped in miraculously, parting the Reed Sea and, equally miraculously, closing it again, to drown the pursuing enemy (13:17 – 14:31). Safe on the other side, they sang a song of victory (15:1–18), the first the Bible records, which celebrated God's just and righteous reign.

The wilderness journey (13 – 24, 32 – 34)

The wilderness was an inhospitable place and, before long, the people were longing to go back to captivity. Yet God's grace continued and provided them with food to eat, water to drink and a navigation system which would not fail. This part of the story is more fully told in Numbers.

More significant still, he also provided them with a law by

which their lives were to be governed. It covered the totality of their lives – its spiritual, moral, social, economic and civil dimensions. Spirituality was not confined to religious rituals in the tabernacle. For these covenant people, all of life was to be a spiritual act of worship.

The law was given on Mount Sinai. Its opening section sets it firmly in the context of their deliverance (20:1). Israel was commanded to live as the law required in gratitude for their freedom. It stipulated the most humane, just and sensible way to live. The opening ten brief commandments (20:1–17, repeated in Deuteronomy 5:6–21) have rightly established themselves as timeless commandments. All but the Sabbath law is repeated in the New Testament. Other commandments relate to the particular circumstances Israel faced at the time or would face when they eventually settled in Canaan. But even these laws are not to be ignored as mere relics of the past. Each law should be examined to discern God's intention so that we can still live today in our different world in a way which pleases him.

While Moses was receiving the law from God, the people, aided by Aaron, his brother and lieutenant, rebelled against God in a massive way and fashioned a golden bull, similar to those they would have known in Egypt, as an object of worship (32:1 – 33:6) How absurd! Yet God's anger against them was turned into a merciful and wise discipline, as a result of Moses pleading for them.

The building of the tabernacle (25 – 31; 35 – 40)

The tabernacle was a portable tent, set up in the centre of the Israelite camp, as the place where sacrifices were offered to God. Here priests would offer worship, secure atonement for sin, strengthen fellowship with God and seek his guidance. It housed the Ark of the Covenant (25:10–22; 37:1–9), which was to be God's throne among the people. It was a box, overlaid with gold, with cherubs at either end, and was later to contain the tablets on which the law was written and some manna (a biscuit-like, honey-tasting substance which God provided for the Israelites to eat in the wilderness). The Ark stood in the Most Holy Place in the tabernacle, but was eventually lost without trace.

The elaborate details concerning the construction and furnishing of the tabernacle may seem laborious to us. But it was important as a visual aid for the faith of Israel and each part of it signified something meaningful. The priests' dress reminded them not to serve God casually, but to approach him with care. The details of their uniform acted as a visual aid to Israel. The High Priest's breastplate, for example, contained twelve precious stones, one for each of the tribes of Israel. Two things stand out. First, the God who delivered them from Israel deserved the best in worship. Anything less would not do. Second, the God who made such demands also equipped his people for the task. Two skilful craftsmen, Bezalel and Oholiab, are spoken of as "filled with the Spirit of God" (31:1–11). This suggests that the Spirit who played a role in creation (Genesis 1:1) is the inspiration for artistry and craftsmanship and is not just the source of religious experiences.

Exodus involves the confirmation of another covenant. God would be Israel's God in return for their obedience to his law. The people agreed and confirmed the covenant with the sprinkling of blood (24:1–18). Their God showed himself to be not an angry, legalistic God, but rather "the Lord, the Lord, the compassionate and gracious God, slow to anger, abounding in love and faithfulness, maintaining love to thousands, and forgiving wickedness, rebellion and sin" (34:6, 7).

Leviticus

Leviticus can fairly claim to be among the least popular books of the Bible but, ironically, it is among the most significant. It is about loving God (1 – 8; 16) and loving our neighbours (9 – 15; 17 – 27).

Instructions about offerings (1 – 7)

Sacrifices were a common way of offering worship throughout the ancient world (and still are in many parts of our world today). Their purpose was as much to express love to God as it was to secure forgiveness for sin. So, first, instructions are given to the worshippers (1 – 6:7). Then the ground is gone over again for the benefit of instructing the priests (6:8 – 7:38).

Five offerings are mentioned. The *burnt offering* (1; 6:8–13) was the basic, all-purpose sacrifice, offered twice daily to God and on numerous special occasions as well. It expressed praise, prayer and loyalty, and sought atonement. The *grain* or *cereal offering* (2; 6:14–18) was "just a gift" and a reminder of the covenant Israel enjoyed. The *peace* or *fellowship offering* (3; 7:11–36) was an optional thanksgiving meal which celebrated the presence of God. The *purification offering* (4:1 – 5:13; 6:24–30) was for worshippers who had unintentionally sinned or been made unclean by circumstances beyond their control. The *guilt offering*, or *reparation offering*, (5:14 – 6:7; 7:1–10) demanded that compensation be paid when wrong had been done.

The sacrifices, like the tabernacle in which they were offered, were a visual aid to the worshippers. They required careful preparation and costly involvement. God was not to be worshipped in the same way as the surrounding nations worshipped their gods: by magic, sorcery, frenzy or ritual. Rather, Israel's God made ethical demands on his people. And when they failed, it was blood that served as the cleansing agent to remove the defilement of sin.

These sacrifices were not truly effective. They were a foreshadowing of the ultimate sacrifice offered by Christ, which would deal with sin and reconcile human beings to God once and for all. The imagery of sacrifice is often pressed into service in the New Testament to explain Christ's work, especially in the letter to the Hebrews.

The beginnings of the priesthood (8 – 10)

Aaron and his family were set apart, in an impressive ceremony, to serve as Israel's priests. They not only offered sacrifices but also taught God's laws, prayed for his people and discerned his will. Not long after their ordination, two of Aaron's sons offered incense to God which was "unauthorised" (10:1–3). While we cannot be sure what that means, the sad incident teaches us important lessons. No one receives automatic protection in the presence of God just because some status has been conferred on him or her. God is a God of dynamic holiness, who always deserves to be served with care.

Variations on a theme: clean and unclean (11 – 15)

Four different issues are grouped together here – food laws (11), childbirth (12), skin diseases (13 – 14) and bodily discharges (15) – under the theme of "clean" and "unclean". Various attempts have been made to work out the reasoning behind these laws. They may have been wise hygiene regulations in view of the hot temperatures in the desert. They may have had symbolic significance about the nature of the community. Observing the rules would certainly have distinguished Israel from the practices of the people around them. The food laws, in particular, would come to be a key way in which Israel preserved its separate identity from others and which bound the Israelites closely to each other. But probably more important than asking for an explanation is the need to recognise, hard though it may be, that if God commanded these laws, his covenant people should obey them rather than dispute them.

The Day of Atonement (16)

The high point of Israel's calendar was the annual Day of Atonement, that is, of being "made one" with God again. Throughout the year, a multitude of sacrifices were offered by worshippers. But this sacrifice was different. Here, the High Priest engaged in an annual spiritual spring-clean, as it were.

Two things made this sacrifice different. The High Priest took two goats, one of which was to be sacrificed. The other, the scapegoat, was to be taken outside the camp, symbolically carrying the sin of the people back to where it belonged, in the abode of the destructive forces of chaos. Then, on this day only, suitably protected, the High Priest entered the Most Holy Place to make atonement for the whole of Israel. Any sin not previously atoned for, or any defilement not already cleansed, would be dealt with in this way. Curiously, the New Testament does not directly link the work of Christ to the Day of Atonement, although it implies a link in passages such as Hebrews 10.

The emphasis in Leviticus on making atonement is still of contemporary relevance. Sin still alienates people from God and leaves them with an actual need, and often a felt need, for cleansing from defilement and for restoration of a relationship with God. Christ, the ultimate sacrifice, is the one to whom the sacrifices of Leviticus point, and the one who makes atonement for us now.

Rules for community living (17 – 27)

If the first part of Leviticus is about loving God, the latter part is about loving your neighbour. Indeed, the phrase, "love your neighbour as yourself", is first found in Leviticus 19:18. The agenda we find here is remarkably up-to-date, even if the details require some unpacking. Note the issues these laws cover: the care of animals (17), the maintenance of family life and the rejection of incest (18), justice in the marketplace, integrity in relationships, care for the vulnerable and disapproval of racism (19), issues of law and order (20), time off for celebration (23), and strategies to ensure economic equality within society (25). That sounds pretty contemporary.

Some of these laws have been subject to a great deal of misunderstanding. For example, the famous "eye for eye, tooth for tooth" law (24:20) is not advocating that justice should always be exacted to the maximum level. Rather, it is designed to restrain the cycle of vengeance in which people easily get trapped and to prevent the escalation of violence. Someone who loses a tooth has no right to take a life in recompense! Read within the context of the wider laws of the day, Leviticus is remarkably person-centred and humane – exactly what we would expect when these laws have their origin in a merciful and gracious Creator.

Leviticus, then, spells out how Israel was to maintain its relationship with God and to organise its common life so as to reflect his holy character (19:1). In doing so, it left us both a legacy of good practice to reinterpret for our own circumstances, and also some sacrificial prototypes which were to be fully developed in the work of Christ.

Numbers

Numbers recounts the story of the 40 years spent in the wilderness. It gets its title from censuses recorded in chapters 1 and 26. It is a sad story of grumbling and folly.

The exodus from Egypt and the journey taken to the Promised Land is, in reality, a complicated series of events and not as straightforward to piece together as many would think. That is one reason why the travelling took so long and the route was not direct. But Numbers makes clear that it was the Israelites' constant complaining that meant that a distance of about 200 miles took them a lifetime to cover, and that the generation who left Egypt, including Moses himself, were denied entry into the Promised Land. The book reveals much about the character of God, but the New Testament uses it almost exclusively as a warning. How could the people who saw God at work so dramatically have grumbled about him so frequently and disbelieved him so spectacularly?

The early organisation of the camp (1 - 9)

The initial census (1) is followed by a description of the way the tribes arranged themselves around the camp (2). The tribe of Levi was special and was assigned to assist Aaron in his priestly duties (1:47–53; 3) In doing this, they were acting as substitutes for all the firstborn males of Israel who, of right, belonged to God (see Exodus 12). Their duties in erecting, dismantling and transporting the tabernacle are detailed (4).

Concerns about the purity of the camp follow (5). Some Israelites wanted to serve God beyond the ordinary requirements and entered into a special vow to do so, involving abstinence from strong drink, not cutting their hair and avoiding contact with corpses (6). They were called Nazirites, the best known of whom was Samson, who lived at a later date.

The rest of these opening chapters include the rich words of blessing pronounced over Israel (6:22–27); the offerings people gave to God (7), the commissioning of the Levites (8:5–26), the second observance of the Passover (9:1–14), and the way in which they would be guided to strike camp and be on the move (9:15–23).

Stories of the journey from Sinai to Moab (10 – 21)

The Israelites left Sinai, in the direction of the Promised Land (10), with the Ark of the Covenant ahead of them and the cloud of the Lord over them. But the grumbling soon started. The people craved the varied menus of Egypt instead of the restricted diet of the desert. God reacted with anger, but it was quickly superseded by his grace. Quail was henceforth on the menu to supplement the manna of which they had grown tired (11).

Moses' own sister and brother then complained, thinking that Moses had got above himself. God quickly endorsed his leadership and punished Miriam for her disrespect (12).

A third failure followed. Spies were sent out to explore the Promised Land. When they returned, the majority report emphasised the might of the peoples whose land God had promised them. Only Caleb and Joshua entered a minority report, urging the people forward. It seems as if the Israelites had forgotten too soon the power of God that they had seen at work as they escaped Egypt. The people's hearts failed them and they wallowed in disbelief (13 – 14).

The catalogue of failures continued. A group of leaders grumbled against Moses and Aaron, although, in reality, they were attacking God. God's judgement on them provoked a more widespread rebellion and a further act of his discipline. Only the prompt action taken by Moses in making atonement saved them from total devastation (16).

The next complaint got even Moses into trouble. This time the cause was the absence of drinking water. To secure an ample supply God told Moses to strike a rock; Moses, perhaps at the end of his patience, struck the rock not once but twice (20:1–13). The lack of trust cost Moses his entry ticket to Canaan. He was to see the land stretched out before him, but never to set foot in it himself.

The journey was aggravated still further by the opposition of the surrounding nations, but the Israelites pressed on, securing a number of victories on the way (20:14 – 21:35).

Stories from the plains of Moab (22 – 36)

Balak, king of Moab, pressed a prophet called Balaam into service to curse Israel. Balaam's track record meant it should have been no problem. But three attempts to do so all failed. Instead, inspired by God, he blessed Israel and predicted the rise of a future king who would defeat Israel's enemies (22 – 24). Another strategy aimed at Israel's destruction occurred when Moabite women infiltrated the camp to seduce the Israelites into idolatry. Decisive action prevented their attempt from succeeding (25). In the rest of the book a couple of significant things are recorded. Joshua is appointed as successor to Moses (27:12–23). Also, as the Israelites stand on the brink of Canaan, the journey is reviewed (33) and future arrangements for the occupation of the Promised Land are contemplated (32 – 35).

Deuteronomy

Deuteronomy makes a fitting conclusion to the five books of Moses. The year is about 1260 BC and the people are about to enter Canaan. Moses gives a "state of the union" address or rather, several addresses! (1:1) He summarises how God has led the people and what they have become. The book's name means "a second law".

The dominant theme throughout is the idea of the covenant, which we will explore more fully below.

The gift of the land

A secondary theme is woven throughout the book. The land the Israelites are about to enter is not their possession by right but a gift of God's grace. That has implications for how they are to live in it. Their lives are to be marked by gratitude and humility. They should never forget their dependence on God and should always conduct their lives in obedience to him (8). No whiff of arrogance nor abuse of the environment could be countenanced. Furthermore, remembering that they once lived as slaves in someone else's land would give them a special care for the poor, the slaves and other vulnerable groups among them (5:15; 15:15; 16:12; 24:18, 22). They were, however, to rid the land of of the "wicked", those who lived contrary to God's ways, and to keep the land pure. If they failed to do so, the purity of their own worship would be corrupted and their continuing existence as God's covenant people threatened (7).

The covenant treaty

Ancient kingdoms entered into treaties with one another, just as governments do today. These treaties, or covenants, conformed to a basic pattern which we can see reflected in the book of Deuteronomy. We have seen how God entered into a covenant with Noah (Genesis 9) and Abraham (Genesis 15 and 17). But the greatest covenant in the story so far is that which he entered into with Israel as a whole at Mount Sinai (Exodus 19). Deuteronomy spells out the terms of that covenant in full, using the classic form of the ancient world.

The preface (1:1–5) sets out the author, date and setting of the treaty.

A historical overview (1:6 – 3:29) of Israel's wanderings in the wilderness follows.

The basic stipulations (4 – 11) follow. The requirement to love and obey God is set out in a general way. In return, the Lord who is God in heaven above, who alone is God and who had demonstrated his awesome power on their behalf, would be their God (4:32–40). The ten commandments are repeated (5). Moses reminds the people that their love of and obedience to God has not always been what it might have been (9:7 – 10:11) in spite of the extraordinary way in which God has "set his affection" on them (10:15). He also points out something of the way in which what it meant to obey God would change when they exchanged their wandering existence in the wilderness for their settled existence in Canaan (7 – 8).

Detailed stipulations (12 – 26) then apply the general principles to a whole variety of particular issues. They cover everything from mourning to feasting, from debt to harvests, and from worship to matters of law and order. Most of these laws are found in the earlier books of Exodus, Leviticus and Numbers.

Arrangements about the treaty document (27) typically come next, setting out how the document was to be preserved, passed on and referred to in the future. Moses ensures that the covenant would be remembered when the Israelites had crossed the Jordan.

Blessings and curses (28) form the climax, spelling out the benefits of keeping the agreement and the penalties for breaking it. Moses reminds the people of the benefits they could expect from God for their obedience, and the curses which would follow if they failed to fulfil their responsibilities.

The conclusion (29 – 34) reports how the children of Israel renewed their commitment to the covenant in a ceremony in Moab (29). Moses pronounces his parting blessing on them, and the succession passes to Joshua (30 – 34).

Looking back . . .

Looking back over the first five books of the Bible, one idea has achieved special significance: the idea of the covenant. God entered into an agreement with Noah, Abraham and Israel, to be their God in return for their loving, obeying and serving him. Unlike other covenants, it was never an agreement between equals, nor were the covenants drawn up for the sole benefit of the people to whom God chose to relate in this special way. His purpose was always that through them, his word would come to others, blessing would flow to the nations, and his salvation would extend to all. We now turn to see how the Israelites got on in keeping their side of the agreement.

Answers:

1. The flood   2. Ishmael   3. The exodus   4. Joshua   5. Samson
6. Solomon   7. Elijah   8. Joash   9. Hosea   10. Hezekiah
11. Ezekiel   12. Ezra

4

The Unfolding Story:
Joshua to Nehemiah

Five key aspects of Israel's story are covered in this chapter, which surveys the historical books of the Old Testament. First, under Joshua, the children of Israel settle, and then, under the judges, struggle, in the Promised Land. Second, Israel reaches the high point of her existence under King David and King Solomon. Third, the kingdom experiences a sad decline as it is split in two and ruled over by many kings who prove unfaithful to God. Fourth, God punishes the people for their sin, by exiling them to Babylon. Last, under Ezra and Nehemiah, the people are restored to Judah. None of this is boring history. It is alive with spiritual truth. It especially traces the fortunes of the people of Israel in relation to how faithful they are to the covenant they entered into with God.

The Unfolding Story:
Joshua to Nehemiah

Picture the Old Testament story as a range of mountains. Peaks, of various altitudes, are interspersed by valleys, some sharper and deeper than others. At one point the range splits into two. Each branch takes its own course, with one petering out altogether, well before the other.

For the children of Israel, entering the Promised Land under the leadership of Joshua was like climbing a steep mountain. Sadly, no sooner had they conquered it than they sank into the "valley" of the judges.

The reigns of King David and King Solomon which followed were like reaching the summits of the Himalayas. Israel was at the apex of her strength and influence. But tragedy struck after the time of Solomon, when the kingdom was divided into two. The larger part of the kingdom, made up of ten tribes, was in the north and was called Israel. The smaller part was composed of the tribes of Judah and Benjamin around Jerusalem, and was called Judah. The temple was situated in Judah and it was there that the direct successors of David reigned. Because of this, the smaller division of the kingdom was of special significance. Although each kingdom had some good rulers, this part of the story consists more often than not of "valleys". God eventually used international forces to punish both kingdoms for their spiritual unfaithfulness. As a result, the northern kingdom disappeared from view around 722 BC. Judah survived a little longer but was ultimately destroyed in 587 BC and its people taken into exile.

That appeared to be the end of the story until, after more than 50 years, a new ruler permitted some of the exiles to return home. The nation began to be restored again and a new temple was built.

All through this time, God was sending his messengers, the prophets, whose preaching needs to be woven into the narrative. Chapter 6 will do this, but first we must look at the unfolding experience of the children of Israel in more detail.

Conquest: the book of Joshua

After 40 years in the wilderness, all those who had left Egypt, except Joshua and Caleb, were dead. Joshua had succeeded Moses (1), and a second reconnaissance mission, during which the spies received the devious help of a woman called Rahab, had encouraged the Israelites to think that God was on their side (2). One barrier remained between them and the Promised Land: the river Jordan. But God miraculously parted the waters there, as he had previously done at the Reed Sea, and so they entered the land with dry feet (3 – 4). Things were never to be the same again. From now on they were going to settle rather than wander; live in buildings, not tents; they would feed off the land and not depend on God's providing them with manna (5:12).

But first, they had to conquer the land, which was already occupied by various tribes. The first strategic victory was won miraculously when the city of Jericho, just across the Jordan, fell (literally) into their hands (6). Their next engagement, however, led to defeat. It was not that God had let them down – rather the reverse: they had let him down. Achan had failed to obey God completely, and consequently God let the Israelites lose the battle for Ai. Once the matter had been dealt with, Ai was destroyed (7 – 8). The book of Joshua goes on to detail the bloody campaigns by which the tribes of Israel conquered almost the entire land and brought it under their control (9 – 13). Although it was evident that "the Lord was fighting for Israel" (10:14), God demanded that they eliminate the existing population in order to ensure their survival. Uncomfortable as we may feel with this, the command injects a note of realism into the story. Tiny and ill-equipped Israel would have had no chance of withstanding the native population unless such a policy had been adopted.

The story of the conquest is not one of unadulterated success for the people of Israel. One lesson which keeps recurring is the need to listen to God. Their occasional failure to do so resulted in problems, whereas careful attention to the details of what God required brought them success (see 7:1–26; 9:1–27).

The second half of Joshua, from chapter 14 onwards, outlines the various areas of land which the tribes were to be allocated. The special arrangements for the cities of refuge and the Levites are included. To us it may read like an irrelevant geography textbook. In reality, it is anything but. Try to imagine the thrill of having some land to call your own after 40 years of homelessness. The nearest most of us would get to it is to recall the day we actually owned our own house! But to Israel it was even more important than that. Possessing the land was a sign of God keeping his promises. He had given them a possession, against all odds, just as he had said he would.

The closing chapters of the book of Joshua record his farewell address to the people (23) and their renewing of the covenant with God (24). The Israelites were eager – too eager – to confirm their desire to serve the Lord who had delivered them from Egypt, protected them in the desert and given them a new land (24:16–18). Unhappily, the next chapter in their story suggests that they would have been wise to take more notice of the cautions Joshua had raised before they rushed into saying they would serve the Lord (24:19–20).

Downs and ups: the book of Judges

The opening words of Judges (1:1 – 2:5) sound an ominous warning note. Israel had often failed to obey the Lord completely when it came to driving out the native population. As a result, the surrounding tribes became a thorn in Israel's side, frequently leading the people into the worship of idols and into breaking their covenant with the living God. From the high point of occupying the land under Joshua, Israel rapidly descended into the valley of disobedience and defeat.

The pattern of Israel's life during this period is first set out in 2:10–19. The people of Israel were still a loose confederation of twelve tribes rather than one united nation and they had no single leader. Without the guidance of a figure like Joshua, they kept going round in circles. The cycle of events went like this:

- The people sinned against God, especially by serving other gods.
- God punished them by letting their enemies defeat them.
- In their distress they cried out to the Lord.
- God raised up a judge who saved them.
- When the judge died, they returned to sinning against God.

The judges, then, were not so much regular rulers as an odd mixture of transient deliverers who rescued Israel when they had fallen into a trap of their own making. If only the Israelites had remained faithful to the covenant they had been so eager to tell Joshua they were going to keep, they would never have got into this repeated mess. That God gave them so many judges is a sign of his patience and grace.

The judges had little in common with each other. Some are only briefly mentioned, whereas the report of others takes up a lot of space. There was **Othniel** (3:7–11), Caleb's nephew who defeated King Cushan-Rishathaim in the north. **Ehud** (3:12–30) is remembered for using his left-handedness to deceive and assassinate King Eglon of Moab. **Shamgar** (3:31) gets a single verse to celebrate his terrific victory against the Philistines.

Although **Deborah** is described as a prophet, she acted like a judge every bit as much as any of the men. She spurred Israel's army into action. But the defeat of the enemy occurred because another woman, Jael, killed Sisera, the fleeing enemy commander (4). This famous victory is celebrated in a song (5).

Gideon (6 – 8) receives a lot of attention for his battles against Midian. He comes over as a man of faith, since he fought the enemy with only 300 men. Yet Gideon was all too human in demanding that God should convince him that he really was on Israel's side. After his success, Gideon resisted the temptations of power but succumbed to the temptations of wealth (8:22–27). Unfortunately, this undid all the good he had done and Israel was back worshipping an idol again. Gideon's son, **Abimelech**, ruled for three years after him. It was a troublesome time which ended in disaster (9).

Tola (10:1–2), **Jair** (10:3–5) and **Jephthah** (10:6 – 12:7) follow. Jephthah "was a mighty warrior" and proved uncompromising in the face of friend and foe alike. His brutal and crude handling of any situation perhaps arose from the rejection he experienced as a child (11:1–3).

Samson (13 – 16) was perhaps the greatest and most curious of the judges. He has been famously described as a "charismatic berserk". He broke all the moral rules, especially when it came to women, and behaved with reckless abandon. He did not enlist an army but fought the Philistines all on his own like a single human bazooka. In spite of it all, God gave him a great victory when he wiped out the whole of the leadership of Philistia as they gathered to worship Dagon, their god. His life stands as a testimony to the grace of God and flags up another important spiritual principle. His great victory was won only at the cost of his own life. Spiritually speaking, it is only as we die to self that we can live for God.

A couple of stories which fit the unsettled time of the judges conclude the book (17 – 21). The real significance of these chapters is the way in which they illustrate the twice-repeated assertion that "in those days Israel had no king; everyone did as they saw fit" (17:6 and 21:25). How was such social and spiritual anarchy to be overcome? Before long, Israel was to move into a new phase. From the valley of the judges, the slopes of the foothills and then the steeper climb of the mountain tracks were to be climbed again and, through the rise of the monarchy, Israel was to reach the summit of its existence.

The early monarchy: 1 Samuel – 1 Kings 11

Samuel (1 Samuel 1 – 7)

The books of Samuel, which were originally one, tell us about the last days of the judges and the early days of the monarchy under Saul and David. Samuel is the dominant figure to begin with and is responsible for anointing both Saul and David as kings.

Samuel, whose story is told in 1 Samuel 1 – 7, is, in fact, the last of the judges. Hannah, his mother, was grief-stricken at her inability to bear children and promised God that should he grant her a baby, she would give the child over to the Lord for a life of service in the sacred shrine at Shiloh (1). When her grief turned to joy (2:1–10), she kept her word and young Samuel was apprenticed to old Eli, which is just as well, because Eli's own sons were unfit to succeed him as priests (2:11–36). The key to Samuel's training was his learning to listen to God (3). The end of Eli's life saw Israel in about as low a state as it had ever been. Defeated in battle against the Philistines, the Israelites tried to reverse the situation by taking the Ark of the Covenant into battle, as if it would work some magic spell. Their action showed once again that they did not understand that God was more interested in their observing the ethical dimensions of the covenant than in their practising some superstitious religious ritual. So the Ark was captured and was still in captivity when Eli died (4). But God is no one's puppet. The Ark was indeed a symbol of God's powerful, holy presence; the

Philistines, when they discovered the havoc it could wreak among them, were soon happy to return it to Israel (5–6).

When Samuel stepped into Eli's shoes, he led the nation in repentance and rid it of its foreign gods (7:2–12). For the rest of Samuel's life, Israel experienced peace, served God faithfully and benefited from his wise leadership (7:13–17). As he grew old, the people expressed their desire for a king so that they could be like all the other nations and have someone to lead them into battle (8). Samuel warned them that their request was not as innocent as it sounded. Not only was it a sign that they no longer wanted to be ruled directly by God (8:8), but kings had a reputation for imposing taxes and feathering their own nests before they protected the interests of their subjects (8:11–18). But the people would not listen. When Samuel took his leave of them, he did the same as Moses and Joshua had done before. He recalled the way God had led them and underlined the need for them to keep the covenant (12).

Saul (1 Samuel 8 – 31)

Saul was chosen as Israel's first king and was acclaimed by the people at Mizpah (9 – 10). He made a promising start. When the Ammonites threatened Jabesh Gilead, Saul united Israel in opposition, organised an army and slaughtered them (11). Before long, however, the flaws in his character began to show. In one stand-off with the Philistines he usurped Samuel's role as priest and offered a burnt sacrifice (13:1–14). On another occasion, he failed to root out the enemy as completely as he should have done (15). Increasingly, he demonstrated cowardice, fear and jealousy (17 – 19). The victories, which were real enough, seem to have belonged more to his son Jonathan than to Saul himself (14). Before the situation degenerated too far, God rejected Saul as king (15:26). In his place, Samuel was told to anoint David (16:1–13), even though it was going to be some years before he obtained the throne.

David became a member of Saul's court but Saul became increasingly suspicious of him and of his triumphs, like his famous slaying of Goliath (17). Before long, Saul's mental state reached full-blown paranoia (18 – 20), so David was forced to flee and live on his wits as a fugitive, eventually in enemy territory (21 – 27). Those who protected him were dealt with viciously (22:6–23) and even his family had to live in exile for their own safety (22:1–5). Yet, twice when David had the opportunity to kill Saul he refused to do so (24 and 26), out of respect for the "Lord's anointed". David preferred to have God vindicate him, as in due time he would do.

The final chapters of 1 Samuel end with some startling contrasts. David, the king in waiting, listened to the voice of God through Abiathar the priest, and chalked up yet more victories (30). In spite of everything, he "found strength in the Lord his God" (30:6). Saul, the king on the throne, on the other hand, failed to hear the voice of God and disobeyed the law by seeking to summon up Samuel, the former priest, through a medium (28). In the face of the enemy, Saul chalked up, not victory, but final defeat – a defeat which cost him his own life as well as that of his sons.

David (2 Samuel)

Surprisingly, **David** grieved over Saul's death and even more over the death of Jonathan, Saul's son, who had been his friend (1). His accession to the throne was far from smooth. Initially, only the tribe of Judah recognised him, while Saul's troops refused to do so. But after much conflict and several assassinations (2 – 4), the nation eventually unified behind David; the elders came together to Hebron to anoint him king over Israel (5:1–5). Only one place now held out against David, and that was the fortress of Zion (Jerusalem). It was still occupied by the Jebusites and difficult to capture. David wanted to make it his capital, to keep the Ark of the Covenant there and eventually to build a temple there. Capturing it, then, was imperative and was to prove the final seal on the legitimacy of his rule (5:6–16).

Central to David's story, and to our subsequent understanding of God's work through Jesus, is the covenant God made with him, recorded in chapter 7. David asked God if he could build a temple as a residence for him. But God refused. He was too big to be confined in any house which humans could build. His refusal, however, was softened by a wonderful promise: David's throne was to be established for ever; his house and kingdom were to endure without end. No wonder David responded in a magnificent prayer of praise! The meaning of this promise was often later misunderstood by the children of Israel. To them it meant that a national and political dynasty was guaranteed permanence. It was an immense shock to them, therefore, when the nation was destroyed and the people exiled. But Christians have seen a deeper meaning to the promise and believe it to be fulfilled through Jesus, a descendant of David, who came to establish a kingdom which will never be overturned.

After briefly celebrating David's victories (8, 10) and noting his compassion towards Jonathan's disabled son (9), 2 Samuel's report on the rest of David's reign is less favourable. The promise God had made was quickly imperilled. Nothing is spared in telling us that this great king committed adultery, which, in turn, led on to murder (11). This called forth a right royal rebuke to the king by the prophet Nathan (12). In addition, effective ruler though David may have been, he seems to have been an ineffective father. One of his sons raped his half-sister while another of his sons, Absalom, set up in opposition to him (13 – 18). David even had to flee Jerusalem for his own safety. He failed as a decisive leader; only after Absalom's death did he end the uncertainty and return to Jerusalem (19:9–39). Absalom's rebellion, however, left a legacy, part of which was to have long-term consequences (19:40–43).

As David reviewed his life, he celebrated the God who had faithfully been his rock, fortress and deliverer (22:2). Yet the picture we're left with is one that reminds us how fallible he was. Right to the last he settled old scores and behaved foolishly in arrogantly conducting a census so that he could brag about his own strength rather than God's grace (20, 24). For all his greatness, we receive the firm impression that he was great because God had made him so, not because of his own abilities and talents.

Solomon (1 Kings 1 – 11)

The story continues in the books of Kings. David chose **Solomon** as his successor; Solomon indeed assumed the throne on his father's death, but not without first dealing ruthlessly with some of the opposition (1 – 2).

Solomon's reign is one of the most ambivalent in the Bible. On the one hand, it began well and accomplished some remarkable achievements. On the other, it descended into corruption and spiritual adultery, leaving, at the end, the unity of the kingdom in tatters.

When he began his reign, Solomon asked God for "a discerning heart to govern your people and to distinguish between right and wrong" (3:9). God agreed to give him wisdom and, impressed by his request, also promised him riches and honour, while warning him to obey the covenant (3:13–14). At first, all seemed well. Solomon exercised wise judgement in difficult cases (3:16–28), showed brilliant organisational skills and administered the kingdom efficiently (4:1–28), spoke many wise sayings (4:32), which are recorded in the book of Proverbs, engaged in embryonic scientific research (4:33–34) and grew wealthy (10:14–29). His reputation stretched far and wide (10:1–13). Unlike his father, he was given permission by God to build the temple; this he did on a grand scale, calling on some of the best resources in the ancient world to enhance its magnificence (5 – 6, 7:13–51). The Ark was brought to the temple, which was opened in an awesome ceremony. The climax of the celebrations came when God filled the temple with his glorious presence (8 – 9), claiming it as his own. At the heart of the dedication ceremonies was the theme of the covenant. God would bless his people if they walked in obedience to the covenant but would punish them if they did not. It was a great time for Israel, the highest point of its existence, and a time when joy abounded because of all the good things God had done for the nation.

Yet, even in the midst of the celebrations, some worrying notes about Solomon's reign begin to sound. To build the temple, he forced his subjects into labour, contrary to the law (5:13–18). The Israelites were back on the road to slavery again – just as Samuel had warned when they had pleaded for a king. And we're told, somewhat ominously, that although Solomon spent seven years building the temple, he spent thirteen years building his own palace (6:38 – 7:1)! It was clear where his real priorities lay. But his ultimate downfall came about through women. 11:1 tells us he "loved many foreign women", each of whom brought her gods with her. So before long, this wisest of all men was behaving in a spiritually foolish manner. His heart "turned away from the Lord, the God of Israel, who had appeared to him twice" (11:9). He conveniently put the covenant away in a drawer and forgot it. But God remembered it and exercised his righteous judgement. On Solomon's death, the kingdom would be torn in two (11:11–13). Never again would it reach the heights it had under David and Solomon.

The divided kingdom: 1 Kings 12 – 2 Kings 25

Rehoboam was Solomon's legitimate heir but showed not a whiff of the wisdom of his father. His threat to rule more oppressively over the united kingdom than Solomon had done precipitated a revolt and the split of the kingdom into two, thus bringing about God's promised judgement (1 Kings 12:1–24). The majority of tribes broke away, leaving Rehoboam to rule over a greatly depleted area, composed of the towns of Judah. Jerusalem was, of course, still in his hands. The other ten tribes of Israel gathered under the leadership of **Jeroboam**. He understood the significance of the fact that they had no access to the temple in Jerusalem, and so he set up a couple of alternative worship centres. In them he placed golden calves, similar to those their ancestors had known in Egypt (1 Kings 12:25–33). Israel's defection seemed complete. The ten tribes had broken away from the divinely chosen throne of David and now had thrown over the faith of their forefathers as well. Such outright rebellion against God could not possibly succeed: Jeroboam's dynasty was not to last (1.13, 14).

Meanwhile, Rehoboam was doing little better. His people also began worshipping foreign gods and, although he reigned for seventeen years, his kingdom was attacked by Egypt and its economy left much weakened (1.14:21–31).

Kings (and Chronicles, to which we will come later) weaves the stories of the kings of Israel and Judah together. Reigns are judged on the basis of whether they promoted the true worship of God or permitted and encouraged idol worship. On that basis, most of the kings were bad. After the rapid descent from the heights scaled under David and Solomon, both kingdoms spent much of the time in the valleys, with the clouds only lifted when there was a ruler who occasionally led his people back to the worship of the living God and to fresh obedience to the covenant.

The story of Israel

After Jeroboam, Israel was led by a number of kings who did evil in the eyes of the Lord. **Omri** stands out only because he built the city of Samaria (1.16:24). He was followed by **Ahab**, whose wickedness was aggravated by his marriage to Jezebel, a non-Israelite from Tyre and an enthusiastic follower of her own religion. Ahab encouraged the adoption of her religion among his people and provoked God to anger more than any of his predecessors (1.16:33). It was during his reign that the prophet Elijah appeared and spoke for God. First, Elijah forecast a drought (1.17) – which hit Baal-worship where it hurt, since Baal was supposed to be in charge of the weather – and then he challenged the representatives of Baal to a showdown on Mount Carmel, at which, as servant of the living God, he trounced them (1.18). Although Ahab successfully fought off an attack by an alliance of kings led by Syria, his spiritual apostasy and moral corruption continued (1.20–21). He was eventually killed in battle after typically ignoring the voice of a prophet (1.22).

Ahaziah followed Ahab and continued to worship Baal. He was punished for it by God, in spite of his abortive attempts to get Elijah to intercede for him (1.22:51 – 2.1:18). Elijah was replaced by Elisha, who performed a number of remarkable deeds during his time (2.2 – 8), including overseeing the healing of Naaman, a Syrian general, from leprosy (2.5). But the nation of Israel continued to be disloyal to God, under Ahaziah and then his son **Joram**, until Elisha anointed **Jehu** as king. Jehu was God's instrument for the destruction of the house of Ahab (2.9 – 10). He also massacred the prophets of Baal and led a partial spiritual reformation, but it didn't go as far as throwing out the golden calves which Jeroboam had made.

From then on, for almost a century, it was all downhill spiritually for Israel. Evil king succeeded evil king, with only the barest minimum recognition of the living God, as when **Jehoash** showed respect to Elisha when he was dying (2.13:14). This was the case even when the nation fared well. Under **Jeroboam II**'s long reign, for example, Israel became prosperous and enjoyed a number of military successes (2.14:23–29) but the people still practised evil and refused to listen to the prophets Amos and Hosea. It was said of every one of Jeroboam's successors that "he did evil in the eyes of the Lord". During this time, Assyria, a new political power, had been growing in strength. The end came for Israel when Assyria invaded the land, laid siege to Samaria and dragged the population off into exile (2.17:1–6). These events were not, however, the mere outworking of international politics. Kings tells us they happened because God had finally lost patience with his stiff-necked people and "removed them from his presence", so that only Judah remained (2.17:7–23). Israel was no more. The year was 722 BC. After that, the ten tribes faded into history.

The story of Judah

Judah lasted longer but was also eventually to experience defeat and exile. How did that come about?

Whilst the overall direction of Judah's spiritual life was one of apostasy and decline, Judah had the benefit of Jerusalem and the temple, and the occasional blessing of good kings, or at least better kings than Israel, which drew her back from the brink and reminded her of the covenant.

Rehoboam briefly remained loyal to God but then set up religious shrines which were unacceptable to him (1.14:22–24). **Abijah** reigned only briefly but continued his father's sinful ways (1.15:1–8). **Asa** (1.15:9–24), his successor, however, was mercifully different. During his reign, he removed the pagan shrines and even deposed the Queen Mother for practising foreign worship. He was plagued by border problems with Israel but entered into wise alliances, with the result that Judah grew in prosperity and strengthened its fortifications. He left Judah a much better place than he had found it. **Jehoshaphat**, his son, walked in his father's footsteps (1.22:41–50). For 25 years he stood against pagan worship, built up a strong military presence, engaged in education and appointed good judges. He did what was right in the eyes of the Lord.

Unfortunately, the same could not be said of his son **Jehoram**, who married into King Ahab's family and encouraged idolatry (2.8:16–24). **Ahaziah**, who reigned very briefly after Jehoram, was one of the same kind (2.8:25–29). For a time afterwards, Judah was ruled by **Athaliah**, his mother. She pursued an aggressive policy of Baal-worship and slaughtered all legitimate opposition, except for one young child, Joash (2.11). Godly leaders acted courageously to ensure the overthrow of Athaliah and the accession of **Joash**, then only seven, to the throne. He reigned for 40 years and initially was a great king, even repairing the ruined temple. But when Jehoiada, the high priest and his wise guide, died, Joash turned and forsook God (2.12).

Amaziah followed and took some corrective action, without completely wiping out idol worship (2.14:1–22). The next king was **Azariah** (2.15:1–7). He is better know as Uzziah because of Isaiah's famous experience in the temple, mentioned in Isaiah 6. He reigned for 52 years and was a good and strong king. Under him the nation experienced military success, growing prosperity, significant advance in its infrastructure and, in large measure, loyalty to God. Sadly, his achievements went to his head and led him into pride. So his success was tarnished at the end, as God disciplined him and inflicted him with leprosy. **Jotham**, whose reign overlapped with his father's, was a good king (2.15:32–38).

The next king, **Ahaz**, however, was one of Judah's worst (2.16). His spiritual betrayal even led him to sacrifice his own children to foreign gods. Facing military opposition all round, he sought protection from Assyria but at the cost of stripping the temple of many of its precious objects. Thankfully, after 19 years, Ahaz was succeeded by **Hezekiah**, one of the best kings Judah had (2.18 – 20). He also had to face the challenge of Assyrian aggression. On one occasion, the Assyrian army came right to the walls of Jerusalem and attempted psychological warfare to get the city to capitulate. But, encouraged by Isaiah who prophesied Jerusalem's deliverance, Hezekiah prayed. That very night, the Assyrian army was miraculously annihilated, without a weapon being used. God had truly kept his covenant. But Hezekiah, like Azariah before him, fell into the trap of pride and also ended his reign under a shadow.

Manasseh, who followed, is a byword for wickedness (2.21:1–18). Kings has nothing good to say of him and records only the way he ruined the nation spiritually, morally and in every other conceivable way. The account of his reign in Chronicles does, however, speak of his repentance at the end and of God's remarkable grace in allowing him to rescue something from the disaster he had caused (2 Chronicles 33). Be that as it may, his son **Amon** perpetuated the old evil ways to such an extent that even his own officials conspired against him and assassinated him (2.21:19–26).

Josiah, his son, was Judah's last hope (2.22 – 23:30). Although young, he was to preside over a spiritual revival in Judah. This began when a book of the law (almost certainly Deuteronomy) was found. Its message was taken seriously and led to the renewing of the covenant, the refurbishment of the temple and the resumption of worship. The people had not known such joy for a long time. Nevertheless, Josiah's reign was only a brief climbing of the hill again before Judah descended back into the valley. The revival was not deep enough to cause the people really to turn back to God long-term, nor to stem God's anger at the way in which they had flouted the covenant for so long in previous times.

Four relatively short reigns follow – those of **Jehoahaz**, **Jehoiakim**, **Jehoiachin** and **Zedekiah** (2.23:31 – 24:20). None proved loyal to God and each increasingly faced the squeeze from surrounding nations. In the power play between Egypt, Assyria and Babylon, it was Babylon who was to win: in 587 BC, after most of Judah had already been captured, Jerusalem was destroyed by the Babylonians. The temple was ransacked and then set on fire, the king taken captive, the royal family and officials executed and the population deported. So we read the fateful words, "So Judah went into captivity, away from her land" (2 Kings 25:21). It was just what the terms of the covenant had promised.

Where do the books of Chronicles fit in?

The observant reader who has been following the Bible along-side the story above may have noticed that a detail about the life of the kings was occasionally included which is not found in the books of Kings. That is because there is a second account of the period of the monarchy in the Bible, in the books of Chronicles. These books cover the same territory as Kings but from a slightly different perspective.

The opening nine chapters consist of lists tracing people's

family history from Adam through to after the exile in Babylon. To us they may appear boringly irrelevant. But we should remember that such lists are about real people. Just think of the interest many show today in tracing their own family trees. They serve as a witness to the faithfulness of God. The rest of 1 Chronicles deals with David's reign. 2 Chronicles 1 – 9 records the reign of Solomon. The rest of 2 Chronicles is about the reigns of the kings of Judah up until the exile.

The fact that the kingdom of Israel is ignored is significant. The Chronicler shares with Kings a belief in the importance of the children of Israel obeying the covenant. But he has particular concerns. He believes that true kingship is only to be found in the family line of David. And he believes that true worship is only found in the temple. The way in which the temple is treated by the kings of Judah therefore becomes the measure of everything in his account. Given this, the Chronicler sometimes gives us fuller accounts than the parallel reports in Kings, and sometimes briefer accounts.

We cannot be sure when these books were written, although it is likely to have been after the Jewish people had returned from exile in Babylon (more of which in a moment). They draw on a wide range of sources and seem to be aimed at giving the small Jewish group who were seeking to rebuild the nation a sense of their history and of what was important about their worship as it was being reconstituted. These books do not pretend to be a neutral reporting of facts. They use history selectively but not inaccurately as a spiritual object lesson.

What about Ruth and Esther?

Two short books which are found in the historical section of the Bible bear women's names and have women as their principal characters.

Ruth is set in the time of the judges but is thought to have been written much later, because it explains customs (4:1–12) which would have been well known if the book had been written earlier. It is the sad but noble story of a woman from Moab.

The family of Elimelech and Naomi migrated to Moab from Bethlehem in search of food. While there, one of their sons married a local girl, Ruth. All the men in the household died, leaving Naomi and her daughter-in-law without any means of support. When Naomi decided to return home to Bethlehem, Ruth was determined to go with her, even though she was under no obligation to do so. For a time, their desperate financial condition continued, but Ruth's loyalty to Naomi was eventually rewarded when, according to the customs and laws of Israel, she married a relative called Boaz, who became her "kinsman-redeemer". Together they had a son who was the grandfather of King David.

So Ruth, the woman from outside Israel, takes her place in the list of those who were ancestors of Christ (Matthew 1:5), together with two other unlikely women, Rahab and Bathsheba. The story shows how God's love extends beyond the borders of his covenant people. It also demonstrates God's great concern to act as a redeemer or rescuer to those in trouble.

Esther enjoys the reputation of being the only book in the Old Testament not to mention God. Even so, his presence is everywhere in the book. It was probably written after the exile and concerns a plot to destroy the Jews, hatched during the Persian period.

By a strange but providential turn of events, Esther, a Jewish woman, became queen. When her uncle Mordecai discovered a plot to assassinate King Xerxes, or Ahasuerus, the intelligence information was conveyed to the king via Esther and the conspirators were caught and hanged. Meanwhile, an official called Haman was setting in motion plans to exterminate the Jews. Xerxes, however, remembered that he had never rewarded Mordecai for his loyalty; when he did reward him it whipped Haman up into a frenzy of hatred. Haman built a gallows on which he looked forward, with some relish, to hanging Mordecai.

Mordecai persuaded Esther to use her influence with the

king, a task which was not quite as straightforward in her day as it might seem to be now. But she combined both feminine charm and diplomatic skill to tell the king what was going on, with the result that Haman was hanged and the Jews were granted freedom and protected status (8:11). The Jews were authorised to take vengeance on their enemies, which they did on the appointed day. Whilst the number killed seems high (9:5–10), it was nothing in comparison with the number of Jews who might have been slaughtered, had Haman's plans come to fruition.

These events explain the origin of the annual Jewish Feast of Purim, when Jews celebrate deliverance from their enemies. It is a remarkable story of God's providential care for his people and a story which, because the Jews have frequently found themselves to be the object of genocide, has continuing relevance.

The exile

Resuming the main storyline, the people of Judah were deported to Babylon in three segments in 597 BC, 587 BC (the year Jerusalem fell) and 582 BC respectively. Exile was to last for half a century, or 70 years in round Biblical terms. Conditions in Babylon do not appear to have been unduly harsh. They lived in what might be described as a liberal internment camp. Even Jehoiachin, the last surviving king of Judah, was released after 37 years in prison and treated with some dignity.

But the exile threw up urgent questions for the people of Judah. What had happened to God's promise that David's family would rule for ever? Why did the Babylonian gods seem to be more powerful in the affairs of the world than their God? How was their God to be worshipped when there was no temple in which to do so, no ark, and no possibility of offering sacrifices as once they had done?

There is no history book which records the Jews' experience in exile but a picture of it can be gained from reading the books of Jeremiah, Ezekiel, Daniel and the latter part of Isaiah. These books seek to interpret the meaning of what was happening in exile. They present it as a punishment for Judah's sin. They provide a sense of realism about the captives' situation but also inspire hope for the future by presenting a vision of a restored nation and temple. The exile, although painful and serious, was not God's last word to his chosen people.

In the absence of the temple cult, other things became important in Jewish worship. In the absence of one kind of sacred space (the temple) the Jews emphasised the value of another kind of sacred space by stressing the importance of Sabbath observance. In the absence of sacrificial ritual, they emphasised the importance of the study of the law. These features came to shape the Jewish faith and left their mark on it long after the exile was over.

The restoration: Ezra and Nehemiah

The exile came to a remarkable end. Babylon fell to the Persians in 539 BC without a fight. A year later, Cyrus, the Persian king, decreed that captive people could return home and their gods could be returned to their own shrines. The Cyrus Cylinder, a cylindrical stone recording this event, can be seen in the British Museum today.

The story of the return is recorded in the books of Ezra and Nehemiah. These constitute one book in the Hebrew Bible and form part of a continuous story with Chronicles, which, having passed over the exile, mentions Cyrus's edict in its closing verses. Unfortunately, the books are a bit difficult to sort out as far as their chronology is concerned. But it would seem that a group of exiles returned to Judah under the leadership of Zerubbabel in 538 BC or thereabouts. Ezra led a further group back about 80 years later. Finally, Nehemiah took a party back in about 445 BC.

In comparison with the size Judah once had been, the number of people returning was small. The need to grow food and rebuild ruins meant that re-establishing the nation was tough. Their difficulties were compounded by the jealousy of neighbouring people. The first group to return made a start on rebuilding the temple but quickly became discouraged. Their efforts had to be rekindled by the prophets Haggai and Zechariah in 520 BC. These prophets challenged the people not to put their own interests first and assured them that "The glory of this present house will be greater than the glory of the former house" (Haggai 2:9). But to the small band of returnees, it certainly did not look like it.

Ezra and Nehemiah record the gradual progress of rebuilding the temple and the city of Jerusalem, as well as the hardship and opposition people faced in doing so (Ezra 3 – 6, Nehemiah 1 – 6). But they do more than that. They also record the building of the returning exiles into a people, a nation, once more. Central to that was their reading of the book of the law, their recommitment to the covenant, their reforming of unacceptable practices and their re-establishing of the Passover feast (Nehemiah 8 – 10, 13; Ezra 9 – 10).

The prophet Malachi gives us some insight into the life of the people after that time. They continued to struggle with spiritual poverty and the need to overcome economic poverty. The visions of Daniel (7 – 12) give us an inkling of what is to come later. Otherwise, the story falls silent – for 400 years. The last word of the Old Testament is one pronouncing judgement yet again. But it is a judgement which is suspended and is conditional on the prophet Elijah returning first, before the judgement falls. That word of slender hope reaches across the chasm of four centuries until the silence is broken: the voice of John the Baptist, the new Elijah, is heard, preparing the way for the coming of the Messiah.

The covenant is about to take on a new form.

5

The Spiritual Writings:
Job to Song of Songs

Five books of the Old Testament, all different from each other, are collected together in a section known as the "Writings". Some of them are also known, because of their style, as "wisdom literature". They reveal the inner heart of Israel's faith in God. In doing so, they express praise and adoration, celebrate love and faithfulness, record victories and miracles and give voice to thankfulness and confession. They also reveal the struggles of faith, as when Job is perplexed by apparently undeserved suffering, the writer of Ecclesiastes by the futility of life, and the authors of some of the Psalms by the injustices of life. Proverbs gives us yet another perspective on the faith of Israel, as it illustrates how fearing the Lord will affect the way we live in the routines of our ordinary lives.

The Spiritual Writings:
Job to Song of Songs

In Jewish thought, the Old Testament was divided into three sections. After the Law and the Prophets came the Writings. It is to these we now turn. The Writings are composed of the books of Job, Psalms, Proverbs, Ecclesiastes and Song of Songs. Although it is obvious that they differ considerably from each other, it is even more obvious that they differ from the rest of the Old Testament. They do not contain the sort of history which we find elsewhere, nor do they report the sayings of the prophets. Three of them – Job, Proverbs and Ecclesiastes – belong to a type of literature which was widely known in the ancient world, called "wisdom literature". The book of Psalms is composed of 150 poems and looks very much a like a hymn book. Song of Songs is a celebration of life and sexuality, and is in a class of its own.

Books of wisdom

Wisdom literature reflects on life. At first sight, it does not contain the sort of revelation from God which can be found in the Law or the Prophets, nor does it trace the events of God's dealing with his people as one finds in the historical books. The teaching of the wisdom books appears to emerge from ground level – from wise people observing both human life and the natural world, and making some almost common-sense observations about it. These books are concerned with how the world works, meaning, in the main, the world of individual humans and their relationships.

Similar books existed among the Egyptians and the Babylonians. In fact, the sayings of Agur in Proverbs 30 and the sayings of King Lemuel in Proverbs 31:1–9 were borrowed from elsewhere. That raises the question as to whether or not these books are really secular books, perhaps with a thin layer of Jewish religion laid over them. But no ancient person would have thought in secular terms, as we understand it today. It would have been inconceivable to leave God out of the picture. Ecclesiastes cannot do so, however hard the writer tries. This book concludes that the world may not make much sense *with* God, but it makes even less sense without him. And Job and Proverbs have God firmly on the agenda. Indeed, the basic idea of wisdom is to have respect for God. "The fear of the Lord is the beginning of wisdom, and knowledge of the Holy One is understanding." This saying, from Proverbs 9:10, could serve as a title for all three wisdom books. The air these books breathe is filled with God.

What is more, anyone who comes to look at these works in depth soon begins to see the multitude of connections between them and the terms of the covenant and the preaching of the prophets.

The wisdom literature, then, is not spiritually inferior to the rest of the Old Testament. Its subject matter makes it wonderfully accessible to people. We can see our own lives and struggles reflected in these writings and identify with the comments, often wry comments, of their authors. They draw us in and open up a godly perspective on life that, left to ourselves, we might never conceive.

Job, Proverbs and Ecclesiastes differ from each other both in terms of style and in their particular subject matter. So let's look at each one in turn.

Job

The book of Job deals with the problem of suffering. It's a moral drama rather than an historical record. It is a bit like a play on the radio which explores a moral conundrum from a number of angles, except that Job mainly records debate rather than action.

It takes its title from the name of its main character. We cannot tell when Job lived. The story seems set in the distant past, probably the time of the Patriarchs, but many of the usual markers which might help us to place it more precisely are missing. Job is a god-fearing and clean-living man who is careful to offer all the correct religious sacrifices, even if they aren't needed. It is implied that, as a result of his keeping of the covenant with God, he is blessed with a large family and a prosperous livestock business (1:1–5). One day, Satan, the Accuser, brings his name up in God's court. He alleges that Job only serves God because of what he gets out of it. Remove all the benefits, Satan claims, and Job would soon be cursing God. So God agrees to Job being put to the test, providing only that Job's own life be spared (1:6–12). Within a short time, a series of calamities fall on Job, wiping out his fortune, his family and finally his own health (1:7 – 2:8). All he is left with is a disgruntled wife and three friends, who are going to prove anything but helpful in understanding what is going on (2:9–13).

Job, of course, knows nothing of the explanation and has no clue as to why such misfortune has fallen on him. But, while refusing to curse God, he naturally expresses his bewilderment and his anguish. It would have been better, he protests, if he had not been born, rather than being born to this.

The main part of the book (3–31) records the conversations Job has with his friends about the suffering he has inexplicably experienced. Each time the friends speak, Job replies to them. The conversation, which becomes increasingly passionate, goes round the circle three times in all. To start with, Job agrees with the generally accepted position that he must have done something wrong to cause his downfall. But as his friends dispense their "wisdom", so he is driven more and more to reject it. His experience tells him that their explanations don't hold water. Something else must lie behind his suffering.

It is difficult to characterise the three friends and their individual arguments. Eliphaz appears to be the oldest and begins respectfully. But he is dominated by the thought of the sinfulness of human beings and so, when Job protests his innocence, becomes more and more insistent that Job must have sinned, even inventing, in his final speech, a catalogue of horrible sins which Job must have committed (22). What comes through Bildad's blustering manner is his great concern to defend the justice, majesty and perfection of God in the face of sinful humanity (see, especially, 25). Zophar is the harshest and most impatient of them all. He tells Job that he deserves to suffer more than he does. Job's friends, who never once demonstrate an ability to listen to him, have a very black and white view of the world, one which Job knows just doesn't fit reality.

Throughout the discussion, Job rejects their arguments. While continually protesting his innocence, refusing to stage a false repentance and mostly expressing confusion, his speeches contain some wonderful glimmers of hope. He is sure that eventually God will come to his aid and vindicate him (19:25–27). He knows that God's ways are beyond human understanding and, consequently, all that people can do is to fear the Lord and shun evil (28).

When his three friends have finished, leaving Job in a worse state than he was before, a fourth person enters the scene: Elihu says very little that has not been said before, but he says it with tremendous passion. He has been described as "the original angry young man" because of his tirade against Job. His rebuttal of Job and his defence of God's greatness and wisdom leaves us with a very unattractive picture of God. To Elihu, God is so mighty that he has no care for puny, whinging, little people like Job. He puts God well beyond the reach of human beings. Job should not expect an answer from God and is foolish to think that God would bother with the likes of him.

Just at that moment, God steps in (38 – 41). He gives to Job the most wonderful panorama of his creation. He reveals himself to be an awesome Creator who has made creatures that Job has never thought of, let alone seen. His strength is such that neither powerful animals nor raging rivers can get the better of him. So Job is indeed reduced in size before God. He comes to terms with his own unworthiness and confesses that he has often spoken without knowing what he is talking about.

Do these chapters say his friends were right after all? No. God's speech to Job is far more gracious than theirs. When God finishes speaking with Job, he expresses his anger at the friends for not speaking rightly of him (42:7–9). But God's final word to Job comes in the form of an action: Job's family are restored and his prosperity doubled (42:10–17). And he is given a good long time to enjoy his renewed good fortune.

Job teaches us how little we know of the mystery of suffering and how unwise we are to pretend otherwise. Suffering is clearly not always a punishment for sin, and to pretend that it is is to speak foolishly and cause unnecessary hurt. We must learn from Job's friends never to let cold, doctrinal correctness get in the way of listening to people and their struggles. Nor must we ever think that God is incapable of speaking for himself.

Proverbs

Although Proverbs 1:1 states that what follows are the proverbs of Solomon, son of David, it is evident that what follows is the compilation of several collections of wise sayings, from different times and places, brought together, perhaps, by Solomon's wise men.

The purpose of the book is to reflect on how ordinary, day-to-day life can be lived in such a way that its path is as smooth and trouble-free as possible. Its central theme is that to live wisely is the most likely way to bring about success and happiness, while to live foolishly is to court trouble, worry, inconvenience and even disaster. But what does it mean to live wisely?

It means to live in "the fear of the Lord" (1:7; 2:5; 9:10; 15:33) since "the fear of the Lord is a fountain of life" (14:27). By "fear", Proverbs does not mean the cringing fear of an abused child, but the loving respect of a child who is secure in its parent's company. It simply means that the God who made the world knows best how we should live within it.

The subject matter of Proverbs, then, is very mundane. It is about choosing the right girlfriend or wife. (It is understandably written from the male viewpoint, given the patriarchy of the time.) It is about how we answer people and use our tongues. It has a lot to say about our emotions, about joy, hope, anxiety, celebrating success and restraining anger, and even more about issues of character such as self-discipline and cultivating contentment. The blessings and dangers of both wealth and poverty are mentioned. It deals with the questions of times and seasons, and suggests that advanced planning is wise. It comments on family discipline and business ethics. It commends industry and derides laziness. Neighbours from hell, and friends from heaven, all get a look-in. Addiction, adultery and alcohol are on the list. So too are love, loyalty and faithfulness. You'll find here how to be a wise king or a wonderful wife. Just about all of life is to be found covered within its 31 chapters.

How can it cover so much? The answer lies in the way it deals with the issues. You will not find here a tidy systematic arrangement of topics which explores them in depth. Rather, its style is to offer advice in the form of short, pithy sayings – compact, general sayings, with no room for careful qualification. Most are just two short lines in length, with the first line backed up by, expanded on, or contrasted with, the second line, all of which are ways of strengthening the point. An example of the first kind is: "Honest scales and balances are from the Lord; all the weights in the bag are of his making" (16:11). Or, "Pride goes before destruction, a haughty spirit before a fall" (16:18). An example of contrasting lines is: "When the storm has swept by, the wicked are gone, but the righteous stand firm for ever" (10:25) "The sluggard craves and gets nothing, but the desires of the diligent are fully satisfied" (13:4). The sayings on the various topics are then peppered throughout the book, without, to us, any terribly obvious sign of organisation.

Proverbs sometimes calls on the help of the animal kingdom to teach human beings how to be wise. Ants, for example, are a wonderful model of industrious organisation (6:6; 30:25). But conies, locusts, lizards, lions, peacocks and goats are all part of the creation and serve as lessons for "the human zoo".

In spite of the scattering of topics throughout the book, the reader becomes familiar with certain characters who crop up again and again. Most obviously, there is the fool. But there is also the seductress, the hot-head, the sluggard, the drunkard, the greedy, the flatterer and the mischief-maker, among others. The book commends none of these, nor their lifestyle. Instead, its aim is to educate people to live wisely like the righteous ones.

The book divides in the following way:

1 – 9	Introductory proverbs and spiritual foundation
10 – 22:16	Various proverbs "of Solomon"
22:17 – 24:22	The sayings of the wise
25 – 29	More proverbs from Solomon
30:1 – 31:9	The wise sayings of Agur and King Lemuel
31:10 – 31	A picture of a good wife

One chapter deserves special mention. In chapter 8, "wisdom" is spoken of as if she is a lady; her virtues are extolled in a hymn of praise. (Wisdom was widely considered to be feminine in the ancient world and thus balanced some of the masculine characteristics, such as strength.) Her value far exceeds any earthly fortune. She has a role in guiding ordinary people and kings alike. Of particular note is the place claimed for her in creation. Her origins stretch back before the foundation of the world: she is spoken of as a special, intimate companion of God who was with him as the world was brought into being. At all times, God has acted in harmony with wisdom. It is not surprising, therefore, if his creatures find themselves living more comfortably in his world if they too live in harmony with wisdom. In this picture of wisdom, the early Christians found something that reminded them of Jesus. In Colossians 1:15–17, for example, they present Jesus as the fulfilment of all that is claimed for wisdom in Proverbs.

The basic message of Proverbs is summed up in these words: "Trust in the Lord with all your heart and lean not on your own understanding; in all your ways acknowledge him, and he will makes your paths straight" (3:5–6).

Ecclesiastes

There is no other book like Ecclesiastes in the Bible. One scholar has called it "the joker in the Old Testament pack". Again, it stands in the tradition of the wise philosophers encouraged by Solomon; it reflects widely and deeply on life, before drawing some conclusions about it. Its title comes from the Greek translation of the Hebrew word *Qoheleth* and means something like "teacher" or "preacher" – this person is mentioned in the opening verse.

Its tone is quickly apparent when, in the opening chapter, it denounces the whole of life as "meaningless". The writer's experience suggests that there simply is no purpose to life and, however hard one tries, it's impossible to make sense of it. He looks at the various solutions people have put forward and concludes that they don't hold the secret to life. Wisdom (1:12–18; 2:12–16); pleasure-seeking (2:1–3); investing yourself in great projects (2:4–11); throwing yourself into work (2:17–23); gaining promotion in society (4:13–16) and the amassing of wealth (5:8 – 6:12) all prove pointless. Time seems fixed (3:1–15) and human beings little different from the rest of the animal kingdom (3:16–22). Fate seems in charge or, even worse, oppression seems to roam freely in the world (4:1–12). Good people often get what the wicked deserve and *vice versa* (8:1–17). In the end all die. The good, the bad and the ugly share a common destiny (9:1–12). What's the point in it all?

Overall, the book paints a very sceptical view of life. But that's not, in fact, the total picture. However much the writer might want to throw over traditional faith, he cannot bring himself to do so. If life fails to add up, it adds up even less if you leave God out of the picture. So, woven throughout his doubt-riddled book, is the voice of faith, which he finds impossible to silence. One phrase, which he uses well over 20 times, is the phrase "under the sun" (1:3, 9, 14 etc.). It acts a bit like a short-hand code. He seems to be saying that life is pointless if you only judge it by what happens "under the sun", that is, on the horizontal level. But when you put the reality of the God who lives "above the sun" into the picture, life looks a little different; things do not prove as pointless.

Far from being an atheist, the writer repeatedly draws attention to the fact that God gives people enjoyment in life. Even if God remains a mystery (3:10–11) and even if he puts human beings to the test (3:18), he also gives them the gift of eating, drinking and finding satisfaction in their work (3:12; see also 2:24; 5:18; 8:15 and 9:7). These soundbites are accompanied by more extended passages where he speaks of God. In chapter 5 he writes of our need to approach God in worship cautiously, for we need to stand in awe of him. In chapter 11, from verse 7 to the end of the book, he encourages young people to remember their Creator before age takes its toll. His final word is one about God bringing everything into judgement.

This sideways look at life, which dares to call into question traditional religious faith, is one which many contemporary people find it easy to identify with. But the book is like one of those visual illusions which can be seen in two ways. Is it a candlestick or two faces looking at each other? Is it a youthful beauty or the haggard face of an old woman? Some people will read it and see its scepticism uppermost. Others will read it and see that what it is really saying is that a deep trust in God wins through, whatever the struggles and enigmas we face in life.

Books of poetry

The Psalms

The book of Psalms consists of 150 poems. "Psalms" simply means "hymns". In the Hebrew it is known as a book of praises. They range from the very short (117) to the extremely long (119). They were written over a long period of time – from the early days of the monarchy to late on in the Old Testament period – before being collected together in their present form. Various ideas have been put forward about how they came to be written. Some scholars have tried to identify the particular historical event which lies behind each of them. But most would now agree that, even if this can be done occasionally, it is an impossible, and probably misguided, task in general. There is no need to box the psalms into past history, since they are timeless in their message and meaning.

It is more likely that the Psalms were gradually collected together and edited to form something of a hymn-book to be used in the temple. If so, they would have had three particular roles to play as God's people gathered for worship. First, many of them would have been used in regular worship as vehicles of praise, thanksgiving or, on occasions, anger and lament on behalf of all the people. This group also includes some of the Psalms which have more of a teaching, meditative role. Second, some of the Psalms would have been used for special occasions; they relate either to the great festivals of Israel or to public ceremonies which involved the king. A third group would have had a more personal use: enabling the individual worshipper at the temple to pray for healing from sickness, ask for help in difficulty, express a vow to God or offer thanksgiving for a particular blessing. The Psalms are very comprehensive, covering a complete range of human experience and engaging with a complete range of human emotion. It is for this reason that so many people have found them indispensable to their Christian lives down the years.

There are various ways in which the Psalms can be broken down into smaller sections. The book itself indicates that it is a collection of five smaller books, possibly in an attempt to echo the five books of Moses. The sections are 1 – 41; 42 – 72; 73 – 89; 90 – 106; 107 – 150. Psalms 1 (and probably 2) form an introduction to the whole book; the final Psalm (150) is designed as a fitting conclusion to the total collection.

Seventy-three are headed "A Psalm of David". But this does not necessarily mean that they were composed by him so much as that they belong to him. They were perhaps written by one of David's staff, collected by them or dedicated to him as king. The same is true of Korah and Asaph, whose names are attached to other mini-collections of Psalms. They may have composed some of the Psalms that bear their names, but others on their staff or even their successors would have composed the rest after a style and in a manner of which they would have approved.

Book 1 is composed mainly of the Psalms of David which, in so far as one can characterise them, seem to be mainly personal in nature.

Book 2 consists of songs associated with the sons of Korah, the worship leaders of Israel, a further group of the Psalms of David and a collection of the songs of Asaph. They are still personal, but not individual in the way that the Psalms in book 1 are, and they have a much more public "feel" to them. They consistently use the title Elohim, that is, God, instead of Yahweh, the more personal name of the Lord.

The Psalms in book 3 are mainly attributed to Asaph, a contemporary of David, who was in charge of the worship in the temple in Jerusalem (1 Chronicles 16). Some of them seem to be alluding to events long after his time, so they may have been composed by graduates of his school and by his successors who were associated with the temple choirs.

Book 4 contains few titles, but what seems to bind them together is the story of the Exodus and God's dealing with his people in the wilderness. It has been suggested that they might have played a particular part in the worship at the Feast of Tabernacles.

Book 5 is more of an assortment, although it does involve a further collection of David Psalms (138 – 145), the Hallel (Hallelujah) Psalms (112 – 118, 145 – 150) and the Songs of Ascents, which the pilgrims would have sung as they made their way up the hill of Zion to the temple (120 – 134).

The poetic nature of the Psalms travels well across the gap between Hebrew and English. The use of repetitions and catchwords, the ways verses develop their thought by a second line either paralleling or contrasting with a first, and the overall structure and movement within a Psalm can easily be discerned. Nonetheless, some elements are lost to us. One device the Psalms often use is that of an acrostic, where each verse, or section of a Psalm, begins with a different Hebrew letter. Psalm 119 is an acrostic. But that, together with many of the word plays, is lost in translation.

The different themes of the Psalms are perhaps best illustrated in the selective, and anything but exhaustive, list that follows:

Praise Psalms
General: 100, 111, 145, 150
Creation: 8, 19, 104
Salvation: 78, 105, 106, 111, 149
Pilgrimage: 24, 84, 122, 134

Royal Psalms
The early Christians applied some of these to Jesus.
2, 18, 20, 21, 45, 61, 72, 89, 101, 110, 132, 144

Psalms of penitence
6, 32, 51, 130

Laments
For the community: 12, 44, 58, 60, 74, 77, 79, 90, 137

For the individual: 42 – 43, 52, 54, 86, 88, 141

Expressions of faith
4, 11, 16, 23, 27, 42, 46, 62, 90, 91, 115, 121

Expressions of anger
35, 59, 69, 70, 109, 137

Working through bewilderment
22, 73

God is the focus of the Psalms. They speak again and again of his nature and his activity. He is the one who creates, rules, rescues, judges, and makes himself known. He is living, eternal, unmovable, holy, righteous, just and powerful. But above all, he is the God of unfailing, covenant love whose word is utterly dependable. The Psalms can claim what they do because of the covenant.

However much the Psalms may have served as the hymnbook for people of the Jewish faith (and still do so), they have an even deeper meaning for those who are followers of Jesus, since many of them find their ultimate fulfilment in Christ.

Song of Songs

Many people find this book the most extraordinary in the Old Testament and are unsure quite what to make of it. The title simply means the "best of songs". It is linked to Solomon but was not necessarily written by him. It belongs to a type of literature which fits the cultured circles of his day.

The book is a series of love poems which concern a bride and a groom, or a lover and his beloved. But since the original lacks any headings or stage directions, as it were, it is not always easy to sort out who is speaking. At times, friends come into the picture, which complicates it even further. The poems are evocative and passionate. They spare no blushes. Set in a pastoral community, they make good use of images from the fields and the animals around. Goats, gazelles and stags all make their appearance. So, too, do raisins, apples and grapes. All the senses are called into use.

There is no clear agreement about how the book is organised. Chapters 1 and 2 record the pleasure the bride and groom find in each other. Chapter 3 recalls a dream the bride had about the coming of her lover. Chapter 4 is the voice of the groom extolling the virtues of the bride and his desire for her. Chapter 5 picks up the bride's dream again but then (5:9 – 6:3) gives way to a discussion among her friends as to why she considers her lover superior to others. 6:4 – 7:9 is a further celebration of the beauty of the bride by the bridegroom. The longing they feel for each other, which is the main subject of the remainder of the book, is summed up by the bride's words in 7:10, "I belong to my lover, and his desire is for me."

The book is an uninhibited celebration of love, sexual attraction and personal intimacy. Pious Christians have sometimes been too embarrassed to admit that and so have often spiritualised its meaning, seeing it as an allegory of the love Christ (the bridegroom) has for the church (his bride). They may not altogether be wrong in reading it this way, even though the book should also be taken at its face value: as a poetic outworking of our male and female sexuality programmed into us by our Creator (Genesis 2:23–24). The reason Christians may not be wrong in applying it to the love of Christ for his church is that the Jews used the Song of Songs in a similar way. Curiously, they read this Song at the start of the Passover celebration. Why? It has been suggested they did so because the Passover liturgy could easily become an empty liturgical ritual, a mere formal celebration of the covenant of God's love for his people. But reading the Song of Songs during the festival would remind Israel that the covenant was anything but a mere formal agreement between a nation and her God. It would, as Eugene Peterson has put it, help people to understand and realise "the covenant from the inside" (*Five Smooth Stones for Pastoral Work*, Eerdmans, 1992, p. 45). It would rekindle the flame of love between God and his people and save the liturgical ritual from lacking the passion which God's gracious kindness to Israel deserved. Once again, although the covenant is not actually mentioned in the text, the idea of the covenant is the background against which it is written.

These five books, although very different from each other, are marked by spiritual wisdom – a wisdom which sometimes grapples with the hard questions of life and sometimes can soar to the heights in celebration. They are of use in personal devotion and public worship. These writings address the inner questions of the spiritual life and are a vital complement to the story told by the historians and the sermons preached by the prophets.

6

The Revealing Prophets:
Isaiah to Malachi

God led the people of Israel by means of kings, priests, wise men and prophets. Prophets stood outside the systems of power and were called to voice God's verdict on the behaviour of his people and the policies of her rulers. They were often deeply unpopular and suffered for their interference. As people, they varied immensely. Some of the early ones worked miracles, some thundered denunciations and some lovingly tried to coax the people back to God. The writings of three major and twelve minor prophets are recorded for us. We explore their message here in the order they appeared in history, not in the order they come in the Bible. This means we can interpret them in the context of their times and understand them in relation to their contemporaries.

The Revealing Prophets:
Isaiah to Malachi

Prophets were people who spoke for God. They did not necessarily foretell the future, although some did. They addressed
the present, expressing God's view about an individual person's
action or a whole nation's way of living. Israel had prophets
long before the emergence of the writing prophets, who are the
subject of this chapter. Moses was a prophet (Exodus 18:15,
18; Deuteronomy 34:10), as was Deborah (Judges 4:4). Elijah
(1 Kings 17 – 2 Kings 2) and Elisha (2 Kings 2 – 13) were
among the best known from earlier times. But there was also
Nathan (2 Samuel 7, 12), Ahijah (1 Kings 11:29), Micaiah (1
Kings 22) and a woman, Huldah (2 Kings 22:14).

We get hints that there were more prophets around than we
know about (2 Kings 4:38; 6:1). Some were thought to be
prophets because of their wild and wacky behaviour (1 Samuel
19:19–24). Some probably sought to be prophets because of the
status it would give them in the eyes of others. This raised the
problem of how to distinguish between a true prophet who really was speaking for God, and a false prophet who was just
dreaming up his own words and claiming they came from God.
Deuteronomy 13 is the key to answering that question. The first
test was whether the prophet encouraged people to be loyal to
God or to follow other gods. The second test was the test of

time. Did their words come true or not? The test was never about how they received their message, whether through dreams or visions, but what the content of their message was.

By the eighth century BC there emerged a group of prophets whose messages were written down and preserved for future generations. Four of them are spoken of as major prophets – Isaiah, Jeremiah, Ezekiel and Daniel (although Daniel is in a slightly different category); twelve of them are known as minor prophets. "Major" and "minor" refers to the length of the books that bear their names. The order in which they come in our Bibles is not the best chronological order. I propose to introduce them in their historical order (as far as we can tell), so that their message can be related more easily to the history of Israel.

Prophets of the eighth century

After a period of relative political calm, from the middle of the eighth century, about 745 BC onwards, Israel and Judah faced increasing threats from the rising power of Assyria. They sometimes looked to Egypt for help, but Egypt was really as much of a threat as Assyria and never served Israel well. Israel's significant location on the trade routes of the ancient world made her prosperous. But this wealth was not shared out evenly, so a few people grew wealthy while others struggled with crushing poverty. Religiously, things looked good, on the surface. The rituals of worship were observed regularly. But two things put the true religious situation in a different light. First, Baal and idol worship continued unhindered alongside the pure worship of God. Second, while the people kept up the observance of the ceremonies, they ignored wholesale the observance of the moral and ethical demands of the covenant. They forgot that God was more interested in how they lived in the marketplace than in the sacrifices they offered in the shrine. Oppression, injustice, dishonesty and immorality were rife. This is the situation into which God sent his prophets.

Amos

Amos – a shepherd, not a professional prophet – was a south-
erner, but he was sent by God with a message of judgement to
the northern kingdom of Israel. He preached around 760 BC
when Jeroboam II was presiding over a period of great afflu-
ence. He spoke at the shrine in Bethel and in the capital city,
Samaria.

Three things stand out in his message. First, God is the Lord
of all nations and holds them all accountable for their moral
behaviour. He is no tribal deity, whose influence is restricted to
Judah and Israel alone. So, as we read in 1:1 – 2:3, the kingdoms around Israel, such as Syria, Philistia and Moab, are
called into God's courtroom to receive their sentence for atroci-
ties they have committed. Judah follows and is condemned for
rejecting God's law and for idolatry. Judah's northern neighbour, Israel, would have warmed to Amos's denunciation of her
neighbours. But Amos's strategy is to tighten the noose around
Israel and so he turns, from 2:6 onwards, to expose her crimes
as well. God will judge the people of Israel too. They will have
no place to hide.

The second main theme, characteristic of the other eighth-
century prophets as well, is that God expects his people to
behave ethically. The covenant is as much about being good,
living honestly, and behaving justly, as it is about offering sacrifices. The people of Israel, says Amos, have ignored that.
They have trampled on the needy and then deprived them of
justice in the courts. They let the rich live luxuriously indulgent
lives at the expense of the poor. They do not seem to know how
to do right and are biased to evil. God is sick of their religious
rituals – in their place he urges them to "let justice roll on like a
river, righteousness like a never-failing stream" (5:24).

The third main theme is that of the Day of the Lord
(5:18–24; 8:9–14). Many people are complacently taking
refuge behind the Day of the Lord, believing it will mean that
God will come to their aid and vindicate them against any

opponents, presumably because they have kept up their religious rituals. But Amos warns them that the Day of the Lord will not bring them the comfort they expect. It will be darkness, not light, "pitch-dark, without a ray of brightness" (5:20).

Amos speaks in urgent and graphic terms. His language is vigorous and vehement. God is a roaring lion (3:4). Virgin Israel is to fall, never to get up again (5:2). The people are reclining at ease in Zion (6:1). God is measuring them with a plumb-line, as if they are a wall, to see how upright they are (7:7–8). They are a basket of ripe fruit, ready for picking (8:1–2). They will experience destruction, a destruction that will be almost, but not quite, total (9:1–10).

He holds out a slender thread of hope. Beyond the judgement, he foresees a day of restoration when "David's fallen tent" will be erected once more and days of secure prosperity will be experienced again (9:11–15).

Amos's message, not surprisingly, caused a panic among Jeroboam's officials, who instructed him to shut up (7:10–17). The demand, however, succeeded only in calling forth further prophesies of judgement from his lips. His prophecies came true when Samaria was sacked and Israel went into exile in 722 BC.

Hosea

Hosea also prophesied to Israel, to which he belonged, around the same time as Amos. The nation was going rapidly downhill. His message, although realistic about judgement, is one which emphasises God's wounded love.

The prophecy is initially shaped by Hosea's own story. God instructs him to marry Gomer (possibly a prostitute), even though she is going to prove unfaithful to him (1). Hosea's own experience becomes a parable for the contemptuous way that Israel, in their worship of the Canaanite deity Baal, is treating God. Even their children's names become a reminder of the situation. God is a betrayed husband, trying to woo his people back into his affection. If given the chance, he would prove merciful (2). Chapter 3 briefly mentions Gomer's return to Hosea and the attempt to rebuild their marriage.

The main part of Hosea, from chapter 4 on, details the charges God has against Israel (4); announces God's judgement against them (5, 8–10, 13); and reports on Israel's stubborn refusal to return to God (6–7). Through it all, God's reluctance to let Israel go is apparent. She need not destroy herself, as she is doing, by her spiritual adultery and moral disobedience. God pleads, like a passionate lover who has been deeply hurt by his partner's behaviour, and like a wounded parent who has been rejected by her children, for Israel to return in repentance to him. Chapters 11 and 14 reveal both the husband-heart and the father-heart of God in the most moving of ways.

Isaiah

The major prophet in this group is Isaiah. The book comes at the head of the prophetic books. Many would consider that appropriate, since it is unmatched in its reach and its vision of God.

Isaiah received his call to prophesy in 640 BC, the year that King Uzziah (Azariah) died. He preached for over 40 years. Like his contemporaries, he knew that his message would not win him popularity. Nonetheless, he felt compelled to serve the one he frequently referred to as "the Holy One of Israel". (This title for God occurs 29 times between 1:4 and 60:14). He prophesied against the background of growing Assyrian power and the downfall of the kingdom of Israel. The empire-building ambition of Assyria had implications for Judah too and exacerbated economic divisions and social injustices among her population. Its growing influence also left its mark on the religious life of Judah. Although temple worship continued, other gods were worshipped at the same time and little heed was paid to the ethical dimensions of the covenant. A brief reformation took place under Hezekiah (encouraged by Isaiah), but it had no lasting effect and its benefits were quickly obliterated by Manasseh.

Isaiah is a long and complex book. It has often been said that it falls into three sections, although there is no universal agreement about this. The sections seem to relate to different periods in Israel's history. They are distinguished by their subject matter and their writing style. Some scholars argue that this means there must have been more than one Isaiah. But such a conclusion is unnecessary, unless one rules out the ability of a prophet to predict the future under the inspiration of God's spirit. The sections are 1 – 39; 40 – 55 and 56 – 66.

Chapters 1 – 39, *the first section*, are set in the days of the kings. They record Isaiah's preaching in Jerusalem. The opening chapters (1 – 5) deal with the sins of Judah and the way in which God will execute his judgement on her. The short song of the vineyard (5) portrays Judah as a vineyard which has received the most lavish care, only to repay its owner by producing rotten fruit. Jesus developed this picture in reference to his own work, in Matthew 21:33–41. Chapters 6 – 12 concern the sufferings which are to be inflicted on Israel. But they contain the hope that a remnant of faithful people will be preserved and eventually ruled over by a wonderful king who will re-establish David's throne and bring peace (7:14; 9:1–7). This is followed by a song of praise. The next chapters, 13 – 23, bring together a collection of prophesies condemning the surrounding nations. No nation is exempt from God's watchful eye, since the whole earth belongs to him. Chapters 24 – 27 stand out as different from the rest. Known as "the apocalypse of Isaiah", they stretch language and imagination to its limits and look forward to the time when God will fully and finally establish his righteous rule. Further warnings follow (28 – 35), both for Judah and for the other nations, but the future salvation of God is also spoken about. The first major section of the book ends with an account of the way Hezekiah dealt with the Assyrian threat (36 – 39).

Throughout this section, Isaiah longs to impart good news to his people, but he knows that integrity demands that he can offer no immediate hope. Indeed, their attempts to shore up alliances with other nations against Assyria only make the matter worse, for they betray a lack of trust in God. But he can foresee a future, once God's anger at their sin is past. Indeed, he is so confident that he causes his words to be written down (30:8–14), so that the future will prove him right.

The second section, chapters 40 – 55, deals with Israel's exile in Babylon. It speaks of the time when punishment will come to an end and the people of Israel will experience salvation. It begins with a message of comfort – a comfort which is well grounded in the power of God (40) who is the helper of Israel (41). They will be restored to their position as servants of the Lord and a light to the nations (42). The language of the first exodus is revived and intensified to portray their return from exile (43:14–21). They are assured that their election remains secure (44:1–5). Stress is laid on the power of God to forecast and also arrange the future, in contrast to the impotent idols which the Babylonians worship, false gods who can do neither (44:6–28; 46). His power is so great that even the pagan King Cyrus of Persia, who authorised the Jews' return, is spoken of as God's anointed one – literally, messiah (45:1). Whether he knows it or not, Cyrus is a mere instrument in the hands of the living God. Even the downfall of Babylon is foreseen (46). And so in chapter after chapter the salvation brought about by the Holy One of Israel is celebrated.

One strand which runs through these chapters is that of the "servant", mentioned in 42:1–4; 49:1–6; 50:4–11 and 52:13 – 53:12. At one level, the "servant" is Israel: these "songs", as they are called, speak of the way in which Israel's suffering played a role in bringing about justice in the world. At another level, Israel clearly does not exhaust the image of the servant. The fullest expression of the image is seen in Jesus, as he himself hinted (for example, Mark 10:45) and as the early church leaders openly recognised (see Acts 8:26–35).

The final section, chapters 56–66, captures the scene back in Jerusalem once the exile is over. Israel has a role in bringing others to worship the one true God (56:1–8). Although written in a faith-inspiring way, these chapters are also realistic. So chapters 56 – 59 deal again with the question of sin and remind the people that it is not religion but a humble spirit and a righteous lifestyle that God desires. The final chapters (60 – 66) are visions of the new Jerusalem in all its glory, of cosmic renewal and of God's judgement on all that is evil .

Micah

Micah preached in the southern kingdom of Judah during the reigns of Jotham, Ahaz and Hezekiah, in about 742–687 BC. He was a contemporary of Amos, Hosea and Isaiah. The cities of Jerusalem and Samaria are the main focus of his message. The sins Amos condemned in Israel were obviously just as common in Judah and invoked God's condemnation there as well. The most brilliant summary of the message preached by all these prophets is found in Micah 6:8: "And what does the Lord require of you? To act justly and to love mercy and to walk humbly with your God."

Micah begins by envisaging the disaster which God is going to bring against Israel and Judah, a disaster he possibly lived to see (1 – 2). False prophets tried to silence him (2:6–11), but their attempt backfired as he roundly condemned rulers, prophets and priests alike for their spiritual complacency and failure to exercise justice (3). The case against Judah and Samaria is set out with transparent force in chapter 6. God does not require more sacrifices from his people. He requires more justice and integrity. The prophet mourns the social disintegration he sees around him (7:1–6) and can do nothing but "watch in hope for the Lord" (7:7).

The dominant colour of Micah's prophecy is dark. But the darkness is incapable of suppressing the light altogether. However despairing he may be, hope cannot be snuffed out. He sees beyond the punishment of the not-too-distant future, to a time when God will rule over a remnant of his people in Zion. The day will come when God will judge the nations who have ridden roughshod over Judah – these nations, in turn, will be punished. Judah will be restored even if, to the human eye, only by a small group of unpromising people (4). The secret of their success will lie in the rise of a new ruler who will be born in the backwater of Bethlehem. This king will shepherd Israel in majestic strength and provide them with security and peace once more (5:1–5). Micah's words are the ones we so often read in Christmas services, since they speak of the coming of Jesus, the baby born to be king, centuries later, in Bethlehem.

The prophecy ends on a hopeful note (7:14–20). God will show himself again to be a God who does wonders, just as he did when he delivered Israel from Egypt. When that happens, the nations which now seem so proud will be humbled and ashamed. And they will recognise that only one God pardons sins and forgives iniquities like that. There is simply no god who is in competition with him (7:18).

Jonah

Most scholars think that Jonah belongs to a later time, but we deal with it here because the only other mention of Jonah in the Old Testament (2 Kings 14:25) places him in the reign of Jeroboam II, and his prophecy concerns Nineveh, which was destroyed by the Babylonians in 612 BC. It is a story, not a collection of addresses.

Nineveh was the capital of Assyria, the nation which destroyed Israel and attacked Judah. It was known for its cruelty. Yet God commands Jonah to go there and preach that he loves Nineveh like he loves his own people; Jonah is to tell its people that they, too, can experience God's forgiveness if only they will repent of their sins. Jonah refuses the assignment and hurries away in the opposite direction from Nineveh, to ensure that he cannot be press-ganged into service. But he does not reckon on the power of God. A furious storm almost sinks the ship he is on; calm is only restored when Jonah is thrown overboard in an attempt to remove the source of the problem (1). Astonishingly, he doesn't drown. God arranges for him to be cared for inside a huge fish for "three days and three nights"

(1:17) and then be spewed up on the shore.

Chapter 2 records the prayer Jonah prayed from inside the belly of the fish, asking God to preserve him.

Once on dry land, he is given a second chance to accomplish his mission (3). He proves an effective preacher and the people of Nineveh, from the king downwards, turn in repentance to God. God has mercy on them (3:10).

Rather than celebrating his success, Jonah stomps off in disgust. Chapter 4 tells us the real reason why Jonah did not want to accept the assignment in the first place. He knew God too well. He knew that God would forgive these wicked people of Nineveh if they repented and, in his thinking, that was not fair. They deserved punishment for what they had done, not compassion. God's grace was outrageous! Where was justice?

Jonah hides from the sun in the shade of a vine, which God uses to teach him another lesson. The vine dies, leaving Jonah without shelter and causing him to grumble more, full of self-pity. God points out that if Jonah can show such concern for a vine, surely he, the Lord, was right to show concern for a great city like Nineveh. If it was wrong for the vine to perish, why should it be right for the citizens of Nineveh to be destroyed?

The question we should be asking of this little book is not whether Jonah was literally swallowed by a big fish and kept safe in its stomach, as many have asked, for that may side-track us from its message.[1] We should ask whether we have learned the lesson that the book teaches. God's grace is scandalous. It reaches out and forgives all sorts of people who do not deserve forgiveness, including you and me. That is the meaning of grace. Grace is love which is undeserved. We should read it as a great missionary tract and accept more readily the mission God has given us to preach the good news to those who do not deserve it.

Leading up to the exile

The eighth-century prophets, whose message stressed the failure of God's people to keep the ethical requirements of the covenant, were followed in the next century by a group of prophets who were increasingly occupied by the theme of judgement, although they each had a particular angle on it.

Nahum

Nahum's brief prophecy, in contrast to Jonah, celebrates the downfall of Nineveh. Nahum warns that it will share the fate of the Egyptian city of Thebes, which was destroyed in 663 BC. So the addresses must have been delivered after that and before Nineveh's destruction in 612 BC. It presents Nineveh's undoing as the result of God's personal intervention in history. Through it, God is putting an end to those who have plotted against him and also avenging his people who, one day, will have their splendour restored.

Habakkuk

Habakkuk struggles with the justice of God. He asks God why he tolerates wrongdoing and why he is silent in the face of wickedness (1:1–4, 12–17). Habakkuk prays when Assyria is still firmly in control of affairs. God replies to him that things are going to occur on the international stage which will cause utter amazement. Assyria's power is not secure and, before long, the Assyrians will encounter the stronger power of the Babylonians – "that ruthless and impetuous people" who are "feared and dreaded" (1:6–7) – who will destroy them.

Habakkuk's complaints are bluntly expressed and his desire for God to do something is intense. Yet, although his challenging of God may be described as robust, he never gives in to unbelief. Throughout, he maintains a genuine faith, which results in the book having much to say about the holiness and glory of God (1:12–13; 2:14; 3:2–16). The outcome of his struggles is seen at the very end of the book, where he voices one of the most wonderful confessions of faith in the whole Bible (3:17–19).

The book is also known for the importance of one verse. 2:4

says, "the righteous will live by his faith." Paul takes up and develops those words in a major way in Romans (see Romans 1:17; 4:1 – 5:1).

Zephaniah

Zephaniah prophesied in Josiah's reign, before Josiah launched his reforms. So the date must be about 640–621 BC. Like Amos, he speaks of the Day of the Lord as a day of judgement against Judah and Jerusalem (1). But before the axe falls, he pleads with his people to "Seek the lord", to "seek righteousness [and] seek humility" in the hope that "perhaps you will be sheltered on the day of the Lord's anger" (2:3). Judgement is also pronounced on the neighbouring nations (2:4–15). Finally, after further charges are brought against Jerusalem's leaders, Zephaniah foresees a time when the shame will be removed from Jerusalem and a humble remnant will experience God's presence there, with joy, once again (3).

Jeremiah

Jeremiah's prophecy spans the last days of Judah and the time of the exile. His ministry is one of uprooting and tearing down, as much as of building and planting (1:10). His prophecy is closely bound up with his own life and personality. In addition to the major book which bears his name, there is in the Old Testament a short book of poems which expresses grief at the destruction of Jerusalem. This is the book of Lamentations. While it does not say who the author is, it was eventually attributed to Jeremiah.

Jeremiah was a reluctant prophet who was never at ease in his role (1; 11; 12; 15; 17; 18 and 20). Something of a depressive, intense character, his life was marred by suffering. God forbade him to marry and have children, in order to signal that Judah had no future (16). Consequently, he bore alone the rejection he frequently faced and the charges of treason which were brought against him (26 – 28, 37 – 38).

When Judah began to fall, Jeremiah could have left

Jerusalem for an easy life in Babylon. But he chose to remain in his homeland. When the Babylonian governor, Gedaliah, was assassinated, the people who had not yet been taken into exile fled to Egypt; Jeremiah went with them (42 – 43). There, as far as we know, he spent his remaining days, writing to those in exile and advising them not to think that God would come to the rescue too quickly; they should rather settle down in Babylon, since they were there for the long haul (25; 29).

Jeremiah's prophecies are characterised by vivid imagery, some of which arises from his childhood days in the country-side. They are also characterised by strange actions, as he con-veys his message through the medium of drama – actions such as deliberately ruining a garment (13), visiting a potter's house (18), wearing a yoke (27 – 28) and buying a field (32). His words were recorded, and put into some sort of order, by Baruch (36; 45).

His complex book may be briefly (and roughly) outlined like this:

1	His call
2 – 4	The sins of Judah and a call to repentance
4 – 10	God's anger and sorrow at false worship
11 – 20	Scenes from Jeremiah's life; prophesying disaster
21 – 29	Rejection of King Zedekiah; prophecies of the exile
30 – 33	Prophecies of restoration
34 – 37	Jeremiah persecuted
38 – 45	The final days of Jerusalem
46 – 51	Prophecies against the nations
52	An account of the fall of Jerusalem

Among the many rich chapters in the book, four stand out. In chapter 7, Jeremiah preaches a sermon at the entrance to the temple, warning Israel not to put false hope in religious rituals. Simply having the temple does not mean they are immune from God's judgement. Chapter 29 contains a letter Jeremiah wrote to the exiles. It contains great advice for Christians who, as a small minority, live in their own secular exile today. Chapter 31:33–34 looks forward to the days when God will bring a new covenant into force; this he did in the coming of Jesus Christ. Chapter 36 is different, and crucial. It is a dramatic account of King Jehoiakim burning the scroll which contained Jeremiah's prophecies and which had been read aloud in the temple. This act symbolises Judah's rejection of the word of the Lord; it sealed their fate.

Obadiah

Obadiah's short vision comes right at the end of this period and has one theme. As Jerusalem fell to the Babylonians, the Edomites, their near neighbours to the south east, did nothing to help them. Their indifference was made worse by the fact that, as descendants of Esau, they were relatives of Israel. Obadiah warns them that, although they may currently boast of their secure position, high in the hills, they are not impregnable. God will punish them in the future for their failure to help their kin. They, too, will experience the Day of the Lord first-hand. This prophecy came true when Edom was overrun in the fifth century BC. By then, as Obadiah had foretold, the Jews had known a reversal of their fortunes and had been restored to Jerusalem.

Joel

It is difficult to place Joel, since there are no clear indications in his messages as to when they might have been preached. But the subject suggests that an invasion by a foreign army is imminent and so it fits the period leading up to the exile.

Joel is spurred into action by an invasion of locusts who consume everything in their path (1). The days are days of darkness. They result in famine, destruction and despair (2). Joel uses this experience as a parable of the Day of the Lord and an early warning of another invading army which is to bring destruction on God's people. Courageously, he announces that the Lord will be at the head of that army, since it will be meting out his judgement against Jerusalem (2:11). Like the other prophets, Joel takes no pleasure in the nation's destruction and pleads with the people to return to God in repentance while there is still time (2:12–17). Fearing that they will not repent, he, like the other prophets, looks beyond the period of judgement to a time of restoration when God will deliver Jerusalem, pardon their sin, dwell among his people and pour out his spirit in a new way (2:18–32; 3:17–21). It was this part of Joel's prophecy that Peter saw as coming to fulfilment on the Day of Pentecost (Acts 2:16–21).

The exile and its aftermath

Ezekiel

As a young man, Ezekiel found himself in exile. His hopes of serving as a priest in the temple seemed dashed. But at the age of 30 (1:1), God called him instead to serve as a prophet (1 – 3).

The first part of Ezekiel's well-structured book has much in common with the message of other prophets, especially Jeremiah, whose younger contemporary Ezekiel was. Chapters 4 – 24 were spoken before the fall of Jerusalem, condemning Israel's sin and warning her of the coming exile. Chapters 25 – 32 contain prophecies against the nations surrounding Israel. Chapter 33 – 37 explain the fall of Jerusalem but also begin to sound a note of hope, which becomes increasingly prominent. Much of this is simply a record of Ezekiel's (sometimes demanding) sermons. But it would be wrong to dismiss him as unexciting.

The later part of the book contains some unique material. In chapters 38 – 39 he prophesies against Gog and Magog. These "apocalyptic" chapters envisage a battle to end all battles being played out between the allied armies of the north and God's people. Against all odds, the evil forces who oppose little Israel are defeated by God's sovereign intervention. Ezekiel portrays their defeat in the most horrific way. Revelation picks up this prophecy and uses it to picture the final defeat of Satan (Revelation 20:7–10). These chapters have been a happy hunting ground for those who want to predict the outcome of contemporary world events, but it is doubtful if they should be used in this way. They are straining to capture in human language God's ultimate defeat of evil.

Chapters 40 – 48 also contain unique material. Here Ezekiel has a vision of the restored Jerusalem, and especially of the temple. The detailed blueprints he gives are typical of the interests of a priest. But he is not simply interested in bricks and mortar, nor in sacrifices and offerings. What excites him most is that the glory of the Lord has returned to Jerusalem (43), and the city is teeming with life again (47).

Ezekiel is more than a preacher. Like Jeremiah, he indulges in prophetic actions – such as those in chapter 4 and 5 where he builds a model of Jerusalem under siege, lies on his side and shaves his head to portray Jerusalem's downfall. But chiefly, Ezekiel is a visionary who perceives things through the eyes of a priest. So his principal visions relate to God's awesome holiness and his dwelling in the temple. In chapter 1 he has a vision of God, reigning on his heavenly throne. In chapters 8 – 10 he records his vision of idolatry in the temple, of the execution of idolators and of God's glory departing from the temple. In chapter 37 he has a vision of a valley of dry bones. God breathes life into his dead and desolate people. From chapter 40 onwards, it is a divine vision that he sees, not a human dream, of the rebuilt temple and, most significant of all, of God's glory returning to it. Fittingly, the whole prophecy ends with the picture of the new Jerusalem, which is now named "The Lord is there".

Daniel

Daniel is considered to be the last of the major prophets in the Greek version of the Jewish Bible. In some ways it is a difficult book.

It is set in the period of the exile but, for various reasons,

many scholars argue that it was not written until two centuries
before the coming of Christ. They do so because it is "apocalyptic" literature, a type of crisis literature which was more
common from 200 BC to AD 200. Apocalyptic literature sets
out fantastic visions of the future, and especially of the last
days, which stretch the imagination. Daniel is the best example
in the Old Testament and is complemented by Revelation in the
New. The book also contains some records of events that are
otherwise unknown. Darius the Mede, for example, (5:31
onwards) is not referred to anywhere else. Some have suggested this might be a code name for Cyrus. A further reason for
thinking the book was written later is that in chapter 11 it clearly refers to events which took place in the days of Antiochus
Epiphanes in the second century BC; many do not believe that
a prophet could have predicted those events four centuries in
advance. But these arguments are not conclusive, and an earlier
date, set in the exile, can easily be defended.

The book falls into two clear sections. Chapters 1 – 6 contain
heroic stories about Daniel and his friends in exile. Chapters 7
– 12 contain visions of the future. Both sections have one clear
message of encouragement: God's people should remain loyal
to God and persevere, even in the face of stiff opposition, for
God is sovereign and will reward his people in the end.

The stories of Daniel and his friends Shadrach, Meshach and
Abednego are well known. These four young men, who have
come from the cream of Jewish society, find themselves making difficult choices in exile. They refuse to compromise their
faith, but this, rather than provoking the wrath of King
Nebuchadnezzar, earns them his respect (1). So they serve
among the elite leadership of the nation. Daniel earns further
favour when he interprets a dream which Nebuchadnezzar's
usual advisors cannot understand (2). But, living in pagan
Babylon, Daniel's friends find themselves before long either
having to worship the King's golden image of himself or dis-
obeying the law. They choose the latter and end up being
thrown into a fiery furnace as a result. But God remarkably

delivers them (3). The king has a further dream about a tree. When Daniel interprets it, he informs the king that his pride is going to cause God to discipline him by inflicting a mental illness on him for a period, a sentence which is fulfilled twelve months later (4).

Later, another king, Belshazzar, sees the fingers of a human hand writing on the wall during a feast. Again, Daniel is called to interpret what it means: he warns the king that his rule has been "found wanting" and that God is going to bring his kingdom to an end (5). That very night the prophecy comes true: Darius the Mede (probably, as mentioned, a reference to Cyrus of Persia) invades and takes over Belshazzar's kingdom.

Daniel's long years of faithful service to the ruling powers make him an object of jealousy and a plot is arranged to get rid of him. Darius is tricked into signing a decree which means Daniel will inevitably be sentenced to death by being eaten alive by lions. But Daniel, like his friends before him, experiences a remarkable deliverance, as God closes the lions' mouths, with the result that he is set free and vindicated (6).

These stories remind one of the much later story of the athlete Eric Liddell, who refused to run for Britain in the 1924 Olympic Games if the race was held on a Sunday. The story has been made famous by the film *Chariots of Fire*. Liddell's motto came from 1 Samuel 2:30: "Those who honour me, I will honour." So it proved to be, for in the finals of the 400-metre race he broke the world record and took an Olympic gold medal. The story of Daniel and his friends, centuries earlier, bears witness to the same truth. Those who live by this spiritual principle will not be disappointed.

The visions which follow look to the future. In chapter 7, the four beasts Daniel sees stand for four successive empires which will wax and wane. The lion is Babylon; the bear is Media; the leopard is Persia. The fourth is a horrendous beast, which outdoes the previous empires by its opposition to God and symbolises Greece. But, as the awful reality of its terrifying power is being contemplated, Daniel perceives another reality, the reality of God's throne and of his victory over those who oppose him. The words in Daniel 7:13 about "one like a son of man, coming with the clouds of heaven" become significant words for understanding the work of Jesus later on.

The next vision, in chapter 8, of a ram and a goat focuses in on part of the previous vision and celebrates the downfall of the Greek empire. In chapter 9, Daniel takes us back to the year 538 and prays for an end to the period of exile, which in round figures lasted 70 years, or a lifetime. In chapter 10, Daniel is given an insight into the normally unseen battle that rages in the heavenlies. God's people, he learns, are the object of such hate that some are out to destroy them. But they are also the object of special protection provided by the archangel Michael. Chapter 11 further details the struggles God's people experience during the Persian and Greek period before, in chapter 12, Daniel finally prophesies their ultimate deliverance.

The visions, no less than the stories, encourage God's people to hold on and remain faithful. If they do, the day of resurrection will come and they will "shine . . . like the stars for ever and ever" (12:3).

Haggai

Ezekiel's grand visions were one thing. The reality for the returning exiles was another. As people straggled back to Jerusalem they found it hard to re-establish themselves, hard even to survive. In the circumstances, they chose to build their own houses first and secure a decent financial foundation for their lives. Only after that were they going to start rebuilding the temple. But into the situation stepped a quiet little prophet called Haggai, in 520 BC. He told them they had their priorities wrong. God's house should come first (1). He did not thunder at them. He gently asked them to work it out for themselves. "Look at the bottom line," he said. They had been working hard but gaining nothing. Perhaps they were working for the wrong things?

Three more messages followed from Haggai's lips. He provided motivation for those who thought the new temple they were building was not a patch on Solomon's temple. The glory of this house, he said, "will be greater than the glory of the former house". Indeed, it is just a foretaste of the end time itself (2:1–9). His next message warned the people of the contagious nature of evil and the need to live clean lives before God if they wanted him to bless them. Again, he argued, it was a lesson their own experience would teach them (2:10–19). His final message (2:20–23) endorsed the leadership of Zerubbabel, the governor, but did so in a way that points forward to the future Messiah whom God would choose to occupy the throne of David.

Zechariah

Zechariah was contemporary with Haggai. His work falls into two halves, with chapters 1–8 recording a series of visions, and chapters 9–14 a series of oracles. The very different style of the two parts has led to the suggestion that it was written by two people. But the concern of both parts is the same. Zechariah's burden is for God's people to live in a healthy state. In order to achieve that, Israel's enemies must be dealt with and Israel's own life must be kept clean and blessed by God. Both the visions and the prophecies are variations on that theme.

For all its difficulty, this prophecy contains a number of gems which have been widely referred to subsequently. The message of the Lord to Zerubbabel (4:6), "Not by might nor by power, but by my Spirit", has been a frequent reminder to Christians of the unconventional way in which God works and of the need to depend on him rather than human resources for success. The arrival of the Messianic king on the foal of a donkey as he enters his kingdom (9:9) anticipates Jesus's triumphal entry into Jerusalem on Palm Sunday. The picture of the shepherd being struck and the sheep being scattered (13:7–8) is echoed in Gethsemane. The 30 pieces of silver paid to Judas for betraying Jesus is foreseen in 11:12. Looking on "the one they have pierced" and mourning for him takes us to the cross of Calvary (12:10). Zechariah's picture of the Lord being king over all the earth (14) informs the vision of the book of Revelation.

If Ezekiel is seen as the architect of the temple's restoration, and Haggai its clerk of works, Zechariah is perhaps the artist. His word-pictures add colour and light, as Joyce Baldwin has suggested (*Haggai, Zechariah, Malachi*, Tyndale Old Testament Commentaries, IVP, 1972, p. 59), to an otherwise more plain account. But, like most art, its style and symbolism communicate to some people with brilliant clarity, while others are left to simply stand and stare uncomprehendingly before the pictures in front of them.

Malachi

The final word in the Old Testament, as arranged in the Christian Bible, belongs to Malachi. This is appropriate because of both its date and its message. The temple has by now been rebuilt and the book's concerns are similar to those of Nehemiah. So it is thought to be dated around 450 BC, making it the latest of the Old Testament prophets. Its closing verses predict that "the sun of righteousness will rise with healing in its wings" (4:2). They look forward to the coming of Elijah, who will prepare the way for the coming of the Lord himself (3:1; 4:5–6). So it looks across the centuries to the coming of Christ and to the covenant of salvation, which stands in contrast to the frequent message of judgement which has been heard in the Old Testament.

Malachi's days seem to be days of spiritual lethargy. The exile has come and gone. The temple has been rebuilt and the major challenges of the restoration faced and overcome. So what now? Without anything to keep them on their spiritual toes, as it were, the people have grown indifferent to God.

The language of love, found in 1:1–5, is the language of international treaties and covenants, not the language of sexual attraction or romantic affection. God is reminding the Jews of his covenant with Jacob in which he elected them to be his special people. Once more, however, they are defaulting on the agreement. The sacrificial animals they are offering are not of the best quality (1:6–14). The priests are misleading the people and causing them to stumble (2:1–9). The nation, as demonstrated by their attitude to easy divorce, is proving unfaithful (2:10–16). They are neglecting to care for the poor and vulnerable (3:5). And they are robbing God by their failure to give him all the tithes and offerings he is due (3:6–15).

Given all this, the Lord is weary of them (2:17 – 3:5) and threatens to come against them again in judgement. The Day of the Lord, fulfilled once through the exile, will come again. This time, the Lord will come in person to his temple.

When that day finally did come, it came in a totally unexpected way. Four centuries later, the voice of John the Baptist cried out in the wilderness for people to prepare the way of the Lord. The Lord did indeed come to his temple. But that is the story of the next chapter.

---

[1] Given the Christian belief that God created the world out of nothing, and raised Jesus from the dead, it is curious that many should stumble over the historicity of Jonah being swallowed and then safely disgorged from the stomach of a large fish. There seems to be no valid reason to question the historical trustworthiness of the account.

7

The Good News:
Matthew to Acts

Central to the whole Bible is the life, death and resurrection of Jesus Christ. The whole Old Testament prepares the way for it and, after the gospels, the rest of the New Testament builds on it. The four gospels record the ministry of Jesus, telling us not only the things he taught and the miracles he did, but also about the opposition he faced which led to his death. They end by recording his coming back to life, three days after his crucifixion, and his triumphing over all his (and our) enemies. The gospels have a great deal in common – especially the first three – as one would expect of accounts which are historically trustworthy. And yet they each tell his story from a distinct angle, giving us a very rich and full picture of "the gospel about Jesus Christ, the Son of God". Acts tells us the story of the early church in the years immediately following Christ's ascension.

The Good News:
Matthew to Acts

Now for the good news. With the gospels, a new day dawns. We enter a new stage in God's relationship with the people of the world. What the Old Testament had anticipated comes to fruition. The prophet who would speak the word of the Lord, who had been foretold by Moses and who was like Moses, only greater, appears. The sacrifices of the temple, which were signposts of a greater reality, are superseded by the reality itself – the sacrifice of Christ. The work of the priesthood comes to fulfilment in the work of one great High Priest. The throne of David is restored and David's great son, Jesus, sits on it to reign over an everlasting kingdom "that cannot be shaken" (Hebrews 12:28). The new covenant foretold by Jeremiah comes into force. The Day of the Lord has arrived.

The focal point of this new age is Jesus. He was born about 4 BC in the days of Caesar Augustus, and crucified in 33 AD when Pontius Pilate was the Roman governor in Judea. The dates tell us we are dealing with historical events, not made-up myths. The very existence of the dates tells us God came into our world and did something new among us. He did not fix things from a distance in heaven but, for a time, he took up residence among us. The change of date, from BC to AD, tells us he is the hinge of history.

126

Four gospels – Matthew, Mark, Luke and John – record the life of Jesus, telling us about his teaching and his actions, his stories and his relationships, his death and his resurrection. They are not straight biographies in our sense today. Which contemporary biographies spend so long on the death of their subject as these do? Nor are they a neutral record of what happened. They are designed to persuade us that he was the unique Son of God and that his life was good news for the world. "Gospel" simply means "good news".

Why four gospels? There are several answers to that question. One is simply, why not? Great figures often have more than one biography written about them. Why should not the greatest figure of history have four gospels written about him? The life of Jesus could not be exhausted by telling it in one book alone. John says that if everything Jesus did was written down, there would not be room in the world for all the books which would be necessary (John 21:25). Also, each writer, although writing for a general audience, was writing, as we shall see, from a particular angle. Without reading between the lines more than is justified, we can see that each author was concerned to let the life of Jesus speak to the particular situation and concerns which his original readers faced. Consequently, the gospel writers selected, from the many things which could be said, those things which were most relevant to their interests and expressed them in appropriate ways.

Neither this selectivity, nor the commitment they showed to Jesus, implies we have cause to question the truthfulness or historical reliability of what was written. The claims writers made about Jesus could easily have been contradicted or disproved when the gospels were published. But they were not. And although occasionally they differ in details from each other, even that does not undermine the trustworthiness of what they wrote. I find it helpful to view the gospels in the following way. The life of Jesus was, as it were, being played out in a public square surrounded on four sides by buildings. The gospel writers were each observing Jesus's life from a different side of the square. They saw, and recorded, the same events, but, since they were all looking from their own particular vantage points, they were bound to see and also express things in different ways.

The first three gospels, Matthew, Mark and Luke, are called "synoptic gospels" because they have so much in common. "Synoptic", literally, means "seeing with the same eye". In practice, it means these three gospels follow the same outline (synopsis) of Jesus's life. Although much debated, it is likely that Mark was the earliest gospel and served as the basis for Matthew and Luke. Matthew and Luke may both have had access to a second source, since they sometimes stand together in differing from Mark. This is a mysterious source called "Q". Q is not the figure who appears in James Bond films! The word comes from the German *Quelle,* which means "spring" or "source". This hypothetical source has never been found and is pure conjecture on the part of scholars. Matthew and Luke each have their own independent sources as well. All the writers would also have used the oral traditions which had collected around Jesus.

John differs from the other three gospels, as we shall see, in many ways. Apart from anything else, John is much more open, right from the start, about who Jesus was than the synoptic gospels are. The last of the gospels to be written, John is more concerned to reflect on and interpret the life of Christ than are the others. But all four gospels share a common aim: they are written to encourage belief in Jesus as "the Christ, the Son of God" (John 20:31).

Matthew: Jesus, the hope of Jews . . . and Gentiles

Matthew comes first in the New Testament not because it was the first to be written, but because it serves as the best pathway from the Old to the New Testament. Traditionally, the author of this gospel was taken to be Matthew the tax collector, mentioned in 10:3.

The gospel's primary aim is to present Jesus as the Messiah for whom the Jews had looked for a long time, so Matthew writes about themes which would be of special concern to the Jews. He explains most clearly how Christianity grew out of the Jewish faith and highlights the points of continuity and discontinuity between them. His gospel also guides the early Christians on how to deal with the issues thrown up by Jews and Gentiles, with their very different backgrounds, living together in the same church. How much respect, for example, should the Gentile believers show to the Jewish law? He guides them by pointing out the relevant aspects of the teaching of Jesus.

He accomplishes all this in a number of ways.

- Matthew quotes more often from the Old Testament than do the others, showing how the life of Jesus fulfils what it promised. Examples can be seen in 1:22; 2:5, 17, 23; 3:3; 4:14; 8:17; 12:17 and 21:4.

- Matthew begins by presenting Jesus as "the son of David, the son of Abraham" (1:1) and tracing his family tree back to those significant Jewish leaders.

- Matthew uses Jewish ways of speaking, for example, referring to the "kingdom of heaven" rather than the "kingdom of God", because this avoided using the sacred name of God directly (see 3:2; 5:19, 20; 8:11; 10:7).

- Matthew writes a lot about the law and its place among believers. The Sermon on the Mount, for example, has much to say on that subject (5:17–20).

- Matthew structures his gospel around five blocks of teaching (5 – 7; 10; 13; 18 and 23 – 25), almost as if providing a new Pentateuch (the first five books of the Bible) for the people of the new Israel.

- Matthew dwells on the tension between God's particular place for the Jewish people and their customs (15:24; 17:24–27), and God's universal love for all. Only Matthew includes the visit of the Gentile wise men at the birth of

Jesus (2:1). His gospel ends with the commissioning of the disciples to preach to "all nations" (28:19).

- Matthew alone includes mention of the church, as if it is already formed (18:15–20).
- Matthew uniquely confirms that the death of Jesus has inaugurated the new age by the occurrence of supernatural happenings on the first Good Friday (27:51–53).

Matthew's gospel is very well designed. Here it is in outline:

1 – 4	Birth, baptism and temptation of Jesus
5 – 7	First teaching section: the Sermon on the Mount
8 – 9	Mainly miracle stories, with a little teaching about discipleship
10	Second teaching section: sending out of the Twelve on mission
11 – 12	Dealing with questions and controversies
13	Third teaching section: parables about God's kingdom
14 – 17	Various miracles and teachings
18	Fourth teaching section: about the church
19 – 20	On the road from Galilee to Jerusalem
21 – 22	Jesus in the temple
23 – 25	Fifth teaching section: teaching about the end times
26 – 28	Crucifixion and resurrection

Matthew's gospel emphasises the need for radical discipleship. Jesus is a teacher who demands total obedience. His rule must come first. It is to be a priority second to none (6:33). The lifestyle of his disciples was to stand out in sharp contrast to the way most people lived their lives; their goodness would need to surpass that of the religious leaders of the day (5:20). Wherever one looked, his disciples were to be different: whether it be in their inner thoughts or outward actions (5:21–37); their attitude to the law or to enemies (5:38–48); their practice of devotion (6:1–18); their handling of money, anxiety and annoying people (6:19 – 7:6); or the foundation on which they built their lives (7:24–27). The calling of a disciple was not a calling to half-heartedness. Nothing less that the highest ideals would do (5:48).

Jesus provoked two reactions by such teaching. First, people responded immediately by expressing amazement that such things should be taught so authoritatively (7:28). Second, they reacted in the longer term by persecuting Jesus and those who sought to live by his teaching. Jesus warned his disciples that those who really followed him could expect an uncomfortable ride from their peers (5:11–12; 7:13–14). But then, as now, the rewards for obedience are out of this world (5:12).

Mark: Jesus, kingdom-making, kingdom-breaking

Mark is the shortest and most vivid of the gospels. Although it includes some of Jesus's most important teaching, it is essentially an action gospel. An early Christian writing states that Mark consists of Peter's memoirs about Christ. John Mark, a nephew of Barnabas, is mentioned in Acts 12:12, 25 and 15:37–39 and, according to 1 Peter 5:13, had a specially close relationship with Peter. If Mark did write down Peter's reminiscences as he recalled them, it would account for the swift-moving nature of the story, why the word "immediately" is frequently used, and its character as an eyewitness account.

Mark is a "lean" gospel. It has no room for anything to do with the birth of Jesus but jumps right into its subject. Here is good news about Jesus Christ, the Son of God, who announces that God's rule is about to be re-established on earth and the reign of Satan is about to come to an end (1:15). The early chapters demonstrate the clash of spiritual kingdoms, as Jesus sets about healing many people, delivering individuals from demons and even raising the dead (1:21 – 5:43). From the start, he encounters opposition from human authorities, as well as from Satan (2:6–7, 23 – 3:6). The level of conflict quickly rises until it reaches its climax in the crucifixion. It is through the cross that Satan's ultimate defeat is to be secured.

Jesus evidently is portrayed doing many wonderful things, leading people to believe that he was the Messiah. But the term "Messiah" was easily misunderstood. There was no way Jesus would conform to the popular understanding of the term and lead an armed rebellion to throw the occupying forces of Rome out of Judea. Consequently, he tried to dampen down false messianic expectations. He did so in a couple of ways.

First, he referred to himself as the Son of Man rather than the Messiah (e.g. 2:10, 28; 8:31, 38; 9:9, 31). The title comes from Daniel 7:13 and refers to the agent whom God appoints to bring about his sovereign rule in the world. Second, he sought to act wisely and not stir up the excitement of the crowd (1:45). He frequently encouraged those who had seen him at work not to tell others about what he had done (1:25, 34, 44; 5:34, 7:36; 8:30, 9:9 etc.). But all this was to no avail. Third, on three occasions he predicted his suffering and crucifixion (8:31; 9:31 and 10:45). His disciples found it hard to square such predictions with what they saw him doing and with their understanding of the Messiah. How could the one who was triumphant over evil and who was establishing God's kingdom with such power be defeated and subjected to death on a cross? What they did not yet understand was that it was through suffering, not by avoiding it, that the Messiah would finally bring about God's everlasting reign.

The tension between suffering and the power of Christ receives special emphasis in Mark. This may be explained by the fact that, as is often assumed, this gospel's first readers were undergoing persecution for their faith and it was written to encourage them.

There was much the disciples did not get right and Mark is not in the business of sparing their blushes. But, significantly located right at the heart of the gospel (8:29) is Peter's confession that Jesus is "the Christ", that is, the Messiah. Even if he went on to spoil it immediately by his overconfidence, his understanding of Jesus was right. He had correctly read the evidence he had seen. Jesus was the one who was bringing about God's kingdom.

Here is an outline of Mark's gospel:

1:1–13	Introduction: John the Baptist and Jesus's baptism and temptation
1:14 – 3:35	Initial activity in Galilee provokes opposition
4:1–34	Jesus teaches in parables
4:35 – 5:43	A series of miracles in Galilee
6:1 – 8:26	Growing opposition, further miracles in Galilee
8:27–38	Peter's confession of faith
9:1–13	The transfiguration
9:14 – 10:52	Jesus instructs his disciples
11 – 12	Jesus in Jerusalem
13	Jesus teaches about the future
14 – 16	His betrayal, death and resurrection

The ending of Mark's gospel is a puzzle. The shorter ending seems to break off abruptly, at 16:8, with the women at the empty tomb left bewildered at what it all means. A longer ending, verses 9–20, which is more in keeping with the book, seems to have been added a little later. It not only reports more confidently on the resurrection but includes the commissioning of the disciples to the task of worldwide mission.

The figure of Christ in the gospel of Mark is a towering figure who, through his cross, defeats evil, releases people from oppression, overcomes the disjointedness of the world and opens up a new day in which all men and women can have access to God and enjoy the benefits of his kingly rule.

Luke: Jesus, the compassionate Saviour

Luke was a doctor and travelling companion of Paul (Colossians 4:14). Unlike the other gospel writers, he was not a Jew, nor an eyewitness to the events of the life of Christ. But, he tells us, he set out to research the life of Christ and set out his story in an orderly fashion. The result is a very comprehensive and beautifully written gospel which not only follows the main outline drawn up by Mark but contains a lot of fresh material as well.

He presents Jesus as a compassionate Saviour who reaches out to make God's grace known to men and women of all kinds, especially those who least deserve it. The God who sent Jesus into the world is a God who, astonishingly, is "kind to the ungrateful and wicked" (6:35).

Luke can be divided into five sections:

1 – 2	The birth of John the Baptist and Jesus
3 – 4:13	John's preaching and Jesus's preparation for ministry
4:14 – 9:50	Jesus's work and teaching in Galilee
9:51 – 19:28	The journey to Jerusalem
19:29 – 24:53	Events in Jerusalem, climaxing in his death and resurrection

In the first two chapters, Luke gives us the fullest account of the birth of of Christ. He fills in the background about John the Baptist (1:5–25; 2:57–80). Only Luke tells us about the songs which Mary (1:46–55) and Zechariah (1:67–79) sang. Only he mentions the political context, the shepherds, the angels and the presentation of Jesus in the temple (2:1–40). And he is the only one to say anything at all about the boyhood of Jesus (2:41–52).

In the second section we have a fuller account of John's preaching than elsewhere (3:1–20).

Luke alone tells us that in the early days of his ministry in Galilee, Jesus paid a visit to his home synagogue in Nazareth where, during the service, he staked his claim to be the fulfilment of Isaiah's words about the coming of a time of God's special grace. His words were met with rejection (4:14–30).

Almost half of the fourth section contains material which is exclusive to Luke. It is essentially a densely packed disciple-ship manual. One of the key methods of teaching which Jesus used was telling parables, that is, stories with a point, which were quite capable of leading the unwary (especially the spiritually arrogant) into a trap. Of the 17 parables in this section, fifteen of them are not found anywhere else. The familiar stories of the good Samaritan (10:25–37), the rich fool (12:13–21), the lost sheep (15:1–7) and the prodigal son and disgruntled brother (15:11–32) are all found only in Luke.

Similarly, the healings of the crippled woman (13:10–17), the man with dropsy (14:1–4) and the ten lepers (17:11–19), plus Jesus's encounter with Zacchaeus (19:1–10), all of which are very significant for his message, are all exclusive to Luke.

The final section inevitably goes over the same ground as the other gospels. But even here Luke has a unique angle on things. Take the words which Jesus spoke from the cross, for example. Luke alone mentions his prayer of forgiveness for those who crucified him, his welcome of the dying thief into his kingdom and his gently commending his spirit into the hands of his father (23:32–46).

Other things are specially characteristic of Luke as well. He has a special interest in people, mentioning more of them by name than his colleagues do. He is particularly interested in those who were outcasts or, like Zacchaeus, were on the margins of society. Women and children receive much more attention than one might expect, given that they were usually written off as unimportant in the days when Jesus lived.

Jesus is a sociable person who eats with Pharisees (7:36–50; 11:37–44 and 14:1–24). Each of these occasions is turned into an important teaching opportunity, with some of Jesus's most radical teaching about his "upside down kingdom" taking place over a meal – hence Fred Craddock's comment that "nothing can be for Luke more serious than a dining table" (*Luke*, John Knox Press, 1990, p. 175).

The themes of prayer, joy and the Holy Spirit all receive a special emphasis in Luke.

All this adds up to a distinctive picture of Jesus. He is the Saviour whose forgiving grace reaches out to embrace men and women of all social classes, all degrees of ritual purity and of whatever ethnic background. The dining table is important, not just because it's a good place to teach, but because it epitomises the social conventions of the day. Only those who were good enough, clean enough and Jewish enough would be on the guest list of the Pharisees. But the guest list for the great banquet in God's kingdom would be composed of the most surprising kind of people: the poor, disabled, disadvantaged, impotent, sinners and impure (14:15–24). The dining table was the place where the accepted social conventions of the day were turned upside down by the one who died to be the Saviour of all.

Acts: Jesus still at work

Luke's gospel is the first part of a two-volume work. The second part is the Acts of the Apostles. Luke was involved in some of its story himself and so writes as an eyewitness. In these sections he talks of "we" (16:10–17; 20:5–15; 21:1–18; 27:1 – 28:16). In the other sections, he applies the same careful research skills as he used in his gospel. Although it is not always easy to fit the events of Acts into the historical framework suggested by Paul's letters, Luke is widely regarded as a fine example of an ancient historian. Acts covers the period from about 30 to 62 AD.

The continuity between the two books is evident. The end of the gospel is left hanging somewhat, as if there is more to come. Then, in the opening words of Acts, Luke picks it up. The "former book", that is, the gospel, was "about all that Jesus *began* to do and to teach". The implication is clear. Acts is about what he *continued* to do, by the power of his Spirit through his apostles. And when Luke is finished telling their story, he makes it clear that is not the end of it either. Luke concludes Acts with Paul in Rome under house arrest. But this is not a cause of concern for, "Boldly and without hindrance he preached the kingdom of God and taught about the Lord Jesus Christ" (28:31). Once more, the implication is clear. Not only is the story one unbroken story of the inbreaking of the reign of God, from the birth of Jesus to the imprisonment of Paul, but the story goes on. It is not finished yet.

Acts records how the gospel spread and became universal good news. Beginning in Jerusalem, it broke out of the confines of Judea and first reached into Samaria and then into the lives of individual Gentiles, before being widely preached around the Gentile world. The climax came when the gospel reached Rome, then the centre of power in the "civilised" world. The book follows the programme Jesus gave his disciples when he told them that, after they had received the Holy Spirit, they would be his witnesses "in Jerusalem, and in all Judea and Samaria and to the ends of the earth" (1:8).

Three things are worth bearing in mind. First, the developments did not take place because the church was perfect. The early Christians struggled with problems of deception (5:1–11) and division (6:1–7). In God's grace he does not wait for us to be perfect before he uses us. Second, the developments did not always take place because the apostles took the initiative or planned them. In fact, initially, they seemed very reluctant to do anything which was going to move them out from Jerusalem. Indeed, it was only because persecution arose and dispersed the Christians that new missionary advances took place (8:1). Third, the growth of the church among Gentiles threw up problems which had not been anticipated and which caused sharp argument. Peter, a good Jew, was confronted with the implications of the Gentile mission in a vision he received in Joppa (10:9–23), but by all accounts, he took some time to work through this fuller understanding of the gospel. The church as a whole later confronted the issues when leaders of the older Jewish churches and the newer Gentile mission came together in Jerusalem for discussion (15:1–35).

The book falls into three main sections:

The obvious theme of Acts is the power of the Holy Spirit. There are five accounts of significant outpourings of the Spirit (2:1–4; 4:28–31; 8:15–17; 10:44–46 and 19:6). Mentioned over 60 times, it is the Spirit who brings the church into being, fills Christ's servants with power for witness, guides and directs the missionaries, empowers the apostles to work miracles, endows believers with the gift of tongues, enables disciples to be joyful in suffering and unmistakably confirms significant new advances in mission by the giving of signs and wonders. In fulfilment of Joel's prophecy, the Spirit gives people visions, dreams, prophecies and words of discernment.

A second important theme is the progress of the word of God. It is mentioned ten times and often, significantly, when the church is struggling with opposition or making a new advance. The word of God seems almost to have a dynamic of its own (see 6:7). God's power, through the combined activity of his Spirit and his word, ensures the gospel bears fruit wherever it goes and whatever obstacles it confronts.

Acts chiefly revolves around the story of two men: Peter, the apostle to the Jews, and Paul, the apostle to the Gentiles. Their lives parallel each other in remarkable ways, not only in their common experience of the Spirit and of persecution, but even to the extent that they are both used to raise someone from the dead (9:36–41; 20:7–12). Luke seems to go out of his way to show that the emergence of the church among the Gentiles under Paul is as legitimate as it was among the Jews under Peter.

But Acts is not essentially the story of Peter and Paul. It is the story of the ongoing work of Christ. Their preaching is not so much about the kingdom – the language of the gospels – as about the king. Their speeches, which are frequently reported in Acts, are full of Jesus and show us how the early Christians interpreted his life and death. Within a few weeks of his resurrection they claimed, remarkably, that the crucified Jesus was "both Lord and Christ" (2:36). Although they expressed the message in a variety of ways, this was their central theme. Jesus of Nazareth was the Lord of the world, with a power which vastly outdistanced the power of the lord Caesar in Rome. And he was the Messiah for whom the Jews had looked for so long. In him, the new age had arrived.

John: Jesus in widescreen

John gives us a different perspective on the life of Jesus from the other gospel writers. He wrote much later and provides a more in-depth reflection on what took place. Although John's gospel records, with the others, several of the events of Jesus's life, such as his cleansing of the temple, miracles, and death and resurrection, it is much more concerned to reveal his life's inner meaning. John, therefore, does not begin with the birth of Jesus at Bethlehem. For him that is much too narrow a canvas. The only way to understand Jesus is to paint his portrait on the widest screen possible – an eternal, cosmic screen. He is the Word who was with God, indeed, *was* God, from the beginning (1:1). The amazing thing is that this eternal Word became a human being and took up residence on earth (1:14).

The distinctiveness of John's gospel is seen in its language, contents and the timing of events. Where the synoptic gospels speak of the kingdom of God, John talks about eternal life. Several of the miracles and a lot of the teaching is unique to this gospel. The others allude to the Holy Spirit but John, who calls him the Paraclete, that is, the "one who stands alongside to give support", develops the Spirit's role in depth. Confessions of faith seem to come earlier and more easily than Matthew, Mark and Luke recall. Timewise, Jesus does not first minister in Galilee and only then go up to Jerusalem at the end, as in the synoptic gospels, but seems to travel back and forth more than once. John places the cleansing of the temple at the start of Jesus's ministry (2:12–25) rather than after Jesus's triumphal entry to Jerusalem. And John seems to think that the death of Jesus took place a day earlier than the synoptic gospels claim (19:14).

None of this means that John is historically inaccurate or that what he writes is a figment of his imagination. Many of the tensions between John and the other gospels can be reconciled. Their accounts are complementary rather than contradictory, with John filling in some of the gaps that exist elsewhere. In fact, there are several pieces of evidence, such as his use of place names, which testify to his trustworthiness. But John makes good use of artistic licence as he retells the story too. The timing of Jesus's death, for example, means that Jesus dies just at the moment that the Passover lambs are being slaughtered in the temple. This is John's way of sending out a signal as to who Jesus really was and why he was being put to death (1:29).

John is a marvellous artist with words. Several themes illuminate his gospel. He keeps writing of life, light, darkness, love, truth, glory and eternal life. His pictures make use of wonderful symbolism. He speaks, for example, of birth and the need to be "born again" (3:1–8) and of the thirst which Jesus alone can quench once and for all (4:10–15). He picks up images from the Old Testament and shows Jesus to be "the lamb of God" (1:29), "the bread of life" (6:35 and also 41) which greatly surpasses the manna which fed the Jews in the wilderness (6:25–59) and "the true vine" which supplants the wild vine of which Isaiah spoke (15:1). He paints in strongly contrasting colours, making use of death and life, darkness and light, hate and love, descent and ascent, unbelief and belief. His original readers, who are thought to be Jewish Christians who were facing a hard time from the Jewish community because of their faith in Jesus, would have found such contrasts particularly appealing.

John loves "sevens" – a significant feature of his gospel is his inclusion of seven miracles and seven sayings of Jesus. These often give rise to long discussions with the opponents of Jesus, who are identified as "the Jews". These discussions then become vehicles for Jesus's teaching.

The miracles are called "signs" or "signposts" by John, who tells us quite clearly that they are included to encourage belief in Jesus as the Christ and Son of God (20:31). Only two of them are found in the earlier gospels. The signs are:

- changing water into wine (2:1–11)
- healing of the official's son (4:43–54)
- healing of the lame man at the pool (5:1–15)
- feeding of the 5,000, then walking on water (6:1–24)
- healing a blind man (9:1–34)
- raising of Lazarus from death (11:44)
- the resurrection (20–21)

The seven sayings are unique to John. They all begin with the words "I am" (which may echo the divine name) and stake Jesus's claim to being the unique son of God. They are:

- the bread of life (6:35)
- the light of the world (8:12)
- the door (10:9)
- the good shepherd (10:11)
- the resurrection and the life (11:25)
- the way, the truth and the life (14:6)
- the true vine (15:1)

Another unique feature of John's gospel comes in chapters 13–17. John reaches the final phase of Jesus's life quite early in his writing. This gives him space to pull back the curtain on the final week of his life and reveal much more than the other gospels do about the time Jesus spent in conversation with his disciples. These chapters make John's portrait of Jesus a very intimate one. They begin with the humbling picture of Jesus washing his disciples' dusty feet, the task of the lowliest slave (13:1–17). They end with the sacred record of Jesus praying to his Father (17:1–26) and talking about his own crucifixion and the future of his disciples. In between, Jesus teaches his disciples about what will happen after he has left them. Twin themes run through the discussions. On the one hand, his departure will cause them grief and their future will be marked by rejection. On the other hand, they will experience joy, as the Holy Spirit is given to guide and strengthen them and to make them fruitful.

An outline of John's gospel looks likes this:

1:1–18	The introduction of Christ as the Word
1:19–51	The beginning of Christ's ministry
2:1 – 12:50	The signs and public discussion of Christ
13:1 – 17:26	The farewell conversations of Christ and his disciples
18:1 – 21:25	The death and resurrection of Christ

John's undeviating purpose is to encourage belief in Jesus, the man, yet the eternal Word, in whom the glory of God shone, as the disciples saw with their own eyes, and through whom the grace of God flowed (1:14).

To sum up

According to Revelation 4:7, there are four living creatures around God's throne: a lion, an ox, a human being and a flying angel. Long ago, Irenaeus (130–200 AD), Bishop of Lyons, used those images as a way of describing the fourfold picture of Christ which the gospels present. They can still be found as images in many older churches in the UK. Matthew, Irenaeus wrote, presents Jesus's human face and presents him as a teacher of righteousness. Mark presents Jesus as the lion, roaring in the face of his enemy. Luke reveals Jesus to be the ox, the compassionate Saviour who bears the burdens of others. John portrays Jesus as a soaring eagle, flying high above the world in the sphere of eternity, yet whose talons can dig deep into its prey and under whose wings its young can find shelter. That is not a complete picture. But it is not a bad way of understanding the gospel portraits of Jesus.

8

The Pauline Correspondence:
Romans to Philemon

The apostle Paul dominates much of the New Testament. After his conversion he was the foremost pioneer evangelist to the Gentiles, establishing churches in many different places in the ancient world. Several of his letters offer follow-up advice to these young churches and deal with specific questions they were facing. Two of them, including Romans, his fullest letter, were written to churches he had not visited. Four other letters offer advice to individual leaders within the church. They cover virtually the whole period of Paul's active missionary travels. Here we look at them in the order (as far as we can tell) in which they were written. No single theme emerges, but a recurring theme is that of Paul's gospel: of God's grace and our need to live by faith in Christ and in Christ alone.

The Pauline Correspondence:
Romans to Philemon

The figure of Paul towers over that of others, with the exception of Jesus, in the central part of the New Testament. He was a Jew, educated in one of the best schools of the day, led by a Pharisee named Gamaliel (Acts 22:3), where he studied the law of Moses. But, because he had been born in Tarsus (Acts 22:3), a Greek university city, and was the son of a Roman citizen (Acts 22:25–29; 23:27), he was also thoroughly at home in the Gentile world. Once converted to Christ, no one could have been better qualified to preach the message of a Jewish Messiah in the cities of the Roman world in a culture which was so thoroughly Greek.

His early life was spent as a bigoted defender of his Jewish faith – he viciously persecuted the followers of Jesus. From his standpoint, Jesus could not have been the Messiah, since he had been executed on a cross and the law said that those who died in such a way were under God's curse (Deuteronomy 21:23). Christians, then, were heretics and traitors who deserved imprisonment, if not worse. So our first introduction to Saul (his Jewish name) finds him playing a significant role in the martyrdom of Stephen (Acts 8:1) and then setting off to root out other Christian troublemakers from the synagogues in Damascus (Acts 9:2). On his way, he encountered the risen

Jesus in an experience which was to transform the rest of his life and turn him from an ardent persecutor of Christ to one of his most fervent champions. Through a disciple called Ananias, he immediately received a commission to be the apostle (messenger) of Christ to the Gentiles (Acts 9:1–19).

In spite of some suspicion (Acts 9:21), Barnabas had soon introduced him to the church leaders in Jerusalem and he set about preaching the gospel (Acts 9:26–30). The precise order of events is not quite clear because, as Paul tells his story in one of his letters, he spent a good deal of time on his own, learning about his faith, before going to make the acquaintance of the apostle Peter (Galatians 1:15–20). But, at least after a three-year training period, Paul started preaching and, soon after, the church at Antioch confirmed his commission and sent him and Barnabas off on a missionary tour (Acts 13:1–3).

Acts records three tours Paul made with various colleagues (see previous chapter), during which he planted churches and went back to visit some of them to give them encouragement and further teaching. He usually worked in the significant cities of the ancient world, such as Philippi, Thessalonica, Athens, Corinth and Ephesus, since the gospel would soon radiate out from these centres of influence. To begin with, he used the Jewish synagogue as a platform, but after much opposition there he turned to use secular venues and appealed directly to Gentiles to follow Christ.

He was a pioneer who never showed any desire to pastor churches which other people had founded. He was always pressing on into new territory. His ambition was to preach about Christ while passing through Rome on his way to Spain (Romans 15:24, 27). He got his wish, if not in the way he expected. The last chapters of Acts tell us how he was taken to Rome as a prisoner to stand trial for his faith before Caesar which, as a Roman citizen, was his legal privilege. Acts ends with Paul under house arrest. As far as we can tell, following that he was released and engaged in further missionary activity, before finally being condemned to death. But the details are unclear, which gives rise to some arguments about the circumstances in which he wrote his later writings.

Paul's letters were a vital part of his ministry. Most of them, but not all, were letters he wrote to churches he himself had founded. They were written either just to encourage people in their faith or to teach them about the gospel more accurately and sort out some misunderstandings and problems which had arisen since he moved on. They fall into three groups. This chapter will look at them in the order in which they were written, which is different from that in the New Testament:

Group 1: Paul's early letters
1 and 2 Thessalonians
Galatians
1 and 2 Corinthians
Romans

Group 2: Letters from prison
Ephesians
Philippians
Colossians
Philemon

Group 3: Paul's last letters
1 and 2 Timothy
Titus

Paul's early letters

1 and 2 Thessalonians

1 and 2 Thessalonians were probably Paul's first letters, written about 50 AD. They were written within a few weeks of each other.

The story of the planting of the church at Thessalonica is found in Acts 17:1–9. The founding members were totally transformed from their previous way of life and were great examples of the gospel (1.1:4–10). But they were subjected to severe opposition (Acts 17:5–9; 1.2:13–16). So Paul, who had been prevented from going to see them in person again (1.2:18), wrote a short follow-up letter by way of support and further instruction.

The tone of 1 Thessalonians is very encouraging (see 1.3:1–13), but Paul saw an obvious need to explain several things which were causing the church difficulties. Some people were putting it about that Paul's ministry was a failure and that he was just using them to his own ends (1.2:1–2). The fact of persecution and Paul's own premature departure from Thessalonica did not sit easily with a message which preached the victory of Christ (1.2:13–20). The lack of sexual purity in the lives of some members, who were perhaps still too much influenced by their background or surroundings, was an issue; Paul urges them to live more holy lives (1.4:1–12). In addition, their expectation that Christ would return in the very near future had taken a sharp jolt, as some members of the church had unexpectedly died; the church did not know how that fitted into the scheme of things. So Paul gives them some very practical instruction about how to live in the light of the second coming (1.4:13 – 5:11).

The second letter continues the warm tone but was written to correct a misunderstanding which was still circulating about the return of Christ. The central part of the letter (2.2:1–12) is difficult because it refers to fuller teaching which Paul had given them, to which we are not party. But it is evident that he is trying to dampen the misguided enthusiasm of some believers who were putting it about that Christ had already returned. Much more was to happen yet, Paul tells them, including a final outbreak of rebellion against God, which would be led by a person who would blasphemously set himself up in opposition to God. Given that this was yet to happen, believers were wrong to give up their ordinary occupations and sit around waiting for Christ's coming. Rather, they should act as responsible citizens and earn their keep (2.3:6–15).

Paul concludes by praying that God might give them "peace at all times and in every way" (2.3:16).

Galatians

Galatians is the sharpest letter Paul wrote. It is written to address a crisis which had arisen through false teaching in the churches of what is today central and southern Turkey. The story of Paul's founding of these churches in Antioch, Iconium, Lystra and Derbe is told in Acts 13:13 – 14:23. His follow-up visits are mentioned in Acts 16:1–6 and 18:23. The letter is among the earliest of Paul's writings and was probably written in the early 50s AD.

The problem was that Jewish Christian teachers had followed Paul to Galatia and told his Gentile converts that, besides faith in Jesus Christ, it was necessary to keep the Jewish law in order to be a true Christian. Even if faith on its own was sufficient to put one in a right standing with God initially, it was not sufficient to keep one in a right relationship with him. For that, obedience to the law was needed. The Jewish law included the requirement for men to be circumcised and also imposed strict rules about whom one could eat with. Both of these are issues in Galatians.

Paul vigorously refutes this position and denies that it has anything to do with the gospel (1:1–9). As evidence, he appeals to his own story and the agreement of the other apostles (1:11 – 2:21); to their own experience (3:1–5); to theological argument about Abraham (3:6–25) and to the scriptural example of Hagar and Sarah, Abraham's child-bearing slave and wife respectively (4:21–31). To insist that the Jewish way of life had to be observed in addition to faith was to say, in effect, that Christ's death was insufficient and had to be supplemented by something of our own works. That would undermine it all. The gospel was about staking one's life on God's promises and his action in Christ, not about trusting in anything we could do.

An important point to emerge is that God had not changed his mind, nor his plan. It was not the case that people could be in a right standing with God before Christ by keeping the law, but after Christ by simply believing. People had never been in a right standing with God, except through believing his promise, that is, by exercising faith, as the story of Abraham demonstrates and as the prophet Habakkuk, quoted in 3:11, taught.

Positively, Paul writes fully on the nature of Christian freedom. Christ came to liberate us from Jewish customs which could only enslave us (5:1) and to give us our full rights as children adopted into his family (4:26–27). The trouble is, freedom easily gets abused and degenerates into licence. So, to prevent any misunderstanding, Paul spells out the nature of responsible freedom, a freedom which leads to service, purity and fruitfulness (5:13 – 6:6). His description here of "the fruit of the Spirit" (5:22 – 23) is among his best-known sayings.

1 and 2 Corinthians

The founding of the church at Corinth took place over 18 months and is reported in Acts 18. One wonders whether Paul ever regretted this project, for it proved to be a troublesome church which bore all the hallmarks of struggling with the influence of pagan surroundings and false teachers. Paul felt an intense love for the church members which was not always returned; this resulted in a tempestuous relationship between them. Reading 1 and 2 Corinthians leads us to believe Paul wrote more letters than the ones we have. And he obviously received letters from them. So what we read is a bit like listening to a partial and one-sided telephone conversation. These letters were probably written in 54 and 56 AD.

1 Corinthians starts with Paul raising some of his own concerns and then, from 7:1 on, turning to answer questions the Corinthians have raised. He has heard about divisions in the church, where groups are clustering around particular Christian leaders (1.1:10–12). This is no light matter for, as he explains, division runs contrary to what the cross is all about and the way God operates (1.1:20-2:16). It also shows a misunderstanding of the nature of Christian leadership (1.3:1 – 4:20). Having said

that, the church does have boundaries: Paul insists that a member who commits incest has crossed the line and should be expelled (5:1–13). He then instructs them to settle disputes internally rather than resorting to the public courts to do so (6:1–11).

Sex and marriage were obviously issues for the church in Corinth, which is not surprising, given the reputation of the city and the religious practices in some of its temples. In dealing with these, Paul advocates sexual purity, gives advice about the nature of a good marriage, commends singleness as a positive option before God if people could cope with it, and gives guidance about divorce, particularly where a Christian is married to an unsympathetic partner (6:12 – 7:39).

Then, Paul gives some finely balanced guidance about how Christians were to cope with attending social events where meals would have involved religious rituals and where the meat would have been offered in homage to idols first (8).

Lots of things were wrong in the church at Corinth. The way the members treated Paul himself was not right (9), nor was the way they behaved at Communion (10 – 11), nor was the chaotic way they conducted their worship (12 – 14), nor was their odd belief that Christ had not risen from the dead (15). In Paul's responses to all these matters we have some rich teaching about the nature of worship, the church as a body, the exercise of spiritual gifts (such as tongues and prophecy but also teaching, helping and administration), the meaning of love, and our future hope. 1 Corinthians provides not so much a manual for individual disciples as a great manual for corporate discipleship and what it means to be the church.

The turbulent relationship continues in 2 Corinthians. Throughout the letter, Paul is answering accusations which are aimed at undermining his ministry. But Paul is not so much engaging in a personal and self-centred defence as giving us a thorough exposition of the nature of Christian ministry. His actions are all tied in to his understanding of God and his calling. So, for example, he doesn't change his mind, because that would be at odds with the God he serves, who is a God of integrity who keeps his word (2.1:12 – 2:4). Paul takes everything back to first principles – to God and the gospel. That is even evident in the middle of the letter where he writes about the collection he is making for the needy Christians in Jerusalem (2.8 – 9). Money was one of the issues between Paul and the Corinthians. Again, Paul shows them how giving to others is not a social convention or a political convenience, but is something which imitates God's grace to us and has deep spiritual implications.

Chapters 10 – 13 are sometimes thought to be a separate letter which has somehow been added on to the previous chapters. Its tone does sharpen, but the questions it addresses seem to be the same. False teachers, from the Jewish stable, have called into question Paul's credentials as an apostle. To them, he is not successful enough, powerful enough, eloquent enough. Paul replies ironically. He also writes in a deeply personal way, revealing some of his own struggles, especially with his "thorn in the flesh" (2.12:1–10). In doing so, he again shows us that Christian ministry, by its very nature, is not about success, but about allowing God to channel his grace to others through our weaknesses. After all, Paul reminds them, at the heart of the gospel there stands a cross where Christ was crucified in weakness (2.13:4).

Romans

The church in Rome was not founded by Paul and when he wrote to them he had not yet visited them. His letter, written around 57 AD, was, if nothing else, a way of introducing himself to them by setting out his understanding of the gospel and by outlining his travel plans. It is the gospel, rather than the travel plans, which occupy the space in the letter. His basic message had already been sketched in his letter to the Galatians. Here it is developed much more fully and without the edge that Galatians contained. His great theme is how sinful people can be "justified", that is, made just or righteous or, in other words, put in a right relationship with God. Romans 3:21–27 contains the essence of his message in concentrated form.

One important thing must be borne in mind as we approach this letter. The big issue is not essentially about how an individual can be saved. It is about whether God was being just in saving Gentiles as well as Jews. The fault line between them ran deep in the ancient world and affected everything. The inclusion of the Gentiles in the church, through the work of Christ, raised big questions, as we have already seen. How did it fit with God's election of the Jews and the special heritage they had enjoyed? Did it mean that God had changed his mind, relating to people through the law in Old Testament times, and through grace in New Testament times? What precisely was the nature of the way God was now working? And, if God's plan was now to save Gentiles, what did the future hold for the Jewish nation? All these questions, and more, are addressed in Romans 1 – 11. After that, Paul turns to the more practical outworking of the faith.

The first three chapters of Romans begin by putting Jews and Gentiles on a level playing field before God. Whatever advantages the Jews may have had, such as the law and the covenant sign of circumcision, they stood condemned by their lives as no better than the Gentiles. The truth is that "all have sinned and fall short of the glory of God" (3:23). Then, in chapter 4, Paul argues that God has always acted on the same basis and has "justified" sinners by faith. Abraham, the great father of the Jewish nation, stood in a right relationship with God (which is what justification means) because he believed God's promises, not because he earned God's acceptance by circumcision or the law. Faith, then, is the means by which all may be justified and have access to God (5:1) – faith, that is, in Christ who died for ungodly sinners. Just as Adam stands at the head of one stream of humanity who are dying because of the sin he introduced, so Christ stands at the head of another stream who live because of the death he died (5:12–21). But those who have faith in Christ have no reason to go on sinning. Rather, they have become slaves of Christ, dead to sin and alive to God's transforming Spirit (6 – 8).

Romans 9 – 11 is often avoided by contemporary Christians as being both difficult and not applicable to them. In reality, this section is the climax of this part of Romans. Here, Paul shows how God can be true to himself and his word to the Jews and yet "graft" the Gentiles onto the tree of faith (11:11–24). Paul robustly defends God's freedom of action and his righteous sovereignty. And he looks forward to the time when Gentile belief will provoke the Jews in a positive way, so that "all Israel will be saved" (11:26).

Romans might be divided as follows:

The Christian gospel: 1 – 11

1:1–17	The servant of the gospel: introducing Paul
1:18 – 3:20	The need for the gospel, for Jew and Gentile alike
3:21–31	The gospel in a nutshell
4	The consistency of the gospel with how God has always worked
5	The benefits of the gospel in reconciliation through Christ
6 – 7	The implications of the gospel in mastery over sin
8	The experience of the gospel in enjoying the Spirit
9 – 11	The future of the Jews in the light of the gospel

The Christian life: 12 – 16

12	Issues of personal character and relationships
13	Political and social relationships
14:1 – 15:13	How to deal with differing opinions in the church
15:14–33	Paul's personal plans and motivations
16	Greetings

Because Romans was not written to engage with a particular pastoral situation, Paul expands his thoughts more freely than elsewhere. So this is the longest and deepest of his letters. It is also among the most difficult to understand in parts; maybe Romans was in Peter's mind when he wrote that Paul's "letters contain some things that are hard to understand" (2 Peter 3:16). But it is worth grappling with, because it reveals the depth of human sin and the majesty of God's salvation more fully than any other New Testament book.

Letters from prison

The second group of letters are known as "the prison epistles" because Paul wrote them while he was in captivity. This probably refers to his period under house arrest in Rome, which happened in the early 60s AD. They come from the middle period of his ministry and reflect the way the church and Paul's thinking had developed since the earlier writings.

We take them in the order we find them in the New Testament.

Ephesians

A careful study of Ephesians reveals several differences between it and Paul's other letters. It contains no personal references to him except the address to the Ephesians in 1:1 and even that is not to be found in all the early manuscripts. Its writing style is more complex and its thought more developed than elsewhere. So some suggest, especially in the light of Colossians 4:16, that it was more of a circular letter than a letter to an individual church. Some also think that it may have been written by one of Paul's disciples, following in the tradition of Paul, rather than by Paul himself. But arguments for that are by no means conclusive. True, the themes show a development on Paul's earlier writings, but they are perfectly consistent with them and in many ways are simply the finest exposition of things which we know excited him.

We read of the start of the church in Ephesus in Acts 19. Ephesus was a centre of magic; when some came to believe in Christ they confirmed their conversion by burning their magic books in public. The letter to the Ephesians mirrors this background and has a lot to say about spiritual power, "rulers and authorities in heavenly realms" (3:10) and spiritual warfare (6:10–18).

Ephesians develops several major themes. It places the gospel in the context of God's eternal purposes and, as John does with Jesus, portrays it on the widest possible canvas. The salvation of the Gentiles through Christ was not an afterthought on God's part, nor his Plan B. It was part of his plan "before the creation of the world" (1:4). But God had kept his plan quiet for some time. Only in recent times had the mystery been revealed and Paul had been called to announce it (3:1–13).

Chapter 2 makes two major things about salvation clear. First, salvation depends wholly on the grace of God reaching out through Christ to the spiritually dead and undeserving. The only requirement placed on them, if they are to receive that grace, is to exercise faith (2:1–10). Second, salvation is not simply about the rescuing of individuals so that they can enjoy heaven, but about God's way of bringing Jews and Gentiles together to form a new humanity. This reconciliation takes place because Christ has made peace by bearing the price of conflict on the cross (2:11–22).

Chapter 3 leads us further, to see that the gospel is not even only about the human race. In the realm of the unseen, there were forces at work in conflict with God which were also affected by this gospel. The existence of a united church in which Jews and Gentiles worshipped together was, therefore, not only a remarkable surprise on earth but a necessary witness for the heavenly realms as well (3:10–12).

Given this gospel, Paul naturally stresses the need for unity in the church in spite of the different backgrounds, personalities and gifts of its members (4:1–16).

The rest of the letter works out the meaning of the gospel for our personal characters and social relationships. It shows how a life which has experienced the love of Christ will clean up its act and behave in a disciplined and socially responsible way. Relationships come into sharper focus still when, in 5:21 – 6:9, Paul writes of how husbands and wives, parents and children, and masters and slaves should find their relationships transformed by Christ. Paul uses a pattern of household rules which were common in the ancient world. A similar pattern is found in Colossians 3:18 – 4:1 and 1 Peter 3:1–7. But even in using a common framework, he invests it with new meaning in Christ.

Ephesians gives us an exalted view of Christ. The whole of creation will be united through him (1:10). His work on the cross was the means by which a new, united humanity comes into being (2:14–17). This Christ already reigns in heaven (2:6) but works through the church on earth. He is to the church what the head is to the body: its source of life, direction and authority.

Philippians

Philippians may well lay claim to being the happiest letter in the New Testament. Paul's relationship with the church there was close and a matter of joy. Philippi was a Roman colony (reflected in the citizenship language of 3:20) in northern Greece; Paul had visited it in about 50 AD when the church had come into being (Acts 16:12–40). The purpose of this letter was for Paul to express thanks for a gift he had received from them (4:10–20).

The church there was not facing any major problem, although there were a couple of clouds on the horizon. One cloud was persecution, so Paul writes to encourage them to be steadfast and tells them what a privilege it is to suffer for Christ (1:27–30), as he himself was doing.

Another cloud was the Jewish false teachers who might cause them to deviate from the true gospel. So he writes to remind them that knowing Christ far outshines any merits they can boast about of their own (3:1–11).

A third cloud was the problem of disunity. The most obvious

evidence of this comes in his appeal to Euodia and Syntyche, two women in the church, to stop falling out with each other (4:2) but there are other hints of it as well. It is a concern for unity which lies behind the "hymn" which Paul uses in 2:6–11 and which is probably the best known part of this letter. The "hymn" sets out the example of Christ, who did not cling on to his divine status but voluntarily relinquished it to become a human being and surrender himself to the most humiliating experience of execution on a cross. But, as a result, God exalted him once more to the highest place in the universe; his name is one which will one day command universal recognition and homage. In Christian understanding, the way to be great is to be humble. And humility is a vital ingredient in the unity of the church. Without it, unity is impossible.

Passion for the progress of the gospel (1:12–26) and for progress in the Christian life shines through the letter (2:12–18; 3:12-4:1). Timothy and Epaphroditus are commended as exemplary Christian workers (2:19–30). Joy abounds. Even death and suffering are not problems for the Christian who faces the prospect of heaven with eager expectation and who longs to reach the goal and receive the prize (1:19–26; 3:12–14). No wonder joy abounds, for Philippians is full of Christ and celebrates the new life which can be experienced through him.

Colossians

Colosse was another place that Paul had never visited. The church there had been founded through the witness of Epaphras (1:7), who was probably one of Paul's converts during his mission at Ephesus, a hundred miles away. He had then taken the gospel home with him. It was because of his connection with Epaphras that Paul wrote to Colosse, probably about 60 or 61 AD.

Its teaching is very similar to that of Ephesians and there are some remarkable overlaps between the two letters. Some see it as a sort of "Ephesians-lite", since it is a little less complex and high-flown than that letter. Unlike Ephesians, it is a more personal letter (especially 4:7–18) and addresses a particular problem which the Christians at Colosse were facing. The key theme is the supremacy of Christ over all other authorities and religious systems – a supremacy which means that there can be no compromise with them and that there is no need to rely on them in any way for salvation.

Colossians was written against the background of an emerging threat from false teaching. Since it is nowhere explicitly described, people have tried to piece it together and have done so in a variety of ways. The mention of wisdom (1:9; 2:8, 23 etc.) makes some think that it stemmed from a Greek philosophy called Gnosticism, which taught that people needed to be specially enlightened into some superior knowledge to be in contact with the divine. Gnosticism also devalued the human body whereas Colossians emphasises the physical nature of Christ and his death (e.g. 1:22; 2:9). (We shall meet this again in 1 John.)

Others think the picture painted in 2:16–23 shows that the threat came from the Jewish synagogue, even though not all the details seem quite to fit.

More recently, it has been suggested that what was threatening to undermine the integrity of the Christian gospel was a mishmash of religious views. Folk religion is usually anything but pure and often mixes a little bit of this with a little bit of that. This would mean that, in their desire to know God and secure his protection over their lives, the Colossian Christians were beginning not to trust exclusively in the work of Christ but to hedge their bets by putting together a portfolio of religion including a bit of Judaism (which included angel worship at the time), a bit of Greek philosophy, a bit of the mystery religions which were practised in the area, and a bit of magical superstition.

Against this, Paul mounts a powerful challenge. Again, possibly using an existing hymn, he writes in the most exalted terms about the supreme role of Christ in creation, the cosmos, the church, and the coming re-creation of all things (1:15–20).

Since Christians now live under his rule, in his kingdom (1:13), why should they fear any powers of lesser status than Christ, and feel the need to take shelter behind them? The Colossian believers needed simply to stand firm, both individually and collectively, in the faith they had been taught (1:21 – 2:7). They should resist the temptation to think that there was some new, "super-improved" version of religion which would serve them better, wherever it came from (2:8–23).

What the Colossians needed, in fact, was not some missing spiritual experience but a greater understanding of the security they had in Christ and an appreciation of how that was to work out in their daily living (3:1–17). Once Paul begins to talk about Christian character and relationships, he soon introduces the rules for living in Christian households (3:18 – 4:1), which we met when looking at Ephesians.

The message of Colossians is summed up in 1:18 where Paul explains that Christ was the first to rise from the dead and pioneered the entry into the new creation "so that in everything he might have the supremacy".

Philemon

Philemon is not so much a letter as a postcard. Philemon was the name of a Christian slave owner who hosted the church at Colosse in his home. One of his slaves, Onesimus, had run away, which was a serious offence in the ancient world and could attract severe penalties. But Onesimus had fled to Rome and there he had come into contact with Paul, had been converted to Christ (10) and had stayed on to serve Paul for a little while. Paul is now sending Onesimus back home and writes a wonderfully diplomatic letter to encourage (not command) Philemon to welcome him back, not as a troublemaker but as a fellow believer.

Paul is confident that Philemon will treat his slave kindly because Philemon has always been generous-hearted in the past and not least to Paul, who had benefited from having Onesimus around for a time.

Although a very personal letter about a seemingly insignificant matter, the letter reveals much about the nature of relationships within the Christian community and their distinctiveness from relationships in the outside world. It may only be a little note but it witnesses keenly to the transforming power of the gospel. The runaway slave who had been a nuisance was now a "faithful and dear brother" (Colossians 4:9).

Paul's last letters

The final three letters, 1 and 2 Timothy and Titus, are often referred to as the "Pastoral Epistles". The story has moved on and Paul faces the prospect of laying down his apostolic role in the church soon and passing the baton on to the second generation of leaders.

Some think these letters were written after Paul's death, again by one of his "disciples" who used his name in a way which is believed to have been an acceptable practice in the ancient world (1.1:1; 2.1:1; Titus 1:1). These scholars argue that the letters reflect a church which has ceased to be a community and become an institution, a set of doctrines which have become fixed and in need of preservation, and a softness towards the world over issues such as wealth, all of which are uncharacteristic of Paul. True, the subjects are different and the style has changed a bit. But the situation facing the church after it had been established for some time was bound to be different from that when the church was newly founded. A wise pastor does not merely repeat what has been said before, but moves on to guide believers through the issues they currently face. There is nothing here which is really unlikely to have come from Paul's pen.

If they were written by Paul, it would seem that he wrote 1 Timothy and Titus after he was released from prison in Rome and during the time when he engaged in missionary activity again. 2 Timothy finds Paul in prison again and awaiting a further trial, which would spell the end. The dates must be mid- and late 60s AD.

We know quite a bit about Timothy. The son of a mixed marriage, he had been taught the faith from an early age (Acts 16:1; 2 Timothy 3:15). After Paul met him in his hometown of Lystra, he often accompanied the apostle on his missionary journeys and was used by him as a messenger. He had become a true spiritual son to Paul (1 Timothy 1:18). Titus, similarly, was one of Paul's partners and used by him especially as a go-between in his relationship with the Corinthian church.

1 Timothy

The church in Ephesus, where Timothy was (1:3), was under threat, so Paul writes to give him advice on how to handle some of the difficulties. The chief threats came from false teachers (1:3–11); immature worshippers (2:1–15); inadequate leaders (3:1–13); legalistic killjoys (4:1–5); widows who had too much time on their hands (5:9–16) and money-loving Christians (6:6–10, 17–19).

The antidote was for Timothy to point out error and teach truth (4:6–16). But if he were to do so effectively, he was warned he would have to give as much attention to the quality of his own life as he would to the content of his teaching (4:11–16). He was also to learn the delicate art of relating to people of different ages and situations so as to open up their ears to his message, rather than being so zealous that they switched off from him (5:1–3).

The tone of the letter is urgent. The Christian life is seen as a fight – one in which there had already been casualties (1:18–20; 6:12). The task of leadership is seen as something to be handled with care because of the many pitfalls that might trip up those who exercise it (e.g. 6:11–16).

1 Timothy has a very high view of God, who is referred to as "God our Saviour" (1:1; 2:3), an eternal and immortal King (1:17), and "the blessed and only Ruler, the King of kings and Lord of lords, who alone is immortal" and worthy of honour (6:15–16). The position of Christ is equally exalted. He is the only mediator between God and humanity (2:5) and the one

whose appearing will signal the end and the summoning of all people to give an account of their lives before God (6:14). No doubt this was deliberately designed to remind Timothy that, whatever difficulties, disappointments or challenges he faced, he was serving a great God who was not only able to equip him for the task but who would also one day reign supreme.

Titus

Titus covers very similar ground to 1 Timothy. He was charged with "straightening out" the situation on Crete (1:5), where he too had to confront leadership deficiencies and teach various groups within the church how to behave in the church.

The letter divides in the following way:

1:1–4	Introduction
1:5–16	The appointment of leaders
2:1–10	The teaching Titus is to give to various groups
2:11 – 3:11	The purpose of grace: to live good lives
3:12–15	Final remarks

Titus shares with 1 Timothy not only a common agenda, but also a common motivation. Here Paul sums it up as waiting "for the blessed hope – the glorious appearing of our great God and Saviour, Jesus Christ" (2:13). The return of Christ should govern how Christians behave in general and how pastors lead in particular.

2 Timothy

Written from prison, this letter gives a moving picture of Paul, whose departure from life is not far away (see, for example, 4:6–18). It is his "last will and testament".

Looking back, Paul thanks God for Timothy (1:1–7) and urges him to remain faithful to the gospel (1:8–18). The reason for Paul's confidence in the gospel lies in his knowledge of Jesus Christ (1:12). It is not shaken by whatever was going to happen to him personally, nor by how unpopular the gospel might become (3:1–9).

In this letter, the images Paul uses to exhort Timothy to faithful service tumble over one another. He is to be:

- a soldier who endures hardship (2:3–4)
- an athlete who keeps the rules (2:5)
- a farmer who works hard (2:6)
- a disciple who remembers Jesus (2:8)
- a worker who does not need to feel ashamed (2:15)
- a dish that has been cleansed (2:20–21)
- a servant who uses gentleness (2:24)
- a student who remembers what he has been taught (3:10–16)
- a herald who announces God's word (4:2)
- an evangelist who shares good news (4:5)
- a friend who visits a lonely prisoner (4:9).

Paul's last letter is characterised by a sense of wonder at God's grace, and confidence in God's power. His life is safe in the hands of "the Lord, the righteous Judge", who will reward him with a "crown of righteousness" on the day of Christ's appearing (4:8). With utter certainty, Paul can look back on his life and lay down his well-used pen, still saying, "to him be glory for ever and ever. Amen" (4:18).

9

The Final Messages:
Hebrews to Revelation

The early church was composed of a wide variety of churches with different needs. In addition to the churches founded by Paul in Gentile areas, there were others, some of which had a more Jewish background. The remaining books of the New Testament reflect this variety. Hebrews explains the gospel in terms which makes sense to those brought up in the Jewish faith. James is a sort of New Testament Proverbs and adopts the style of Jewish wisdom literature. Although the letters of Peter have much in common with Paul's, they, together with Jude, reflect a more Jewish complexion as they deal with questions of discipleship and suffering, and warn against false teachers. John's letters are dominated by the meaning of love. Revelation is apocalyptic and unlike anything else in the New Testament. It encourages the church to remain faithful to God, by showing Christians who are undergoing severe trials and temptations the full picture of God's battle against his enemies and God's ultimate triumph. It is a fitting climax to the New Testament and points forward to the new creation.

The Final Messages:

Hebrews to Revelation

After Paul's letters, there are nine "books" which complete the New Testament. They are very different in length, style and purpose. Hebrews and Revelation are long; 2 and 3 John are very short. James, Peter, John and Jude are clearly written as letters. Hebrews was probably originally a sermon; Revelation is a prophecy. They are written to different groups of Christians and each has a different agenda.

For all their differences, these final messages have a number of things in common. None of them are addressed just to a single church but to a wider readership, which has meant that the books, at least those from from Hebrews to Jude, have sometimes been referred to as the "General" or "Catholic" (universal) epistles. Subsequently, their teaching was considered to be of significance beyond their initial readership as well, and so they were included in the canon. They were all also thought to be written by apostles. This gave their words special weight: since they came from people so close to Jesus, it meant people should sit up and take notice of them. Today, people debate the question of who did write Hebrews, 2 Peter and Revelation – but more of that later.

Hebrews

Although the last chapter of Hebrews contains some personal notes, there is nothing else to say it is a letter. In its original language it sounds as if it was composed to be heard, rather than read, so many now suggest it was a (very long!) sermon.

Its theme, throughout, is the superiority of Jesus Christ to anything which has gone before or which might be considered in competition with him. Its purpose is summed up in the words: "So do not throw away your confidence; it will be richly rewarded. You need to persevere so that when you have done the will of God, you will receive what he has promised" (10:35–36).

The first readers of Hebrews were Jewish Christians who were trying to relate their new faith in Christ to all that they had been taught in their scriptures. Therefore, much of it is composed of an explanation of how the old sacrifices and priesthood came to fulfilment in Jesus Christ, who is the ultimate sacrifice and great High Priest, and were therefore done away with by him. To 21st-century Gentiles this may seem quite remote. To first-century Jewish believers it would have been absolutely vital. And, if we are prepared to invest a little time studying it, for us today it will still pay rich dividends. It will lead us to many fresh insights into Jesus and to a deeper understanding of him and what he achieved.

The original readers were experiencing mild persecution (12:4; 13:3) because they had become followers of Jesus. Before long, a wedge was driven between Jews and Christians and they were driven apart, even though Jesus had been a Jew and the first Christians had still worshipped originally in the temple (see Acts 3:1). The inclusion of Gentiles in the church and their loose attitude to observing Jewish customs (which Paul spent so much time writing about) was considered unacceptable to good Jews, who therefore thought that following Jesus was an act of treason. Jewish Christians were expelled from synagogues and cut off from family and friends. The readers of Hebrews were asking whether it was worth it. With no temple to go to, no sacrifices to offer and no priests to rule over them, the Christian faith could seem pretty abstract in comparison with the Jewish faith. Wasn't it better, some were asking, to admit the mistake and go back to the synagogue?

To answer these uncertainties, Hebrews adopts both a positive and a negative approach. Positively, it sets out to show the superiority of Jesus to anything Judaism had to offer. Indeed, it aims to prove that the Jewish religion was one big signpost pointing to him. It also builds in a number of positive encouragements to following Christ, such as holding out the hope of finally laying down all the burdens of this life and entering into God's rest (4:1–13). Another positive encouragement comes when it is pointed out just how the great heroes of the faith from former times were cheering the readers on in the race they were now running (11:21–40). Negatively, there are a number of passages where the author warns his readers, sometimes quite sharply, of the danger of "drifting away" (2:1–4; 3:7–9; 4:11–13; 5:11 – 6:12; 12:25–29). These warnings usually follow on from some constructive teaching and set out, in no uncertain terms, the danger of ignoring what has just been said.

We can chart a course through Hebrews like this:

1:1–4	Christ superior to all God's previous messengers
1:5 – 2:18	Christ superior to angels
3:1 – 19	Christ superior to Moses
4:1–13	Christ superior to Joshua
4:14 – 7:28	Christ superior to the High Priest
8:1 – 9:28	Christ's superior covenant
10:1–31	Christ's superior sacrifice
10:32 – 12:29	The call to confidence and perseverance
13:1–25	Final warnings, encouragements and greetings

Hebrews is anonymous; no one can be sure who wrote it. To begin with, many attributed it to Paul, but that was never fully accepted. Its approach is so different from Paul's that it is unlikely he wrote it. One good suggestion is that it was written by Apollos, who is mentioned in Acts 18:24–28. This author's knowledge of the Hebrew scriptures, and his polished Greek, would certainly have equipped him to write Hebrews. But the authorship remains a mystery.

The "sermon" assumes that the Jewish temple and the sacrificial system is still in operation. Since all that came to an end when the Romans destroyed the temple in 70 AD, it must have been written before then, probably in the late 60s.

We should not be too quick to lock Hebrews up in a display case, as if it were a relic of some past time but of no value today. Quite apart from some of the wonderful passages, such as chapter 11, which do not get bogged down in Jewish ritual and which speak clearly to any time and culture, there are many people in our world who seek to know God through religious rituals, angels and priests (although today many would call them counsellors, therapists, trainers or gurus). So Hebrews is not limited to those of a Jewish background and still speaks aptly to our age.

James

There are several people with the name of James in the New Testament. The author of this letter was almost certainly James the brother of Jesus, who became the key leader in the church in Jerusalem (Acts 12:17; 15:13–21; 21:18). Any other James would have needed to qualify his name at the beginning of the letter in a way that the brother of Jesus did not. A sceptic during Jesus's lifetime, James came to believe when Jesus appeared to him after the resurrection (1 Corinthians 15:7). When he writes this letter he describes himself, significantly, as "a servant . . . of the Lord Jesus Christ" (1:1).

Many consider this letter to be inferior to other letters in the New Testament. It took some time to secure recognition – even Martin Luther described it as an "epistle of straw". It mentions

Jesus only twice (1:1; 2:1) and some say these references add nothing to the letter, which, apart from them, could be a Jewish tract. There is nothing here that you couldn't find in numerous Jewish writings, and plenty you could. But, even though James does not quote Jesus directly or say anything about the events of his life, as we might have expected, a careful reading of James reveals that time and again he is reflecting on the words of Jesus, alluding to them in his own words and applying them to his readers.

Who were his readers? James himself describes them as "the twelve tribes scattered among the nations" (1:1). One way of understanding the church was to see it as the new Israel (Galatians 6:16). So here were Christians who were living away from home in many different parts of the Roman world, but who almost certainly had a Jewish background. We also know that the economic situation meant some of them were really struggling to make ends meet (1:9–11; 5:1–11).

The letter reads just like one of the wisdom books of the Old Testament. It is not a carefully structured systematic or theological argument but a spiritual reflection on a number of practical concerns in life, such as suffering, money, anger, relationships and the tongue. One thing seems just to lead on to another; indeed, James is not above circling back over a topic he has already mentioned. But it is not a chaotic book whose subjects are chosen at random. They are chosen because of their significance for the original readers. And, unlike Proverbs, although he includes short, pithy sayings, he usually opens up a subject in a little depth before passing on to the next one.

James makes brilliant use of word-pictures. He writes vividly about stormy seas, withering flowers, shabby tramps, bits in the mouths of horses, small sparks that set forests ablaze, corroding silver and being fattened for slaughter. He also uses biblical illustrations to make his point. Abraham, Rahab, Job and Elijah all make their appearance.

Here is an introduction to practical Christian living. It

covers the ground like this:

1:1–16	Facing trials and temptations
1:17–27	The religion that pleases God – practical Christianity
2:1–13	Favouritism is unacceptable in the church
2:14–26	Believing and doing – how they fit together
3:1–12	Our troublesome tongues
3:13–18	Two kinds of wisdom
4:1–3	Trouble in the church
4:4–12	Friendship with God
4:13–17	Planning tomorrow
5:1–6	Justice for the wealthy who are unjust
5:7–12	Patience
5:13–20	Prayer and healing

James 1:27 is often thought to summarise the letter's whole message: "Religion that God our Father accepts as pure and faultless is this: to look after orphans and widows in their distress . . ." But the rest of the verse, which is often ignored, is also important: ". . . and to keep oneself from being polluted by the world." To James, the crucial issue facing his readers is whether they were going to shape their lives according to the world's ways or according to God's. It is God's wisdom (3:13–18) and his friendship (4:4) that matter.

1 Peter

1 Peter is a letter about suffering. Peter refers to his readers as "strangers in the world", suggesting that others made them feel that they did not fit in. He also speaks of "the painful trial" (4:12) they were suffering, which was the result of local opposition rather than an organised persecution by Rome. His purpose is to provide them with encouragement so that they might persevere and also to explain to them more fully about a Christian approach to suffering. There is much more in the letter than this, but this theme weaves its way through everything

Peter writes here. So, for example, when Peter writes about the rules for household living, as does Paul, he puts a particular spin on it and is concerned to explain how slaves should react when they are unjustly punished (2:19–20).

The letter was written by the apostle Peter from Rome (referred to symbolically as Babylon in 5:13). Tradition has it that Peter was based in Rome in his later years and was executed there by being crucified upside down when Nero persecuted the church in 64 AD. So this letter was probably written in the early 60s. There are a number of very personal touches in the letter. He writes of the resurrection with the conviction of an eyewitness (1:3). He mentions witnessing the suffering of Christ, as he introduces how to be a good elder (5:1–2). His conversation with Christ on the lake shore at Galilee after the resurrection (John 21:15–19) must surely have been in his mind as he wrote about eldership. When he tells his readers to be clothed with humility, did he have Jesus in mind being clothed with a towel as he washed the feet of the disciples (John 13:4)?

An outline of 1 Peter:

1:1–12	The Christian hope
1:13 – 2:3	The call to holy living
2:4–10	The church under construction
2:11 – 3:12	Living "the good life"
	2:11–12 as strangers in the world
	2:13–17 as citizens
	2:18–25 as slaves
	3:1–6 as wives
	3:7 as husbands
	3:8–12 in general
3:13 – 4:19	Dealing with suffering
	3:13–22 suffering when you are in the right
	4:1–11 do not give up
	4:12–19 suffering as sharing with Christ
5:1–11	Advice to elders and young men
5:12–14	Final greetings

The impressive thing about Peter's exposition of suffering is that he keeps bringing it back to Christ. We can face it, he says, because we have a hope in Christ which no one can take away from us (1:3–9). We can put up with it even when it is wrong, because that is exactly what Christ did (2:21–25). We can bear it, providing we know in our conscience that we are suffering only because we have made Christ Lord and are obeying him in everything (3:13–22). We can understand it as sharing in Christ's own sufferings (4:12–19). Over all this we can stand firm, knowing that the purpose of his suffering was to bring us to God (3:18) and that the end is near when all will stand before the Judge (4:5–7). On that day, those who have suffered unjustly will finally receive justice.

2 Peter

The tone and subject of 2 Peter is very different from that of Peter's first letter. It seems to repeat well over half of the letter of Jude, which has given rise to doubts as to whether Peter really was its author. And yet it bears the hallmarks of being written by him. It refers to his conversation with Christ, recorded in John 21 (1:14), and to his being an eyewitness of the transfiguration of Christ (1:17–18), as well as alluding to some of Christ's teaching. The change of situation and subject matter would have a significant impact on the way Peter wrote and may be sufficient to account for any differences between the two letters which bear Peter's name. When we also take into account that the early Christians did their homework carefully on the origin of the letters and believed they were only including in the canon those which were genuinely from the hands of the apostles, there is ultimately nothing to convince us that it was not from Peter's hand.

The letter, however, jumps straight into its subject and, apart from Peter's name, gives us no clues as to when and where it was written. No personal news is included. The damage being done by false teachers is its overwhelming concern. So it has no time for the niceties.

The letter begins by encouraging its readers to make their "calling and election" more secure (1:10). The way to do this is to build up their spiritual muscles by doing some spiritual exercise. They need to put some effort into their faith (1:5–9). This is not because there is anything lacking on God's part. Indeed, putting in spiritual effort would be a waste of time except that God has supplied them with everything they need to grow successfully to spiritual maturity (1:3–4). To attain that maturity, they also need to base their faith on the prophesies of Scripture which have been inspired by the Holy Spirit, and avoid being misled like spiritual infants by whatever the latest, exciting but potentially false, teaching is that is doing the rounds.

The main argument of the letter comes in chapter 2 where Peter denounces the false teachers, describes them as arrogant and self-indulgent, and prophesies their destruction. His confident prediction of their judgement is based on stories of judgement from the Old Testament.

Mention of future judgement leads Peter, in chapter 3, to do some teaching on the return of Christ. In this he has a twofold purpose. First, he counters the cynics who ridiculed belief in the second coming and gives his readers some good grounds for expecting it. Second, he shows them how this future Day of the Lord should have an impact on their lives in the here and now. Like 1 Peter, he demonstrates here a real concern for holy living. "Since everything will be destroyed in this way, what kind of people ought you to be? You ought to live holy and godly lives, as you look forward to the day of God and speed its coming" (3:11–12).

1, 2 and 3 John

1 John does not tell us who wrote it. 2 and 3 John say they were written by "the elder". The language and teaching of these letters are so similar to that of John's gospel that traditionally they

were thought to be written by the apostle John. Life, light, truth and knowledge are all mentioned here, as they were in the gospel. The claim, in the opening verses of the first letter, to be an eyewitness to events of Christ's life seems to confirm this view. If so, the letters were probably written in John's old age, when he was living in Ephesus. These letters are among the latest writings in the New Testament and by the time he wrote them, John was probably the only apostle still alive.

1 John is a pastoral letter with an emphasis on love and joy. But it should not be misinterpreted as a soft touch. John is writing because false teaching is being spread in the church; it has therefore become necessary to give people guidance as to how they can distinguish true from false believers. The false teaching bore some of the characteristics of a philosophy later known as Gnosticism. (We have already mentioned Gnosticism in reference to Colossians.) This philosophy taught that special "knowledge" was necessary to be in touch with God. It also taught that only the spiritual was good, whereas anything material was evil. That had all sorts of implications. It meant Jesus could not have been a real person because God would not have been able to pollute himself by taking on a human body. Some also took it to mean that if only the spirit counted, then you could do what you liked with your bodies, including living immoral lives, because it would not matter to God. Shades of this false teaching are still around today.

John emphasises his authority and writes quite sternly about the false teachers. They are "antichrists" (2:18; 4:3) and liars (2:22) who belong to "the world" and not to God (4:4–6). He wants his readers to enjoy to the full the blessings of being children of God. But they cannot do that while the false teaching continues to disturb them. So, how can they sort out truth from falsehood?

To answer that, John devises three basic tests which can be applied to any teaching. John mentions them more than once, sometimes combining them, which gives the letter the feel of being circular in its argument.

First test: Behaviour
Does the teaching lead people to obey Christ's commands?
(2:3–6; 2:28 – 3:10)

Second test: Experience
Does the teaching lead people to love others? (2:7–11;
3:11–18; 4:7–21)

Third test: Doctrine
Does the teaching lead people to believe Christ was truly a
human being?
(2:18–27; 4:1–6)

His aim throughout is to encourage his readers to be certain of
their faith, not to hope it is so, or wish it to be true, but to know
it is. The word "know" occurs 26 times in the NIV translation
of this short letter. When the tests are applied, there is no need
for believers to be insecure about their faith; full assurance is
possible.

2 and 3 John are very short letters which go over the same
themes as the first letter. But they are more personal, are
addressed to individuals and mention the subject of hospitality,
which was an important issue in the early church. If there is a
difference between them, besides a difference of recipients, it is
that 2 John stresses love and 3 John stresses truth. 3 John
shows us that truth is not about believing a set of mental propositions but something on which you build your whole life. So it
speaks of being faithful to the truth (3), continuing to walk in
the truth (3), and working together for the truth (8).

Jude

In this short letter Jude lambasts false teachers with all guns
blazing. Jude, the younger brother of Jesus and James, had
planned to write a pleasant letter dwelling on the theme of salvation (3) but the false teachers were putting the church at risk

and so he had to write instead to encourage his friends "to contend for the faith that was once for all entrusted to the saints" (3). This was not a faith you could amend or improve upon when you felt like it.

The false teachers, who are obviously members of the church (4, 12), are described in terms which are very similar to 2 Peter: they are insolent grumblers who reject authority, are arrogant, sexually immoral and self-indulgent. Judgement is heaped upon their heads, again using the Old Testament to provide the precedents.

Jude's letter is urgent but not panicky. His friends are "called, . . . loved . . . and kept" by God (1) and so are more than adequately equipped to fight back against the offensive of the false teachers. Three weapons are provided for them to mount the counter-attack: the apostolic faith, the Holy Spirit and the love of God. They are to build themselves up in their most holy faith, to pray in the Holy Spirit and to keep themselves in God's love (20–21).

Revelation

The book of Revelation usually provokes one of three reactions: great excitement, great controversy or great bewilderment. It is unlike any other book in the New Testament and is open to wide interpretation. It describes itself as a revelation (1:1) and a prophecy (1:3). However difficult, it promises to bring blessing to those who read it and take it to heart (1:3; 22:7).

The author identifies himself as John. Traditionally, that was taken to refer to the apostle John. The book was written from exile on the island of Patmos (1:9), when the church in what we now know as western Turkey was suffering persecution. The evidence suggests that this was during the reign of the Roman emperor Domitian in 95 AD.

It is written in an "apocalyptic" style. The Greek word for "revelation" is *apokalypsis*. This was a kind of crisis literature which was quite common between 200 BC and 200 AD. An Old Testament example is found in the last part of Daniel. It unveils the hidden secrets of the cosmos and the purposes of God in history, by using visions which are full of weird pictures and amazing symbols. It is wrong to think that these visions can be reduced to flat reality. They are much more like abstract art than an architect's plan. They are poetry rather than prose. The images are there to stir up imagination rather than to define things tightly. Nonetheless, they are intelligible to those who read them, providing a few basic keys of interpretation are understood.

One key is the way John uses numbers. Seven frequently occurs and is the symbol for fullness, completeness or perfection. So the seven churches (1:4 – 3:22) represent the whole church. The seven bowls of wrath (15:1 – 16:21) represent complete judgement. And when the seven spirits of God (5:6) are sent out into all the earth, it means that God is holding nothing back. In contrast, six is one short of deity and perfection. The symbol for the beast is 666 (13:18) because he foolishly pretends to be God but lamentably falls short. This number, too, might have been a symbolic way of talking about the emperor Nero, who viciously persecuted the church. The reason we think this is that, in the ancient world, letters of the alphabet could be translated into a numerical value and, once you do that with the name Nero, the letters add up to 666. Twelve is the number of the tribes of Israel, which is mirrored by the twelve tribes of the New Israel. 144,000, (14:1, 3) therefore, is not a literal number but a thousand (that is, a huge number) times twelve times twelve. It speaks of the massive number who make up the redeemed.

Another important key is the Old Testament. Revelation contains some 400 quotes or allusions from 24 Old Testament books and it makes full use of key Old Testament symbols, such as Babylon (14:8; 16:19; 17:5; 18:2, 10, 21). Babylon, the site of the tower of Babel (Genesis 11:1–9) became, in later history, the symbol of all great world powers which oppressed

God's people. So Babylon could signify the city which was persecuting the church of John's day, or any similar centre of power since that time, without it being named. The lion and the lamb have an obvious Old Testament background too.

We must remember that the letter was first written as an encouragement to its original readers, so that they could persevere under persecution. So we must first of all read it through their eyes. But its message is not limited to them; it is included in the Bible because it is valuable for us too. Some try to relate its various chapters to the progression of world history, usually with a view to claiming that they are living at the very last moment of time before the final judgement and coming again of Christ. But all attempts to do this have so far been proved wrong and it is almost certainly not the way in which the book is meant to be read.

It is more profitably understood as pulling back the curtain on recurring world events, to show the unseen realities which are behind them and which are really governing the world throughout the period between the ascension and the coming again of Christ. We can tell this is the way we are meant to read it, because the events do not all happen one after the other. Seals 1 to 6, for example, follow one after the other. But before the seventh seal is broken, the sequence is interrupted and another slice of reality is inserted which obviously is occurring simultaneously. Revelation often flicks, as it were, from one television channel to another, to view what is happening in parallel elsewhere in the universe, rather than unfolding history in a neat, chronological order. But Revelation also makes clear that history is not trapped in an endless cycle of events from which there is no escape. History is working towards a climax.

This all adds up to the book having a powerful impact. The church might be under threat and attack but the reality is that its enemies are defeated and judged. Caesar, or any other world tyrant, may appear to be in control, but the one who breaks the seals and initiates God's final judgement is the Lamb who was slain (5:1–14). The throne of God is secure. The plan of God cannot be thwarted. The message is that, whatever our experience of evil now, the time will come when God will triumph over all wrong; evil and its henchmen will be banished, and God will live in peace again among his people.

Much of Revelation is patterned on a series of seven. It is difficult to provide more than a rough guide, since the sequence is disjointed in places and a lot of fine details need to be added, but a basic outline goes like this:

1	A vision of the exalted Christ
2 – 3	Letters to the seven churches
4 – 5	A vision of heaven
6 – 7	Opening of the seven seals
8 – 11	Sounding of the seven trumpets
12 – 14	Vision of the seven signs
15 – 16	Execution of the seven plagues
17 – 18	Celebration of the fall of Babylon
19 – 22	Seven scenes of God's final triumph

It is hard to think of a more suitable way to conclude the Bible than with the book of Revelation. It looks back to the work of Christ and his cross. It looks up to the hidden realities of our world. It looks forward to the coming day when God will rule over all. It inspires worship, excites hope, stimulates faith and strengthens perseverance.

It also brings us full circle. The story of God's dealing with his creation began in a garden where God enjoyed perfect harmony with men and women. But this was destroyed by sin, with the result that God and human beings could no longer live together. The long story of God's gracious dealing with humanity leads to a new creation where the harmony is restored and he lives again among men and women. On that day, Eden will not only be reclaimed but surpassed. "Amen. Come, Lord Jesus" (22:20).

10

One Story or Many?
Diversity and Unity in the Bible

The Bible seems to contain such a varied collection of writings, covering different times, styles, themes and emphases that we need to ask whether it is any more than a collection of interesting but fragmented documents which is full of inconsistencies and lacks any overarching unity and coherence. After exploring some of the reasons why its diversity is to be understood and valued, this chapter suggests that a number of common themes run throughout the Bible, all of which demonstrate that any developments which occur in them are developments which fit into a pattern and make consistent sense. The Bible finds its greatest coherence in Christ.

One Story or Many?
Diversity and Unity in the Bible

After an action-packed holiday, the moment comes when the photos are developed and the family members sit around to look at them. The photographs bring back great memories but also sometimes cause confusion. It is amazing how much of the holiday has already been forgotten. "Did we do that on Tuesday or Wednesday?" "That's Scarborough," says one member of the family. "No, it isn't, it's Whitley Bay," says another.

Our long journey through the Bible has now been completed and possibly, by now, you are feeling that you don't know your Hosea from your Habakkuk, your Thessalonians from your Ephesians. Don't worry. The more you read it, the more its different parts will become familiar to you. But our purpose in this chapter is to stand back and ask how it all fits together. Is the Bible just a collection of snapshots which are taken at different points on the journey and which do not particularly relate to each other or are there overarching themes which bring it all together and make it a coherent message from God?

The question is important to help us see the wood for the trees. It is also important because many today deny that the Bible has a unified message. What began as a healthy enquiry into the distinctive contributions of the Bible's different authors has ended with the Bible being seen as a collection of loosely connected writings, without any overall coherence. So some speak of Paul's gospel, or of Peter's gospel, or of John's gospel but can no longer speak of "the gospel". This process of fragmentation has resulted in there being no coherent, meaningful revelation from God in which we can trust.

Hebrews 1:1 deals with the Bible's diversity and unity neatly: "In the past God spoke to our ancestors through the prophets at many times and in various ways [there is diversity], but in these last days he has spoken to us by his Son [there is unity]." The diversity of God's communication to us finds its unity in Christ.

Creation may help us to understand this. Surely, the God who made the wonderfully complex and varied world in which we live is more than capable of communicating with people in their different situations in more than one way. He is anything but a monochrome God. So why should we think that his communication has to be reduced to a single style, use a single medium, or endlessly repeat a single monotonous message? But creation is neither random, contradictory, nor chaotic. It was out of chaos that God brought order, meaning and coherence, by his word. In like manner, the God who communicates in the Bible does so in a wonderfully varied set of ways and yet he does so with a unified message which makes sense and fits together into a meaningful whole.

Celebrating variety

The Bible is a very varied book. There is nothing to be afraid of in this but rather much to celebrate. Think of why this should be so.

Variety due to its history

The story told in the Bible covers at least 2,000 years of history. The Bible's early chapters tell of tribespeople in the ancient world, wandering around a desert during the time of the great Egyptian civilisation. They then become a settled urban community under their own kings. The scene moves on to the rise of the Assyrian and Babylonian empires, which eventually take these people captive and displace them from their homeland. Restoration back to an emaciated Jerusalem follows under the Persians. In between the Old and New Testaments, other civilisations come and go. Persia gives way to the Greeks, whose culture exerts a powerful influence throughout the civilised world and whose seductive impact threatens to undermine the Jewish faith from within.

By the time the New Testament opens, the Greeks have been put in their place by the Romans – yet another form of civilisation rules the world. It is characterised by law and military rule but brings a sort of peace to the ancient world. It is in this culture that the good news of Jesus flourishes. That gospel, which relates to a man who grew up in an area about as remote as possible from the centre of civilisation, spreads out from Jerusalem until it infiltrates, and at first threatens and then transforms, the great cities of the Roman Empire, including Rome itself. There is bound to be diversity. The world in which the Bible is set and to which it speaks keeps changing.

Variety due to progressive revelation

Some ask, however, whether the message, not just the setting, of the Bible changes dramatically over time. The sort of thing such questioners usually have in mind is that the Old Testament seems to be all about law, whereas the New Testament is all about grace. Some say that there even appear to be two Gods spoken of in the Bible. The God of the Old Testament is one Person: awesome, holy, happy to command his people to engage in warfare and genocide, and spending a good deal of time being angry. The God of the New Testament is three Persons (Father, Son and Holy Spirit): friendly, loving, commanding his people to be peacemakers and to love their enemies, and spending a great deal of his time being forgiving.

In answer to such questions, we must first insist that these pictures of God in the Old and New Testaments are gross caricatures, so gross as to be indefensible. Later in the chapter, we will look at the way in which a unified picture of God runs throughout the Bible. There are not two Gods in the Bible but one.

Yet, having said that, there clearly are differences in emphasis and approach which still need to be considered. One way in which theologians have done so is to talk about "progressive revelation", that is, God gradually making himself known in history. God does not reveal himself all at once. What God discloses of himself gets fuller and fuller as time goes by, until it reaches its ultimate point in Christ.

The idea is really quite simple and can easily be understood when we think of the relationship between a parent and a child. I am the same person today that I was when my son was born. Of course, I have changed a bit over the years, put on weight and gone grey. (God does not change in this way, because he is not a human being but immortal and not subject to the ageing process.) But basically, I am the same person as I was when my son was first born. Yet our relationship today is different because the way in which we communicate with each other has developed over the years. When he was a very small child and was on safari around the room, about to do something dangerous, I did not stop to reason with him, man to man. If he was heading for a red-hot poker (which I hasten to add he never did), I would have shouted at him, to frighten him and distract him away from the object he had set his mind on. Later, when communication developed, I could spell out the law to him in a cooler manner – "Don't touch the poker, because it's hot" – and back it up with sanctions if necessary. Later still, I could reason with him and explain the folly of picking up a hot poker by introducing him to the laws of physics. (Well, I could, if I knew them!) Earlier, he would not have been able to grasp them and it would have been a futile exercise on my part. And so on. Communication develops and becomes fuller as people grow up.

As with human relationships, so it is between God and his

creation. The fact that an infinite, eternal God communicates with his finite creatures at all involves him "accommodating" to our limitations. Over time, he accommodates in different ways, so that people at various stages in salvation history can understand. Yet, at each stage, God makes enough of himself known so that his revelation of himself is sufficient, until he makes himself most fully and completely known in the coming of Christ. One stage of revelation is built on another. Nothing is wrong with the earlier stages or in need of correction. They just need to be developed and unpacked more fully and clearly.

A particular example of this might be seen in the way in which the blessings of God in the Old Testament are measured in material terms, such as wealth and a long life. These concrete ways of measuring his blessing recede into the background in the New Testament, as people come to appreciate the spiritual blessings there are in Christ (Ephesians 1:3). This is just like the child who measures a parent's favour initially by the size of her pocket money but comes increasingly to appreciate the less tangible aspect of parental love as she grows.

The time of the patriarchs mirrors the close relationship between a parent and a very young child. Then, as the child grows, under Moses, comes the time of the law. During adolescence, the law is explained more fully by the prophets, through whom God reasons with his people (see Isaiah 1:18). Then, "when the time had fully come" (Galatians 4:4) and adulthood, as it were, had been reached, the ultimate form of communication took place in Christ. The Bible teaches us that nothing further is necessary after Jesus, except that the Holy Spirit would spell out the meaning of some of the things he had said and done (John 16:12–15).

Variety due to its writers and readers

Over the length of time involved, people were bound to write in different ways about different issues. We no longer write today (mercifully) in the way Samuel Pepys did when he wrote his diaries about the Great Plague and Fire of London in the 1660s.

Chapter 1 spoke of the varied gifts and styles which the authors and editors of the Bible brought to their task; all of these people were rooted in their own time and culture and consequently, to some extent, were inevitably shaped by the days in which they lived.

They were also writing for different audiences, concerning the issues which were important to them. The questions which occupied the readers in Jerusalem during Solomon's reign were very different from those of the exiles in Babylon. No wonder Proverbs is different from Jeremiah! The needs of people living in one of the cities of the Roman empire who mainly had a Gentile background were very different from those who were steeped in the Jewish faith. No wonder Corinthians is different from Hebrews! These factors were bound to add to the Bible's variety.

Variety due to the wonder of the gospel

When it comes to the New Testament, yet another factor needs to be introduced. Paul speaks of the "riches of Christ" as "unsearchable" or "inexhaustible" (Ephesians 3:8). He is saying that however much you contemplate the grace of God, and however many ways you invent to express it, you will never come to an end of the process. It defies complete understanding and can never be reduced satisfactorily to a few simple sentences. It is always possible to examine God's grace from different angles; new dimensions of it are always being discovered. It can always be put in innovative ways for fresh audiences, using original words for new generations. There is a single reality in the gospel but that single reality demands a multitude of ways to understand it.

Variety due to its being a living communication

There is a further reason to thank God for diversity. It is the diversity which makes the Bible a real and living book. It is not a boring, systematic manual from God, which provides an encyclopaedic but wooden answer on everything. It relates to the real world, speaks of the diverse fortunes of men and women and communicates in living ways. At its heart, it is about the relationships between God and the people he made. Relationships are dynamic, ever changing, never static. Although you can find useful insights into human relationships in psychology, management or sociology textbooks, we all know that real life never happens in textbook fashion. Novels often give us more insight into the complexity and changeableness of human relationships than textbooks do (and they are usually more enjoyable to read). The Bible is much too alive to be compared to an academic textbook and so is bound to be diverse. Its diversity means that we can all find points of entry and identify with it somewhere.

Celebrating unity

Good relationships are dynamic but not haphazard. Good relationships need freshness and originality, but they also need continuity and stability. Marriages may fail if they grow stale; one of the major factors in staleness may well be that the partners have never grown as persons in their own right or in their relationship. But they equally may fail if one partner keeps changing the way they behave or their ideas of who they think they are. Then, the other partner doesn't know where they stand. To wake up married to a plumber one day, a pop star another, a politician on another day and a preacher on yet another day would put a strain on most marriages. To keep changing one's mind about how one is going to spend money, discipline the kids or whether one supports Liverpool or Manchester United is likely to test most relationships. Continuity, as well as change, is important.

The Bible may have two Testaments and 66 books but it exhibits continuity. It does not contradict itself but shows itself to be a connected work, marked by a certain progression, where the elements are woven together to make a coherent picture. The New grows out of the Old as a flower grows from a seed. And, just as you don't plant marigold seeds and find pansies growing, so the New is a consistent development of the Old.

We may illustrate this by briefly looking at seven key themes which run like a thread throughout the Bible.

God

The Bible is consistent throughout in what it teaches us about God. From beginning to end he is One and Three, holy and gracious, compassionate and just, powerful and merciful.

The basic declaration of faith for the people of Israel was, "The Lord our God, the Lord is One" (Deuteronomy 6:4). God was unique and indivisible in his solitary supremacy in the universe. People may have worshipped other deities but the reality was that these deities had no real power and were not in any way to be compared with him. The New Testament affirms these same truths about God in 1 Corinthians 8:5–6.

Yet this one and only God says, "Let *us* make human beings" (Genesis 1:26). Here we get a brief glimpse into God also as a divine community, communicating to himself. Messengers of God suddenly appear in human form on occasions in the Old Testament, anticipating the time when "the son of God" would appear and dwell among people (Joshua 5:13–15; Daniel 3:25). The Spirit of God comes on people and equips them for various tasks, even if only temporarily. These faint impressions form a much clearer picture in the New Testament, where we find God making himself known as Father, Son and Holy Spirit. So Christians continue to affirm that there is one God (1 Timothy 2:5) who makes himself known in three persons (2 Corinthians 13:14).

It is true that God is pure, majestic and awesome in his holiness. But the basic and often-repeated statement about God in the Old Testament is that he is "The LORD, the LORD, the compassionate and gracious God, slow to anger, abounding in love and faithfulness, maintaining love to thousands, and forgiving wickedness, rebellion and sin" (Exodus 34:6 and eight other references). Yes, he shows himself to be opposed to sin but he always shows himself to be a God of grace and love. John's deceptively simple claim that "God is love" (1 John 4:16) could have been written at any time. He is love from beginning to end.

Yet he is also holy and powerful, no less in the New than in the Old Testament. The way his majestic holiness expresses itself may change but it is just as real. His judgement on sin is still experienced dramatically in the early church (Acts 5:1–11), preached by the apostles (Romans 1:18; 5:9; Colossians 3:6; 1 Timothy 1:9–11; Hebrews 12:28–29) and, most of all, awaited by the prophets (Revelation 6 – 20).

Throughout the Bible, this one God is, as P. T. Forsyth called him, "the Holy Father" who balances his love with his faithfulness, his righteousness with his peace (Psalm 85:10), without denying his character in any way.

Creation

Another thread that runs throughout the Bible is the theme of creation. It is especially evident in the opening and closing chapters of the Bible, but it makes frequent appearances elsewhere and even more frequently, forms the backdrop when other things are being discussed.

Creation is an act of God and carries all the hallmarks of being his handiwork. It is vast and varied, colourful and complex, precise and orderly, good and bountiful, alive and mysterious. He brought it into existence by his own power, unaided (Isaiah 40:9–31). So it rightly belongs to him, exists for his pleasure and is at his disposal.

The Bible never leaves this vision of creation behind. John, Paul and Hebrews all draw attention to Jesus as the one by whom, through whom and for whom creation was made (John 1:1–4; Colossians 1:15–17; Hebrews 1:2). Paul adds the thought that its continuing existence and well-being depends still on Christ sustaining it.

All this means that the creation is important to God. The

material world is not something from which to escape as soon as possible to some higher realm of the spirit or to some ethereal heaven. It is in the material world that God relates to men and women, the crown of his creation. The care of the physical creation has been entrusted into their hands and continues to be our responsibility now. And it is in the theatre of creation, in a body, that Jesus lived and died to redeem it from its fallenness.

Creation needs redeeming because it suffered when men and women declared independence from God; as part of God's judgement on humanity, the ground became cursed (Genesis 3:17–19). From then on, planet Earth behaved in a distorted and disjointed fashion, out of sorts with its maker, with the people who live in it and even with itself.

Central to the Christian vision of the future is the ending of these "frustrations", as Paul calls them in Romans 8:20. He compares our present situation on earth to going through the agony of labour. The experience is painful, even extremely painful, but is worth it because of the new life which is produced as a result. Pain is a good sign, then, because it gives us hope for the future. So it is to the creation of a new earth, not just some mysterious parallel realm called heaven, to which Christians look – to a creation put back in its rightful relationship with God (2 Peter 3:13). Revelation gives us an insight into what living in this recreated heaven and earth will be like (Revelation 21 – 22).

This redemption of creation takes place, just as much as the reconciliation of individual sinners to God, through Christ's physical death on the cross (Colossians 1:20). It is a further outworking of the spiritual principle, which is often illustrated in the natural world, that life comes out of death.

Sin

Sin is more than breaking God's commandments. The Bible uses a host of terms to describe it. It is failure, trespassing, pollution, wrongdoing, fallenness, getting lost, straying from the right road, missing the mark, being held captive and infidelity, as well as rebellion. In essence, sin comes between us and God and causes our relationship with him to be broken (Genesis 3:1–24). It infects our very nature from birth (Psalm 51:5) and brings death and destruction in its train (Genesis 3:14–19; Romans 6:23). Alienation from God, from each other and from creation results.

In the Old Testament, the law and the sacrifices provided a way of containing the problem of sin, but not of finally curing it. The law restrained people from wrongdoing but could not change them on the inside. The sacrifices provided atonement in the short term, until further sin demanded they be repeated, but they could not bring cleansing or forgiveness once and for all. Neither the law nor sacrifices could fundamentally remove the alienation and reconcile God with human creation. They could only point forward to a time when God would himself provide the real solution. They were "a shadow of the things that were to come; the reality, however, is found in Christ" (Colossians 2:17).

The mission of Christ was to reconcile men and women to God (2 Corinthians 5:18–21). He did this by confronting and overcoming sin, not by side-stepping it and the problems it caused. His strategy was to exchange places with us. In spite of his own perfect sinless life, he took on himself our sin, and its consequences, as he died on the cross and rose again to life, dealing with it once and for all.

Covenant

As we travelled through the books of the Bible, the idea of the covenant often came to the fore. By way of reminder, a covenant is a treaty or agreement made between two parties. God made covenants with Noah, Abraham, Israel and David. Although the particular details varied, in essence the covenants declared that he would be their God, protecting, defending and blessing them in return for their keeping their side of the agreement, which required them to live in obedience to his laws. When the Psalms speak of God's "unfailing love" or kindness, as they frequently do (Psalm 6:4; 18:50; 32:10; 85:7; 107:8, 15, 21, 31), they are speaking of the love spelled out in the covenant to which God was always true. The other side of the agreement was also just as clear, however. Failure to observe the terms of the covenant would result in God withdrawing his blessing and people experiencing his curse. Much of the Old Testament aims to trace the fortunes of the people of Israel in relation to their keeping of the covenant. Their persistent and growing failure to keep it eventually resulted in the curses being meted out, in the form of the exile.

Jeremiah prophesied that one day a new form of covenant would come into being, which would replace the first covenant and transform people from the inside so that they walked in obedience with God (31:31). The New Testament speaks of the work of Jesus as bringing this new covenant into existence. Covenants were usually sealed with blood: the new covenant was sealed with the blood of Jesus (Luke 22:20; Hebrews 9:15–22). This is a superior covenant to all previous ones (2 Corinthians 3:1–18; Hebrews 10:15–18) and results in those who enter into it experiencing complete forgiveness for sin, security in their relationship with God, release from condemnation by the law, and the transforming power of the Holy Spirit within.

Kingship

The reigns of David and Solomon, for all their imperfections, demonstrate what good kingship should be like. Under their rule, the people of Israel knew prosperity. The nation was at ease with itself and enjoyed a fair measure of equality and harmony within its borders. Their enemies were defeated and Israel's boundaries were extended. The oppression of Egypt was behind them. The oppression of their own despotic kings and of Assyria and Babylon was still to come. It was an ideal period in their history.

Their true king was, of course, God, the sovereign ruler of the whole earth (Psalm 47:7). Any earthly king of Israel, who was sometimes called a "son of God" (Psalm 2:7), was merely God's representative. It was when a king forgot that and got above himself that the trouble started.

The gospels use the idea of kingship as a major framework by which to interpret the work of Jesus (Mark 1:15). Against their own best interests, people had conspired with God's enemies to reject his authority. It was a misguided bid for freedom. What they did not realise was that God's enemies were their enemies too and that, rather than gaining independence, their decisions brought them under a new government, that of Satan, which reduced them to slavery once more. The gospels show that, through Jesus, God's rule is re-established. He begins to reclaim the earth, his rightful possession, and throw out the satanic opposition who have been ruining his creation and enslaving his people. God's kingdom is one where justice, liberty and righteousness prevail.

The gospels are full of talk about the kingdom. The letters are less so, although the term is not entirely absent in them (for example, 1 Corinthians 4:20; 6:9–10; Colossians 1:12–14) and the idea, if not the language, is still common (for example, Hebrews 2:14). The letters spend more time on the person of the King himself and on his church, which is the community of the King and the showcase of his kingdom, than on the wider concept. But they never lose the vision that what Christ did was to inaugurate the process which will climax one day in God's rule being fully and finally established throughout his creation, recognised and submitted to by all (1 Corinthians 15:24–28; Philippians 2:9–11; Hebrews 12:28). Revelation envisages that time most fully, and graphically describes not only God's final triumph but the nature of the kingdom to come.

From first to last, the Bible resounds with the shout that "God is king" (see Isaiah 52:7).

God's people

God made men and women so that he could enjoy a relationship with them. When sin destroyed that relationship with humanity as a whole, God chose particular people to whom he could relate in a special way. Noah and his family were one such group (Genesis 6:9) but Abraham is the most significant person in this regard (Genesis 12:1-3). Abraham and his descendants, the children of Israel, became God's elect people.

The idea of "election" often leads people to think that it implies superiority or some sense of divine favouritism and protection, no matter how people live or what they do. But this is a gross misunderstanding of the Bible's teaching about election. There, two things are very clear from the start, both of which undermine such an arrogant misrepresentation of the idea.

First, God does not elect people because they are particularly special, superior or deserving. Deuteronomy 7:7 nails that lie on the head. He chooses people not because of their qualities, but simply out of love. Grace is the basis of election from Genesis to Revelation.

Second, people are elected primarily *for* a purpose, not *to* a status. Their election is with a view to their accomplishing a mission. God said to Abraham that he had been chosen so that "all the peoples of the earth would be blessed" through him (Genesis 12:3). Isaiah speaks of Israel being chosen as the servant of God in the world, so that they could be a light to the nations (Isaiah 42:1-7; 44:1, 2; 49:1-7). The emphasis is mainly on the outward aspect, of their fulfilling their responsibilities in the world, rather than the inward one, of their enjoying the privileges of relationship.

The people of Israel failed to fulfil their responsibilities as God's special people, so God devised a new way of choosing a group of people who would relate specially to him and be his own. Under the new covenant, Israel is set aside, at least temporarily (see Romans 9 – 11, which speaks of their place in God's long-term plan), and Christians are spoken of as "elect" (Ephesians 1:11; Colossians 3:12; 2 Timothy 2:10; Titus 1:1; 1 Peter 1:2; 2:9). God's new people are chosen still on the basis of grace, but they now consist of all those who put their faith in

Jesus Christ, rather than being people of a particular nation. The new people of God, then, are from every ethnic, racial and language group. The inclusion of non-Jews among God's elect people is an astonishing and startling development and becomes central to the proclamation of the gospel by the apostles (Ephesians 2:19–22; 1 Peter 2:9–10).

But election is still for a purpose. His church, as his new chosen people are sometimes called, exists to demonstrate to the rest of humanity, and to the unseen powers of the world, the reconciling and transforming power of the gospel (Ephesians 3:7–11). Their task is to make disciples and to bring the nations to obedience to Christ (Matthew 28:19; Romans 16:26).

Salvation

The word salvation (together with related words) threads its way through the Bible as firmly as a silver strip threads its way through a banknote. Remove it and what is left is worthless. It first occurs in Exodus 15:2 where, after Israel cross the Red Sea, Moses and Miriam celebrate Israel's deliverance and declare that the Lord has become their salvation. Its last occurrence is in Revelation 19:1 where a great multitude in heaven declare that salvation "belongs to our God".

Salvation means deliverance, rescue, setting free from oppression, and being released from bondage so that life might be lived in accordance with God's original design. So the word is naturally associated with the great events like the exodus and the return from exile (Isaiah 46:13) and with personal experiences of deliverance, such as those David knew in his encounters with wild animals and enemies (2 Samuel 22:1–4).

These are great salvation events in their own right. But they are also pointers to the greater salvation which we can experience through the death of Jesus Christ, and through him alone (Acts 4:12). Death, it should be pointed out, was the means, right from the start, by which salvation was obtained (Genesis 22; Exodus 12; Isaiah 53 and Hebrews 2:14–15). Christ's "great salvation" (Hebrews 2:3) delivers us from sin and rescues us from the clutches of our enemies, namely the accusations of the law, Satan and death (Romans 5:12 – 6:14; 1 Corinthians 15:54–57 and Hebrews 2:14–15, again).

The Christian has to speak of salvation in two tenses. First, it is something we are already experiencing (2 Corinthians 6:2; Philippians 2:12). But our experience of it is partial for, second, it is a salvation which is yet to come and to be realised fully (1 Peter 1:5, 9; Revelation 12:10). That is why, for the moment, being a Christian can sometimes be an uncomfortable experience, one where we are still struggling against sin and the power of Satan and will experience a physical death. We are a bit like the children of Israel in the wilderness. We have been delivered from Egypt but have not yet entered into the Promised Land. But the day will come when these tensions are past and we enter fully into our inheritance (1 Peter 1:4).

One title for God, affirmed throughout the Bible, is that he is "God our Saviour" (Psalm 65:5; 68:19; 79:9; 1 Timothy 1:1; 2:3; Titus 2:13). Without betraying any unease, the New Testament can equally affirm that Jesus Christ is "God our Saviour" (Titus 1:4; 2:13; 2 Peter 1:1). Salvation is what God is all about, in the Old as much as in the New Testament. The message is one.

Bringing it all into focus

We could go on developing other themes which witness to the unity of the Bible. But one important thing remains to be said. The unity of the Bible comes into focus in Jesus. In the words of a contemporary writer, Mike Riddell, "Jesus is the centre, the heart and the fulcrum of scripture" (*God's Home Page*, BRF, 1998, p. 42). Without him, it makes no sense. He is the pivot on which the whole teaching of the Bible turns. In the words of a great theologian, Karl Barth, "The Old Testament points forward, the New Testament points backward, and both point to Christ' (*Homiletics*, Westminster/John Knox, 1991, p. 81).

As we have seen, the Old Testament anticipates his coming. The great events, such as the exodus, are like models of the real thing, like an artist's elementary sketch of a great painting. The prophets are constantly straining forward and predicting the coming of a great king or deliverer who will bring salvation and establish peace and a just regime. The sacrifices are mock-ups of the sacrifice of Christ. The great laws reveal the moral perfection of God to which we can never attain. But Jesus lived them to perfection throughout his life of compassion, integrity and inner purity. Lesser laws, which have long since fallen into disuse, Jesus brought to completion in a different way. Take those, for example, relating to skin diseases which rendered people unfit to worship God. Jesus fulfilled these laws by touching the unclean and making them clean and whole, so that they could join once more in the worship of God.

Everything strains forward to him. Without his coming, the Old Testament is like a building half finished, a musical phrase left incomplete, a great project never fully realised, a financial deal never closed. But what the Old Testament began, the work of Christ completed. So the uncomfortable sense of being in a state of suspense because the story is only half completed is overcome. The work of the Old Testament was brought to a wonderful climax in Christ.

It is just as true, but perhaps a little more obvious, that the New Testament goes on to spell out the meaning of the life of Christ more fully. One major way in which it does this is by spelling out the implications of Christ's coming for his follow-ers. That means that everything we read later in the New Testament can be traced back to him. But its relevance is not limited to the disciples alone. It spells out the meaning of Christ's life for the rest of the world as well. It does this in a number of ways. First, it does so by issuing an invitation to people to accept his gospel. Second, it does so by sending out warnings to people who utterly refuse his gospel. Third, it does so by holding out a promise about the future when God will *manifestly* reign supreme and unchallenged in his cosmos.

Jesus pointed out to some of the "biblical scholars" of his day that they were totally misguided in their study of the Scriptures because they missed the whole point of them. "You diligently study the Scriptures," he told them, "because you think that by them you possess eternal life. These are the Scriptures that testify about me, yet you refuse to come to me to have life" (John 5:39–40). The same mistake is possible today. Some are excellent scholars of the book but never seem to come to know and relate to Christ himself. Salvation does not lie in the knowledge of the book but in the knowledge of the one of whom the book speaks. John Stott uses a helpful illustration to point out the folly of stopping with the book and not going on to Christ himself. He writes:

> To suppose that salvation lies in a book is as foolish as supposing that health lies in a prescription. When we are ill and the doctor prescribes some medicine for us, does he intend that we should go home with the prescription, read it, study it and learn it by heart? Or that we should frame it and hang it on our bedroom wall? Or that we should tear it into fragments and eat the pieces three times a day after meals? The absurdity of these possibilities is obvious. The prescription itself will not cure us. The whole purpose of a prescription is to get us to go to the chemist, obtain the medicine prescribed and drink it. Now the Bible contains the medicine for sin-sick souls. It specifies the only medicine which can save us from perishing. In brief, it tells us of Jesus Christ who died for us and rose again. But we do not worship the Bible as if it could save us; we go to Christ. For the overriding purpose of the Bible is to send us to Christ and persuade us to drink the water of life he offers. (*Christ the Controversialist*, IVP, 1970, pp. 101–2)

We must never forget that the whole of the Bible points to him. And unless we come to him and trust him with our lives, all our knowledge of the book will be worth nothing. He is the key that makes sense of the rest. He is the focus and the unifying factor of it all. He is the living Saviour.

11

The Authority of the Bible

The Bible has exercised extraordinary influence down the centuries, an influence which far outweighs that of any other ancient book in the world. Why should this be so? The answer is because it is the book of the living God and is his revelation of himself to his world. As such, it is marked by both his truthfulness and his authority. But how can a human book be so authoritative? Christians have answered that question by referring to the idea of inspiration – an inspiration which also logically leads us to assert that the Bible is without error in all that it teaches. The contemporary world questions all "received" authorities, including that of the Bible. So are there additional arguments we can use to defend the Bible's authority? This chapter points a way forward.

The Authority of the Bible

We turn now to the next important question about the Bible. Having looked at how it reached us and what it says, we now ask why it matters. Why has it exercised such an influence down the centuries? And why do Christians, in particular, spend so much time reading and studying such an ancient collection of books and invest it with such significance?

The short answer to these questions is that the book gives all the signals of being a communication from God. It carries with it, therefore, his authority as well as the stamp of his character. If God has spoken, we, his creatures, are wise to pay attention. We would be foolish in the extreme to ignore what he says. But has he? How do we know?

This basic question breaks down into a number of other related but separate questions, which we will briefly review. Four come to mind: the question of revelation, of inspiration, of infallibility and of authority.

Revelation

Revelation means that God discloses himself, that he makes himself known to his creation. He does so, as we are told in Hebrews 1:1 (which was quoted in the last chapter), in different ways at different times. One way in which theologians have handled this variety is to distinguish between his "general" and his "special" revelation.

God makes himself known in a general way to all his creatures. Note that we are talking here not of man's attempts to search for God, which may give rise to all sorts of religious expressions or spiritual experiences, but of the initiative God himself takes in revealing himself to us.

Creation

God reveals himself, first, through creation. While some cool-headed scientists may reject the notion of a Creator in favour of theories that the world came into being either because of some inexplicable, random event or by a long process of evolution, many other competent scientists, together with countless other people, look upon the world and detect within it the signature of a Creator. Its awesome nature, elegant design, sense of order and the place of human beings at the centre of it all suggest not only that there is a Creator, but also that we can discover something about him. Psalm 19:1–4 puts it like this: "The heavens declare the glory of God; the skies proclaim the work of his hands. Day after day they pour forth speech; night after night they display knowledge. There is no speech or language where their voice is not heard. Their voice goes out into all the earth, their words to the ends of the world." (For those who wish to explore this theme further, I commend *The Message of Creation* by David Wilkinson, *The Bible Speaks Today*, IVP, 2002.)

Moral law

God also discloses himself in the law he gave to Israel and in the moral law which is written within human nature universally. Despite occasional exceptions, and although cultural variations and different emphases exist, there is a basic morality which people of all times and cultures have acknowledged. Similarly, there is an instinct for God within human nature.

Human beings seems curiously incomplete without some way of relating to God. As Ecclesiastes 3:11 claims, it would appear that "he has set eternity in the human heart". Even in the most secular of societies in the Western world, unbelievers find themselves compelled to pray when they face major personal milestones such as the birth of a child, a wedding or a bereavement. They do so even more when they face a calamity. This was the case after September 11th 2001, and following the death of Princess Diana. Where does such an instinct come from? What does it mean? Paul argues in Romans 1:18 – 2:16 that both of these human characteristics – morality and the instinct for God – suggest that all people have some knowledge of God and that they reveal his otherwise invisible qualities so that they can be clearly seen by all.

History

Others will argue that God reveals himself through historical events like the exodus, the return from exile or, even, the cross. From one perspective, that is, of course, perfectly true. Sometimes, real events are overwhelmingly convincing. So, when Daniel accurately interpreted the dreams of Nebuchadnezzar, the king immediately acknowledged that Daniel's God was the only living, sovereign God worthy of worship (Daniel 2:47; 4:34–37). But here we must introduce a note of caution. To see these events as a revelation of God requires that we look at them from the standpoint of faith. We saw, for example, that when Cyrus released the Jews from exile in Babylon, he did so, according to Isaiah 45:1, because he was acting as God's Messiah, God's anointed one. But the contemporary records which his civil servants left behind do not give any such interpretation. The living God of Israel does not merit a mention. It is obvious, as Hebrews 11:6 puts it, that "without faith it is impossible to please God, because *anyone who comes to him must believe that he exists . . .*".

All historical events require interpretation. Some interpretations are better than others. Some can be dismissed as false because they do not fit the facts, while the evidence drives us to reach certain other conclusions with confidence. It is not the case than we can make what we like of events. But neither are they quite as unambiguous as we would sometimes like to think. Even so, many events reveal God for those who have the eyes to see him.

Jesus

In addition to revelation, through which God makes himself generally known, there is revelation in which he makes himself known in a special way. This revelation is as full and final a disclosing of God as human beings need or can bear. It comes through Jesus (John 1:1–17; 14:5–10; Hebrews 1:1–3). He is the Word of God, the singular communication from God himself.

The description of Jesus as "the Word of God" is interesting. It is odd to describe a person that way. It must mean that God is making an announcement to people through Jesus, that he is a "word from God". It is a reminder that God communicates through the use of words. The apostles often spoke about this gospel as "the word that was preached" (1 Peter 1:23, 25; see also Acts 8:25; 1 Thessalonians 2:13). But it means more than this. Jesus not only preached, but also brought about, good news through his life and death.

What has this got to do with the Bible? Simply this. We must never try to drive a wedge, as some do, between the person of Christ and his words. God reveals himself both in the person of Christ and in the teaching of Christ. It comes in the form of a person and in the form of words, information and propositions which that person speaks. The words he spoke do constitute the core of Scripture but also, additionally, lend authority to other parts of Scripture.

Jesus fully acknowledged the authority of the Old Testament and sought to live in submission to it. His life, as the temptations show (Matthew 4:1–11; Luke 4:1–13), or his preaching in Nazareth demonstrates (Luke 4:14–21), was shaped deeply from within by the Old Testament Scriptures (see also Matthew 26:54). He showed respect for what the Old Testament taught, referring to it either as the "word of God" (Mark 7:13) or as spoken "by the Holy Spirit" (Mark 12:36), and rebuking those who did not take it seriously enough. Only at one point does Jesus *seem* to do anything other than authenticate the Old Testament as being the word of God and carrying his authority. In the Sermon on the Mount Jesus repeatedly says, "You have heard what was said . . . But I tell you . . ." (Matthew 5:21, 27, 31, 33, 38, 43). In fact, the tension is more apparent than real. He is not contradicting the Old Testament texts which he quotes, but giving them a deeper interpretation than was popular in his day. Just before this section of the Sermon, in fact, Matthew had stressed Christ's fulfilment, not rejection, of the Old Testament (Matthew 5:17–20). What Jesus says here is perfectly consistent with his undeviating attitude that the Old Testament was the word of God.

The gospels then, together with the Old Testament, are to be seen as an authentic revelation from God, whose validity is founded on none other than Jesus Christ himself. But what about the other parts of the New Testament? How can they be authenticated as a revelation from God?

The same arguments we have used to this point can be extended to embrace the rest of the New Testament. Jesus led his apostles to believe that the Holy Spirit would teach them the meaning of his words and unpack them more fully, once he had been taken from them (John 16:12–15). The church was founded on the teaching of these apostles (Acts 2:42; Ephesians 2:20). Everything within their writings is a consistent unfolding of what Jesus did and said. From a relatively early date, they certainly viewed the writings of the apostle Paul as on a par with "the other Scriptures" (2 Peter 3:16). This is an amazing claim. They almost immediately viewed Paul's writing as more than the interesting opinions of a noble preacher. They were writings which carried such spiritual authority that they were included within the collected writings of

Scripture itself.

God, then, has revealed himself in a general way to all his creation, in a special way through Christ and, consequently, in a clear way through the Bible.

Inspiration

Since the Bible is written by such different people over such a long period, how can we be sure that it is a reliable word from God? Christians have traditionally answered that by referring to "the inspiration" of the Bible. Inspiration is a slippery word. We speak of a composer as inspired and even sometimes of a speaker we have heard as being inspired. We mean that they perform well above the average and have powers that seem to lift them beyond the ordinary world. When it comes to the Bible, we mean something a little more precise.

When writing to Timothy, Paul encourages him to continue to live and teach the Christian faith as he had learned it. He gives Timothy a couple of reasons for doing so. First, Timothy knows he can trust those who taught it to him. We may think, somewhat arrogantly, that we believe nothing unless we have proved it for ourselves. But the truth is that most of us believe what we do about a whole range of things because someone we trusted and admired taught us to believe it. We don't have the time or the ability to engage in first-hand investigation about everything before we accept it. If our teacher proves to be untrustworthy, for whatever reason, we begin to doubt what we have been taught. But Timothy has no reason to do that.

Second, Timothy should continue in the path he is on for a practical reason. The "holy Scriptures" which he has known since infancy have proved "able to make [him] wise for salvation through faith in Jesus Christ" (2 Timothy 3:15). Note the close connection again between the Scriptures and Christ. They are effective in bringing people to Christ and making God known.

Then Paul adds an extraordinary claim. In the New Revised

Standard Version it reads, "All Scripture is inspired by God . . ." (2 Timothy 3:16). The New International Version gives a more precise translation of the word "inspired" when it says, "All Scripture is God-breathed . . ." Paul uses here an extremely unusual word, possibly even one that he invented to convey what he meant. The very life of God himself has been breathed into the words of the authors of Scripture. Consequently, their words possess his authority and partake of his trustworthiness.

Peter says something very similar in his second letter. Peter's concern is to distinguish the true prophets of the Old Testament, whose prophecies came to fulfilment in Jesus, from the many false prophets whose words were dreamed up in their own heads. "Above all," he writes, "you must understand that no prophecy of Scripture came about by the prophet's own interpretation. For prophecy never had its origin in the human will, but prophets, though human, spoke from God as they were carried along by the Holy Spirit" (2 Peter 1:20–21). To be "carried along" is to be inspired, impelled by the Spirit of God. It conjures up the picture of a ship coming to life and floating gracefully across the sea to its destination because its sails have been filled with the wind and it is being carried along by a power outside itself.

The Bible is never concerned to tell us anything about the mechanics of this inspiration. It is surely not possible to conclude, from our reading of the Scripture, that God overrode the minds and personalities of its human authors and editors to ensure its accuracy. The sort of spirit-possession which some religions exhibit is not consistent with what we know of the way God works (see 1 Corinthians 14:32–33) and does not fit with the writing of coherent documents. Equally, the idea that God used people merely as a word processor into which he dictated the script does not fit well with the Bible as we know it. The human element of the authorship is all too real.

If we cannot be too dogmatic about the method of inspiration, whilst rejecting a dictation theory of it, we must also be equally careful not to speak of inspiration in too loose a fashion. Inspiration means much more than God vaguely influencing someone who had a gift for writing in a general way, or illuminating the minds of others with a few ideas, on which they then built, using their own thoughts and notions. That would lead to an interesting set of religious documents, or even privileged opinions, but not to the Bible as a book moulded by the character and authority of God, and still less to the Bible as the word of God.

Blending divine inspiration with human authorship is not as difficult as people have sometimes thought. James Packer calls it a "concursive operation", by which God works "in, with and through the free workings of man's own mind" (*Fundamentalism and the Word of God*, IVP, 1958, p. 82). Although it is not a perfect example, he notes that we recognise the divine and human natures in the person of Christ without feeling the need to argue that the one obliterates the other. The divine nature does not make Christ inhuman and the human nature does not make Christ fallible or a sinner. If the divine and human can coincide in Christ, why should they not also do so in his word, the Bible? As I have written elsewhere, "We affirm both the fully divine and fully human natures of Christ. So, too, Scripture can be both divinely inspired and humanly authored. God worked in and through human writers to cause his revelation to be recorded faithfully, capitalising on, rather than overriding, their setting, skills and personalities, which were God-given, in any case" (*Who Are the Evangelicals?* Marshall Pickering, 1994, p. 84).

Infallibility and inerrancy

If the Scripture is inspired by God, then, it is logical to conclude that it is also infallible. Infallible means that it does not mislead us in any way; it does not deceive, but, on the contrary, it is fully reliable and trustworthy. A God who "cannot lie" will surely inspire the authors of Scripture to speak in a totally trustworthy fashion (Number 23:19; 2 Samuel 7:28; Psalm

12:6; Matthew 24:35; John 10:35; Titus 1:2; Hebrew 6:18) and provide us with a completely dependable record of himself.

The use of the word "infallible" with regard to the Bible goes back at least to the Reformers of the 16th century. But in the 19th century a group of theologians came to use a different word about the Bible: they described it as not only infallible but also "inerrant", that is, free from any error. The latter sought to bolster the Bible's authority in the face of attack from liberals, and to say that "the Scripture in the original manuscripts does not affirm anything that is contrary to fact" (Wayne Grudem, *Systematic Theology*, IVP & Zondervan, 1994, p. 90). The use of this word has caused a great deal of controversy, even among those who credit the Bible with a very high degree of authority. What are the issues here?

As soon as we say the Bible is inerrant, we must ask what we include in the scope of its inerrancy. Does it mean that details of geography and history are all 100% accurate? And what about the dating of the earth or what appear to be its "scientific" statements? How do we handle apparent contradictions? Was there one angel at the empty tomb, as Matthew 28:2–5 suggests, or two, as Luke states (24:4)? And what do you do about some of those large and incomplete numbers in the Old Testament or the dates which do not tie up? Did David and his men kill 700 charioteers, as 2 Samuel 10:18 claims, or 7,000 as 1 Chronicles 19:18 says? And what about the very occasional and minor bits, for example in Proverbs, where the Hebrew is not altogether clear or where the earliest manuscripts differ?

Those who argue for inerrancy are usually careful to qualify the claim in a number of ways. They argue that it is the original authored documents which are free from error, but they accept that there may have been errors made when these documents were being copied. They argue that the text must be rightly interpreted and due account taken of the time when it was written.

Many inerrantists would also argue, rightly, that some of the questions above are hardly major issues since we can often reconcile apparent contradictions. We can accept that incidents may be reported differently from different viewpoints and so may include minor variations. It is understood that numbers can be rounded up or calculated on a different scale from that we might use today, without being wrong. Many of the minor issues that are often raised can be quickly resolved by the application of a bit of common sense. Those who have looked into the so-called inconsistencies in Scripture often testify to the way in which difficulties can be resolved, leading them to a renewed, not weakened, sense of the reliability of the Bible.

That still leaves a big area for discussion. All inerrantists believe that the Bible is totally free from error in the things it teaches, that is, in the things about God and the faith. But they would differ in how far such perfection stretches and whether it includes history, geography, science and so on. Some are limited inerrantists and believe that it is primarily the theological teaching of the Bible which is without error. Others are full inerrantists and believe that every part of Scripture is without fault. Full-blown inerrantists argue that where, for example, science appears to contradict the Bible, or archaeology does not confirm the Bible's claims it is because our knowledge of science or archaeology or whatever is incomplete – one day, when we have fuller knowledge, all will agree with the Bible. There have certainly been a number of historical details in the Bible whose accuracy scholars have questioned, only to have them confirmed in the light of further research or subsequent archaeological discovery.

Others believe that, however well-meaning the desire to bolster the trustworthiness of the Bible by describing it as inerrant, it is better to limit ourselves to talking about its infallibility. The reason they argue this is because they believe "inerrancy" is not an entirely appropriate word. Inerrancy is an appropriate word for the writing of factual reports. But the Bible, although it contains facts, and plenty of them, is much more than just a book of facts. It contains poetry and stories, quotations and discussions, dreams and visions. For these types of literature the simple question of truth or error is not always appropriate. For example, we still speak of the sun rising, when we know very well that it does nothing of the sort. Psalm 19:6 uses this same way of speaking. The sun "rises at one end of the heavens and makes its circuit to the other; nothing is hidden from its heat". So is that an inerrant statement or not?

We must be careful that this debate does not divert our energies from obedience to the Bible's teaching. But the very least one can accept as Christian orthodoxy is, in the words of the Lausanne Covenant of 1974, that "we affirm the divine inspiration, truthfulness and authority of both the Old and New Testament Scriptures in their entirety as the only written word of God, without error in all that it affirms, and the only infallible rule of faith and practice".

Authority

All this leads us to a consideration of the authority of the Bible. The claim that the Bible is a revelation from God, inspired by the Holy Spirit and infallible (or inerrant), adds up to a pretty powerful case that it is a book of great authority to which we should pay careful attention. For centuries this was unquestioned. The Bible was regarded as the supreme rule in the church, both for what Christians were to believe and for how Christians were to behave. Its voice was to be consulted first before all other authorities; its teaching was to be obeyed and it was looked to as the definitive guide for Christian living.

Why, then, is its authority not recognised so much today, even in the church?

Authority questioned

Some 200 years ago or so, advances in knowledge meant that people began to read the Bible through more sceptical lenses. Its authority then came under the microscope. People had previously been content to accept unthinkingly the teaching of books and individuals which occupied a significant place in the wisdom which had been handed down to them. But then, as the so-called Enlightenment period progressed, the place of traditional authorities came to be challenged: people began to accept only what they could reason or prove to be true for themselves. From then on, everything was to be doubted.

So, for example, the Bible speaks of miracles. Since miracles were not an everyday occurrence in 18th-century Europe, people began to ask whether they had ever taken place. Any miracles which had been claimed to happen in the modern world were capable of rational explanation, of being explained away. So why should the ancient miracles not be explained away? Did God really destroy Jericho, or was it a happy coincidence that it suffered an earthquake as the soldiers of Israel were seeking to capture it? Did Jesus really feed 5,000, or was it that the crowd all followed the example of the little boy with loaves and fish – and shared their lunches with others?

The Bible also began to be treated in exactly the same way as any other book from the ancient world. It was subject to "historical criticism", so it was analysed into the various sources which lay behind it, with its accuracy doubted at every point. It was compared with other ancient sacred books and its uniqueness called into question. Other ancient books spoke of creation, reported flood stories and had laws something like those of Israel. So what was special about the Bible? It ceased to be seen as a book from God and became instead one among many compositions produced by merely human authorship.

The scepticism which arose can be answered point by point. Much time and energy have been devoted to doing so, as both the historical accuracy and the theological and philosophical soundness of the Bible have been defended. If, for example, one accepts that the greatest miracle of all, the resurrection, happened, then lesser miracles are really not such a problem. And the Bible does not claim, with the possible exception of the time of Christ, a miracle a day. Events still do occur occasionally which can only be explained by divine intervention, even today. And while the Bible does have a lot in common with other ancient books, careful examination reveals just how different it is from them. None of them yield the coherent revelation of a living God in the way the Bible does. The way to answer the sceptics was not less study of the Bible but more.

Nonetheless, in spite of the answers, the Bible was held suspect in many universities and theological colleges. Consequently, many clergy and ministers were taught to undermine its authority and integrity. This has left its mark in the churches where they have been in leadership, and the result is a widespread suspicion of the Bible. This has taken its toll and left the church profoundly weakened.

The current scene

But things move on. Many of the "Enlightenment" ways of looking at things are themselves now being doubted and called into question. Profound changes are going on which, because we are in the middle of them, are not always easy to understand. The idea used to be that science, and subjects such as history, were really true or objective, while Christianity was a matter of opinion, of bias or merely of values, which could not be proved true. More recently, however, it has been recognised that there is no area of knowledge that does not owe something to tradition and the way people have constructed their understanding of the field. So science is not necessarily superior as a way of knowing truth, and history is not quite as objective as it used to be. There are always new scientific frameworks which call the old interpretations into question. New physics gives way to old physics because science, like faith, is a matter of interpretation within a set of assumptions. Historical interpretation is always being revised. So the teaching of the Bible need not be seen as an inferior sort of knowledge to other teaching.

In addition, the very idea that we can arrive at one universal truth is now often considered impossible. There may be, people say, one truth for me and another different truth for you. But, in reality, we know this argument is nonsense. If a person walks across the road into the path of an oncoming car travelling at a certain speed, the car will make the same impact on a pedestrian of roughly the same age and weight, whoever that person is. Truth is truth and that is the basis on which we live our lives much of the time.

On the positive side, the existence of the supernatural dimension is no longer such a problem for many people these days as it was. People do not need convincing that the world is more than a material world. They are quite happy to entertain the reality of supernatural beings and happenings in a way in which previous generations were not.

And, rather than being concerned about historical questions, it is what the book says, at face value, rather than how it was composed, that is important. What matters to many people is whether what the book says works, rather than whether it is true, at least in the first instance. It is the story of the Bible that attracts them, rather than its ideas or propositions.

Extrinsic and intrinsic authority

Where does all this leave the Bible's authority? Authority comes in different shapes and sizes. There is extrinsic authority and intrinsic authority. Extrinsic authority is an authority based on something outside of what is said, that is, we may accept a statement as correct because of who says it or where it comes from. We may not always understand why something is said, but we believe it or obey it because of the one who says it. Traditionally, that has been the way Christians have viewed the Bible. As this chapter has explained, it is a book of authority because it comes from God and is inspired by him.

We may also recognise something as authoritative because of its intrinsic merits, that is, because a statement makes sense to us or strikes a chord with us. For example, if we are ill, we may accept a diagnosis and treatment on the authority of the medical consultant. That would be extrinsic authority. But we may equally accept the advice of a well-meaning friend who has no medical training, because it fits with what we know about our condition and because of the friendship we have with them. That would be intrinsic authority. (This is the illustration used by Richard Bauckham in *Scripture and Authority Today*, Grove Books: Biblical Series, 12, 1999, p. 3). Authority has a lot to do with the quality of relationship we have with people.

If people called extrinsic authority into question during the time of the Enlightenment, they do so even more in the post-Enlightenment times in which we live. But they recognise intrinsic authority and are prepared to submit to it. If people are introduced to the life-relatedness of the Bible, they will come to acknowledge its authority. The problem occurs when it is taught as if it does not deal with the real issues people face in life. Intrinsic authority is relational. So, if people are introduced to Jesus and begin to make his acquaintance, they will soon want to go on to explore the things he said, what led up to his coming and how the meaning of his life was unpacked by those who knew him. He is the clue.

The place to start with the authority of the Bible is with Jesus, not with an abstract argument which insists its authority must be accepted before it is read. Once people know him, they will go on to enter the wider biblical story of creation, fall, grace and redemption and to recognise its worth. The authority of this grand story, tied up as it is with the history of a particular nation, will open them to other aspects of the Bible's message, such as the commandments, which they may initially wish to reject.

Another aspect we should note, in this connection, is that the Bible is the book of the Christian community – the quality of relations within that community will lead people to investigate the Bible further or close it for ever.

The Bible carries with it an intrinsic authority to which we can appeal today.

In a sense, this is what the Bible itself said all along. Earlier in the chapter, we looked at the first part of 2 Timothy 3:16 as we were considering the Bible's inspiration. But it is time now to look at the rest of that statement. After saying that Scripture is inspired by God, Paul continues, ". . . and is useful for teaching, rebuking, correcting and training in righteousness, so that God's servant may be thoroughly equipped for every good work". Its authority lies in its usefulness. The Bible should be read and followed because in it Jesus speaks, because it speaks to our condition and because it has power to create change.

Sufficient authority

Note also that Paul writes of Scripture as a sufficient resource from God to bring salvation and produce godliness. We do not need to look elsewhere. The way in which this works in our lives may vary. There are themes on which it speaks clearly and unmistakably to help us correct our behaviour and develop our relationship with God. There are many subjects on which God has made his thoughts plain and the answers to our questions are there.

But there are other matters where it is not so straightforward. Many of the questions we face today are not directly addressed in the Bible, since it was written many years ago. How then can the Bible still be sufficient and authoritative for us? One helpful idea is that we should read it not only as an answer book, but also as a book that helps us work through our problems and become wiser persons. Brian McLaren has suggested we might come to it much as we come to a mathematics book. He asks whether such a book is "valuable because it has the answers in the back? No, it's valuable because by working through it, by doing the problems, by struggling with it, you become a wiser person, a person capable of solving problems and building bridges and balancing your chequebook and targeting the trajectory of a rocket to Mars." (*A New Kind of Christian*, Jossey-Bass, 2001, p. 53). That is certainly not the whole story (the fact is that a maths book does have the answers in the back (or the teacher's does!); there are right and wrong conclusions which can be reached. But the point is taken. The value for the pupil is having the method demonstrated and some examples given which helps him or her to work it through. So the Bible helps us to work through issues and build towards wise conclusions about contemporary life. This is a helpful way of looking at how, in part, we should use the Bible; it is also a further part of the mosaic, showing that the Bible is authoritative.

So why, in spite of severe questioning, do we believe the Bible to be a book which carries authority and to which attention should be paid? There is no single answer to that question. One answer will convince one sort of person while another will convince others. When they are added up, however, they make a powerful case for the authority of the Bible.

The Bible is authoritative because:

- it is a revelation from God
- it has its origin in his inspiration
- it is characterised by his trustworthiness
- it is a book which contains his words to us
- it contains a reliable historical record of his dealing with his people
- it is the book of the people called Christians
- it is a book which speaks to the human condition universally
- it is a book which proves useful
- it is a book which works, as those who live by it know.

Above all, it is the book of Jesus. If we know him, then our relationship to him will compel us to get to know his book too.

12

The Impact of the Bible

Some say the Bible cannot be used because it justifies tyranny and oppression. Those who have used it in this way have clearly not read its liberating message and have been quite wrong to use it to support injustice. In fact, the Bible has had the most extraordinary impact for good wherever it has been read with integrity. Here, we explore just a few of the stories that could be told of the way in which it has been used to set oppressed people free and to transform whole societies for the better. We also look at the impact it has had on sustaining individuals through great difficulty, challenging them to forsake sinful lives and deficient world views and transforming them into more Christlike people. One of the many reasons for believing in the Bible is that wherever it is read and believed, it has such a positive effect.

The Impact of the Bible

This chapter takes our consideration of the usefulness of the Bible further by considering the impact for good which it has had in the world. The Bible matters because it is God's inspired word. And because it is his inspired word, it is useful (2 Timothy 3:16). If we really believe that he addresses the world through it, it should not surprise us that its message is just exactly what men and women need. Over the centuries it has had a beneficial effect on those who have read it, sometimes transforming the lives of individuals and sometimes releasing whole societies from the grip of destructive oppression.

Here, we select just a few stories to illustrate that the Bible matters because it is the most beneficial guide to building healthy lives and wholesome societies.

Its power to bring liberty

The rise of fundamentalism in our day has caused many to dread the influence of any kind of religion and the sacred books which belong to it. A popular view would have us believe that the Bible is an instrument of oppression and that we are best off without it. Going back to the Bible, people fear, might well mean stoning adulterers or rebellious children, executing homosexuals, enslaving women and living by the rule of "an eye for an eye". Sadly, some people do use (or rather misuse) the Bible in this way and advocate these policies in the name of God. But they can only do so by violating some basic and sensible principles about interpreting the Bible for today, which we will look at in chapter 14.

In this atmosphere it would perhaps surprise many to learn just how much the Bible has been an inspiration to movements of liberation down the years. While some have used it to justify their rule of oppression, more have used it to combat injustice, challenge oppression and stir up people to overthrow tyranny. Let me give you a few examples.

The Stuarts ruled Britain in the 17th century, exercising an iron grip on church and state alike. Their position was bolstered by a doctrine called "the divine right of kings". Kings were considered to be God's regents on earth; to challenge them was to challenge God. Unquestioning obedience was therefore required.

The Bible played a crucial role in the downfall of the Stuarts and of the concept of the divine right of kings as well. Rulers had often feared what would happen if the Bible was available to ordinary people and had therefore sought to keep it from them. But, since Elizabeth's reign, Bibles were in wide circulation. What followed proved that the fears of the powerful had been justified: the Bible rendered their thrones less secure. In 1612, for example, Thomas Helwys, one of the earliest Baptist leaders, wrote a book which he dedicated to James I called *A Short Declaration of the Mystery of Iniquity*. In his dedication he bravely reminded the king that he was a mortal man and not God. He then proceeded to make a case for religious liberty and freedom of conscience. In everything, his thinking and argument was thoroughly moulded by the Bible. For his trouble, incidentally, he was sent to Newgate Prison, where he died some four years later.

While those in power continued their attempt to use the Bible to bolster oppression, others read in its pages of how God was on the side of the oppressed and stood against tyranny. Radical politicians called into play the great biblical symbols of Egypt, the Philistine yoke, Babylon and the antichrist, using them in their speeches, preaching and writing. The bishops of the church were compared to the Pharisees of Jesus's day. The people sought a new exodus. They were inspired by a vision of the Promised Land – a land of plenty for all – to dream of what was possible. The power of kings was tamed, especially after Charles I was executed in 1649 and, in a fitful way, the people gradually gained greater liberty.

The complex role played by the Bible in this major stage in the emergence of a democratic society in Great Britain during those days of Cromwell, Winstanley, Bunyan and Milton has been exhaustively explored by the historian Christopher Hill in his book, *The English Bible and the Seventeenth Century Revolution* (Penguin, 1993).

A more recent example comes from the Second World War. As Hitler grew in influence, he gained the uncritical support of the majority in the German Church who were captive to the forces of politics and culture around them. The church was theologically weak and many of its leaders had long since ceased to shape their thinking and preaching by the Bible. They just soaked in the prevailing cultural trends of their day, putting up no resistance.

In 1934, however, a group of Protestant Christians issued the Barmen Declaration, which became the rallying cry for the Confessing Church which opposed Hitler. Largely written by Karl Barth, it rejected "false teaching" which acknowledged the authority of any people or powers other than Jesus Christ, "as he is attested to us in the Holy Scripture". The six clauses which followed were all supported by New Testament texts.

It was their commitment to the message of the Bible which released these Christians from compromising with the tyrannical power of Nazism and being sucked into the culture in which they lived. It gave them courage to stand against it and provided them with a foundation from which to criticise it. Without the Bible, they would have had neither the incentive nor the ability to do so. Alister McGrath comments on the significance of this in these words: "In this situation, the evangelical emphasis on the authority of Jesus Christ *as he is revealed in Scripture* (rather than as he is constructed by human interest groups or power blocks) is profoundly liberating" (*A Passion for Truth*, Apollos, 1996, p. 35). Here is yet another example of a submission to Christ leading to freedom from submission to tyranny.

Stories from different ages and continents would confirm the Bible's liberating power. The Bible was banned in many communist regimes because it was seen as a subversive book which would undermine the authority of "the party". I well remember a Romanian church leader who preached in my church during the Ceauşescu era saying that his nation was being invited the next year to celebrate 40 years of communist rule. But, he remarked, our leaders do not know their Bibles: 40 years was the time allotted to being in the wilderness, at the end of which entry to the Promised Land took place. "They are inviting us," he claimed, "to celebrate their downfall." His prophecy was astonishingly accurate. Within 18 months Ceauşescu had unexpectedly fallen and the Bible's imagery had once more become real in the experience of Romanians.

In Korea, during the days of Japanese occupation, the Bible was considered equally subversive and, although banned, provided the Koreans with hope. To take another example, it quickly becomes evident just how crucial the Bible was for many people in South Africa during the days of apartheid when you read a book such as Allan Boesak's commentary on Revelation called *Comfort and Protest* (St Andrew Press, 1987). In Latin America too it has fed liberation movements with energy. Without doubt, the Bible has been an instrument of liberty down through history, but never more so than in our contemporary world.

Its power to transform societies

The Bible does not only provide people with the means of critiquing what is wrong. It also gives directions so that strong and healthy societies can be built.

The story of the mutiny on the *Bounty*, in 1789 is well known. What is less well known is a chapter in its sequel. The mutineers chose to land on Pitcairn Island, where they lived in obscurity until receiving visitors from the outside world in 1808. Then the story of their dreadful experiences began to emerge. To begin with, life was a degrading mess, with immorality and drunkenness rife. Many of the women and children found it so hard to bear the behaviour of the men that they separated from them. Most members of the community lost their lives through either disease or violence. Then two of the mutineers, Edward Young and Alexander Smith, started to read the Bible. A change came over them and, in turn, through their leadership, a change came over the whole of the small community which still survived. So, by the time they were rescued, their rescuers recorded that they had found "the most perfect Christian society ever seen". A card recording this is preserved in the Greenwich Maritime Museum. The transformation from an anarchic society in disintegration into a wholesome community took place because of the influence of the Bible.

On a grand scale, the same is true of Victorian Britain. I know it is popular to denigrate the achievements of the Victorian era and assume that the moral reformation which took place then was superficial and had a great deal of evil under the surface. It is also popular to denigrate those who pioneered the changes as hypocrites. No doubt the reformation was far from complete and its leaders had their blind spots and were anything but perfect. But all objective observers must applaud the tremendous change for good which came over Britain during Victoria's time. William Wilberforce (1759–1833) and the Clapham Sect, who led the long and often discouraging movement to abolish slavery, were inspired to do so by the biblical doctrine of humanity. Their reading of the Bible meant that they could not dismiss black people as an inferior species but saw them rather as people made in the image of God and, in the case of Christians, as brothers and sisters in Christ. Wilberforce's own disciplined devotional life, in which the reading of, and submission to, the Bible was central, fuelled his reforming work. The fact that this great social reformer also played a major part in the founding of the Bible Society is all of a piece.

The seventh Earl of Shaftesbury (1801–1885), in whose memory the statue of Eros in Piccadilly Circus, London was erected, led a host of reform campaigns and set up a series of institutions for the betterment of poorer members of society. He described himself, in 1845, as "an Evangelical of the Evangelicals" and attributed most of the great philanthropic movements of the century to them, motivated, as they were, by the teaching of Scripture. During his time, a multitude of societies and city missions were formed, all inspired by the Bible; these led a host of ordinary Christians to work among the most disadvantaged in society. The verdict of the *Edinburgh Review* of 1853 was that this was what led to the gradual dissipation of the darkness which had enveloped Britain at the start of the century.

While voices critical of the missionary impulse of the last couple of centuries may clamour for attention, a balanced assessment shows just how many wonderful improvements in health, education, social justice, agriculture and industry have taken place because the missionaries were obedient to a call from God and the teaching of the Bible. The relationship between the missionary movement and imperialism is, frankly, complex, but the origins of the missionary enterprise are undoubtedly to be found in a biblically inspired vision of a world that could be different. As one recognised authority in the field has written about these biblically-driven missionaries, they "went out to the field convinced that the preaching of the cross was both what the 'heathen' needed to hear and also *the only agent capable of effecting regeneration in individuals and society*" (Brian Stanley, *The Bible and the Flag*, Apollos, 1990, p. 62).

Take another recent example. An elder of the church in Myanmar recently commented, "We never imagined it possible to have the Bible in our own language. But when the Falam Bible was made available we discovered the wonderful riches of reading God's word in our own language. It was so good we could not stop. We now realise that the Bible freed us from the 'slavery' and domination of other ethnic groups. We have come to realise that we are special, one of the races God has created. How ever can we thank you (the translators) enough?" (Quoted from Vinoth Ramachandra and Howard Peskett, *The Message of Mission*, IVP, *Bible Speaks Today*, 2003.)

Bible translation has, incidentally, often had the important side-effect of preserving a people's culture and ensuring the survival of its language.

Where it is taken seriously, the teaching of the Bible still transforms communities and societies.

Its power to sustain individuals

Some of the most moving testimonies concerning the value of the Bible come from people who are going through suffering. As a pastor, I have frequently heard people speak of how the Bible has sustained and guided them in times of trouble and has proved to be the channel through which they have heard the comforting, strengthening and instructive voice of the living God.

I remember chairing a conference for Terry Waite at which he described his experiences as a hostage in Beirut. He never realised that the years he had spent participating in Anglican worship would stand him in such good stead in captivity. The regular recital of the liturgies of the book of Common Prayer meant that he had learned much of Scripture by heart. He had done so in the language of the King James Version which, as he pointed out, has a poetic quality which makes it comparatively easy to memorise. It was, he said, his ability to recall the Scripture he had memorised that had kept him going through the years of loneliness.

Martin Niemöller's testimony was similar. He was a pastor in Berlin during the Second World War. As President of the Pastors' Emergency League, he led the opposition to Hitler on behalf of the city's ministers, with the result that he was arrested and sent to a concentration camp. He spent eight years, from 1937 to 1945, in the camps, latterly at the notorious Dachau. Afterwards he testified:

> The Bible: what did this book mean to me during the long and weary years of solitary confinement, and then the last four years at Dachau Cell-building? The word of God was simply everything to me – comfort and strength, guidance and hope, master of my days and companion of my nights, the bread which kept me from starvation, and the Water of Life which refreshed my soul. And even more, solitary confinement ceased to be solitary. (Quoted in Jim Graham, *The Giant Awakes*, Marshalls, 1982, p. 26.)

David Watson's experience was different but his testimony was the same. A well-known evangelist in the 1970s and 80s, his ministry revived a redundant local church in York and he had a global itinerant ministry which saw thousands converted and blessed by the Spirit of God. At the height of his powers he went to his doctor to get a routine prescription for asthma, only to come out of the surgery under a cloud. Totally unexpectedly, his doctor suspected he might have a malignant cancer. Shortly afterwards, further investigations confirmed the diagnosis and he was given, as he called it, "the death sentence". The usual unpleasant and debilitating treatment which cancer patients receive did little to stave off the inevitable, and he died not too long afterwards. In his book *Fear No Evil* (Hodder and Stoughton, 1984), in which he tells the story of his final months with transparent honesty, he records the value of the Bible in sustaining him during his suffering.

As a theological student at Cambridge, David Watson had been exposed by his lecturers to a sustained attack on the authority of the Bible. He had had to work through whether he believed that what the Bible taught was trustworthy or not. Now, in his own final days, he knew his confidence in it had not been misplaced. He writes of his faith in the living God being strengthened during his time in hospital as he chewed over "the endless assurances and promises to be found in the Bible". He comments:

> God's word to us, especially his word spoken by his Spirit through the Bible, is the very ingredient that feeds our faith. If we feed our souls regularly on God's word, several times each day, we should become robust spiritually, just as we feed on ordinary food several times each day, and become robust physically. Nothing is more important than hearing and obeying the word of God (p. 39).

The Psalms in particular became his constant companion. "As I read or prayed through those psalms, I was conscious of my tensions unwinding, my fears disappearing, and once again of the Lord's love surrounding me" (p. 48). They gave him protection from the dreadful things you imagine in the small hours of the morning when you are alone and facing a terminal illness. And they helped him through the periods when he faced the silences of God, as so many of the Psalmists had been there before. The title of his book is aptly chosen from Psalm 23. His faith was challenged, but it never really wavered because it was bolstered by the nourishment of the Bible.

Its power to change individuals

A sceptic might say that those who are determined to find comfort through the Bible will do so but, in reality, such comfort might be no more than wishful thinking on their part, arising out of their own inner resources rather than being the voice of God. It is easy to claim such scepticism, of course, when you are not personally facing suffering. When you are, things are different.

What is less easy to dismiss are the many occasions when the Bible challenges a person's lifestyle or beliefs and brings about an unexpected, even unsought, change. It has a capacity to shed light on wrongdoing and, by convicting individuals of it, to lead them to repentance and change. It also has a capacity to push normal boundaries, inspire faith, encourage people to experience the Holy Spirit and believe in God answering prayer, beyond what many would expect. This is the sort of effect Hebrews warns us that the Bible can have; Hebrews 4:12 says this: "God means what he says. What he says goes. His powerful Word is sharp as a surgeon's scalpel, cutting through everything, whether doubt or defence, laying us open to listen and obey" (Eugene Peterson's translation in *The Message*).

That is exactly how Augustine (354–430), subsequently one of the great bishops of the early church, experienced it. Augustine had led a profligate life as a young man. Even though he knew of the Christian faith through his mother, Monica, who was greatly distressed by the way he lived, and from Bishop Ambrose, he had no personal commitment to it. Then one day, as he records in his *Confessions*, a great surge of grief overtook him for the unhappiness his way of life was creating. While in tears, he heard a boy or girl's voice repeatedly chanting in a nearby garden, "Pick it up and read it, pick it up and read it." He took up a Bible and read the first chapter he came across. It opened at Romans 13, which spoke of the need for Augustine to clothe himself with Jesus Christ and not to gratify the desire of the sinful nature. As he read on, he discovered that even those who were weak in faith were acceptable. It was exactly what he needed to hear. No passage could have been more appropriate. It entered his soul like a spear and led immediately to his conversion and a total reformation of his life. His mother was overjoyed. It was reading the Bible, and reading the Bible alone, which brought about the repentance and transformation of his life which other messengers of God had failed to produce until then.

One of the other great figures in the history of the church is Martin Luther (1483–1546), whom God used to lead the Reformation of the church in Europe and who therefore became the founder of Protestantism. As a Roman Catholic theologian, lecturing at the University of Wittenberg, Luther struggled for years in a state of spiritual dissatisfaction and had no assurance of personal salvation. His anguish was resolved as he was alone, meditating on the Bible in his study in the tower of Wittenberg University one evening, probably in about 1518. He was already fully acquainted with the Bible and had previously lectured on the Psalms, Romans, Galatians and Hebrews. However, he had not yet resolved the central knot in interpreting it, namely, what the Bible meant when it spoke of the "righteousness of God" being "revealed". That evening it came to him. The righteousness of God was not the terrifying instrument of reproach or the impossible standard which he had been seeking to reach by his religious rituals. It was rather a gift from God by which sinners are put right with God (justified) and which is received by the exercise of faith. In that moment he felt, as he put it, "that I was altogether born again and had entered into paradise itself through open gates". The secret of the transformation had lain in his study of the Bible where "a totally other face [other, that is, than the terrifying judgement of God] of the entire Scripture showed itself to me". He ran through the rest of Scripture from memory and discovered in it confirmation of salvation as a free gift of God to those who have faith.

As one historian has concluded: "This was the divine–human encounter which preceded the movement for reform, and from which it sprang. A man, a Bible – and God. When God aims to act, it is always through his Word and its impact on personality" (A. Skevington Wood, *Captive to the Word*, Paternoster Press, 1969, p. 51). The "always" may make this something of an overstatement. But the essence of the claim is true.

To the names of the great and the well known, the names of a multitude of others, ordinary and unknown, could be added whose lives have been transformed by an encounter with God through the Bible. Some years ago, I was asked by the Bible Society to write a small book called *Using the Bible in Evangelism* (1985, 1993). Before I did so, I thought I should do some research and find out not only how people did use the Bible in evangelism, but to what extent the Bible had been used by God as the chief means by which people came to know him and live for him. I was amazed how easy it was to collect stories – stories which I could verify – of people who came to faith primarily through the Bible and often through the Bible alone. Some had no religious background; some had a great deal of church experience. Some had started at the beginning because they did not know where else to start; others began with a gospel. Some were in prison, some in hospital, some in classrooms; some were even on a leisure break. I should not have been surprised, since I knew from my own experience of pastoral ministry that the Bible is an effective tool of God for personal transformation, more effective than we often assume.

When John Finney engaged in a major research project in the 1990s about how people came to faith, he asked them what were the main factors and what were the supporting factors in their journey. Not surprisingly, it was the influence of individual people – family and friends – that headed the list in respect to both questions. But what was surprising was how often people commented on the Bible. 5% of women and 7% of men named it as the chief factor in their coming to faith; for 27% of people it was a major supporting factor. These figures may not seem high, but on both counts they were much higher than for other literature, drama, music, TV and radio, in which the church invests huge amounts of time and money. And, in terms of a main factor, the figure was just as high as for any of the church's activity. The research also suggested, ironically, that people did not have as many problems with the Bible as Christians think they should. 87% of those who had read it found it "very helpful". Perhaps we should have more confidence in the Bible as the living word of God, able still to bring people to faith in Christ and to transform lives, moving them from brokenness to wholeness.

The cumulative impact of the Bible is both massive and constructive. It has shaped whole cultures and transformed total societies for good. It has convicted many of wrongdoing and pointed still more to the Lord. It has healed marriages, given direction, provided strength, redirected vocations and saved lives. It has an intrinsic authority to which, if we are wise, we will give heed.

We end with two quotations, one ancient and one modern, which aptly summarise the impact of the Bible and encourage the church to use it confidently today.

Justin Martyr (100–165) was born to pagan parents and studied the philosophies of the ancient world extensively, but he found them wanting in comparison with the "one sure worthy" philosophy of Christ. He became a great advocate for the faith and wrote concerning the Bible:

> I would wish that all, making a resolution similar to my own, do not keep themselves away from the words of the Saviour. For they possess a terrible power in themselves and are sufficient to inspire those who turn aside from the path of rectitude with awe; while the sweetest rest is afforded those who make a diligent practice of them.

A. M. Chirgwin wrote much more recently, yet he reaches a similar conclusion by a different route. In his *The Bible in World Evangelism* (SCM, 1954), he wrote:

> (The) evidence of history is impressive . . . the times when the Church has gone to its evangelistic task with the Bible open in its hands have been precisely the times when it has won many of its greatest conquests. The Bible has in fact been at the cutting-edge of its advance (p.64).

Later in the same work he wrote:

> It has proved its ability to speak to men of every condition, country and culture. It is the weapon par excellence of the Church's warfare which, if wielded, may have a large part in winning the world for Christ (p.148).

C. H. Spurgeon, it seems, was wise when he advised that we should no sooner defend the Bible than we would defend a lion. Rather we should release it, let it go, and watch it defend itself.

13

Interpreting the Bible

How can people appear to make the Bible say so many different things? If they are all reading one Bible, how can Christians differ over so many issues? Can we not read what it says straight off the page? Well, not quite. Everyone of us has to interpret what we read in the Bible, just as we do with other books. Even the most ardent literalist engages in interpretation. But there are good and bad ways of interpreting the Bible. This chapter explores some of the key principles of interpretation and gives some frameworks for helping us understand the Bible's teaching. It mentions some recent ideas about interpretation, before reminding us that understanding the Bible is not quite the same as understanding other books because of the active role of the Holy Spirit as our teacher.

Interpreting the Bible

My grandfather was a wonderful Christian believer and I owe him a lot. He was one of those people who read the Bible through pretty literal spectacles. He was not concerned with the "ifs" and the "buts". If the Bible said it, he believed it and that settled it. But the truth is that however much he claimed to be taking the Bible's teaching at face value, he, like everyone else, interpreted what he read. We all do – even the most literal among us.

Let me illustrate from our family life in the 1950s or early 1960s. Deuteronomy 22:5 says, "A woman must not wear men's clothing, nor a man wear women's clothing, for the Lord your God detests anyone who does this." On the basis of this verse, my grandfather would have expressed strong disapproval if any female member of my family had appeared in his presence in trousers for, in his mind, they were men's clothes and the Bible forbade women to wear them. (The men, it has to be said, had no inclination to wear skirts or dresses so the problem did not arise the other way around.) Two things of interest stem from this trivial insight into our family history.

First, my grandfather was reading the text straight off the page, or so he thought. But several things obviously never occurred to him. It never occurred to him that this might be a reference to transvestism. His mind was probably too pure to contemplate such a practice. Nor did it occur to him that what were men's clothes in one culture looked suspiciously like a woman's clothes in another. Men in Old Testament times appear to have worn something much more akin to how women's dresses look today than to our jeans or trousers.

Second, there are some other interesting verses in Deuteronomy 22 which, for some reason, he did not feel obliged to enforce. Verse 8 says, "When you build a new house, make a parapet around your roof so that you may not bring the guilt of bloodshed on your house if someone falls from the roof." My grandfather happened to be a builder and I know a good number of the houses he built, none of which have a parapet around them. Why not? Verse 12 says, "Make tassels on the four corners of the cloak you wear." But I never saw a tassel anywhere on him! How was it that he could select one verse and apply it at face value, while ignoring other, equally plain, commands nearby?

I mean no disrespect to him. The fact is, whether he recognised it or not, he engaged in interpreting the Bible, just as the rest of us do. The question is not whether we interpret Scripture but whether the way we do so is well founded or not.

The need for interpretation

Questions of interpretation are at the heart of many disputes and divisions in the church today. Should women be ordained to the ministry or not? Is homosexuality a sin or does its condemnation belong to a past age, like the rule that forbade the Jews to eat pork? Why do we ignore Jesus's clear command to wash each other's feet (John 13:14), whereas we regularly obey his other command to eat bread and drink wine in a communion service (Luke 22:19)? And when Paul says that an elder must be the husband of one wife (1 Timothy 3:2) does it mean, as some believe, that no unmarried person can be an elder in the church or is that saying that if someone is married they must be monogamous? And what does "Wives, submit to your husbands" mean: unquestioning, unthinking obedience, no matter how unreasonable or unjust? And should we still stone those who live sexually promiscuous lives (Deuteronomy 22:20–22), or those who blaspheme (Leviticus 24:15–16), or rebellious sons (Deuteronomy 21:18–21)?

The list could go on. You can see how important interpretation is. Some interpretations will lead us to read the Bible as an oppressive book which justifies the powerful in abusing those beneath them in horrific ways, in the name of God. That was the experience of those I mentioned in the introduction who felt that the Bible could not be used today because it had become an instrument of tyranny. Other interpretations, such as those I alluded to in the last chapter, lead us to read the Bible as a liberating book which forges a path towards justice and dethrones the powerful from their seats. Are all interpretations equally valid? Are there ways in which we can judge between good and bad, right and wrong interpretations? Can we arrive with any degree of certainty at what the Bible means and how it applies today?

The basics of interpretation

Understanding the meaning of the Bible is not something we have just had to start doing. It has always been important. The Levites, in Nehemiah's day, "read from the Book of the Law of God, making it clear and giving the meaning so that people could understand what was being read" (Nehemiah 8:8). The Psalmist regularly prayed for "understanding" (Psalm 119:27, 34, 125, 144). There is a recognition here that understanding the Bible may not always be easy. How we interpret the Bible as we have it in front of us is the big question being asked today. As we ask it, new perspectives on how we interpret what we read are arising. Here we can do no more than give some basic, almost common-sense, guidelines.

The most important thing is to try to understand what the

Bible meant in its original setting before we come to ask what it means for the world in which we live. If we are going to do that, we have to ask a number of fundamental questions.

What did the words originally mean?

The same word can mean a number of different things. "Bank" may refer to the built-up earth that keeps a river in place, or to a place where I keep my money safe, or to the act of placing my money in a bank. The word "fox" might refer to an animal, or be used metaphorically, or used, as a verb, to describe how I have confused you in this book. When Jesus refers to Herod as a fox (Luke 13:32), he is not speaking literally but using the term to draw attention to Herod's craftiness. How the word is used in its setting will often define its meaning. So, when we read words in the Bible, especially some of the "big" words – "faith", "righteousness", "justified" or "redemption" – we need to ask what they meant when they were first used in their context, rather than assuming that they have one fixed meaning or that we use them the same way today.

Where do the words fit?

Words form sentences which form paragraphs and have a place in an unfolding story, argument or poem. Once we have worked out the meaning of the crucial words, we need to stand back from them and see where they come in the whole sweep of the passage of the Bible that we are dealing with. The context is important. Martin Luther once warned of the folly of taking verses out of context by saying, "If this is to be the way, I can prove from the Scripture that bad beer is better than good wine." We can prove anything we like unless we set the words in their surroundings.

An example already referred to is that the Bible says, "There is no God". True enough. But these words need to be set in their context if they are not to be grossly misunderstood. What the text actually says is, "Fools say in their hearts, 'There is no

God.' They are corrupt, their deeds are vile; there is no-one who does good." (Psalm 53:1) This example is obvious, but there are many less obvious ones. To illustrate, some people quote verses spoken by Job's friends as if they were gospel truth. They are in the Bible, aren't they? Yes. But their setting in Job will show just how misguided many of their statements were.

Some years ago there was a TV advertisement which began by showing a man pushing a woman violently on a street. It looked as if she was being mugged. But then the camera pulled back and we saw the wider scene. In fact, she was about to be knocked over by a car, and the supposed mugger was her saviour. Things need to be seen, and read, in context.

What is the historical and cultural context?

To understand what words mean we must set them not only in their literary context but in their historical and cultural context as well.

If you are looking at questions of family, for example, it would be unwise to assume that the way we shape family life today is the same as it was when Israel lived in extended families, clans and tribes, or when families in Roman times lived in households. Are we sure that when we engage in teaching about family issues, marriage or divorce, we are comparing like with like when we lift things straight out of the Bible and apply them to today? Similarly, the Bible has a lot to say about working as a slave but little directly about working in a modern post-industrial society. Are we right to take the words to slaves and apply them "neat" to our age? Before we make superficial applications of the Bible to today's world, we must delve into what concepts like these meant in their original social context, otherwise we may misunderstand and misapply the Bible's teaching.

The question of context may sometimes be a very broad one. So, in reading much of the Old Testament, we need to understand whether the passage is set in the days before the monarchy, during the monarchy or after it, before we can make sense of it. Are these words applied to Israel in the wilderness? If so, what continuing impact did they have after they had settled in Canaan? What continuing impact did they have in exile or after the restoration?

But the historical context can help us with details too. The knowledge of the water system of Jerusalem (which is set on a high hill) helps to make sense of how David's men conquered it in 2 Samuel 5:6–8. Similarly, the knowledge that water was delivered to Laodicea from hot springs two miles away from the city, and that it had cooled down from its 95-degree temperature to being lukewarm by the time it arrived, makes sense of Revelation 3:16.

What is the theological context?

Just as important is the theological context. Where does the passage being studied fit in the scheme of things, as far as God's unfolding revelation is concerned? Is it a part of the Old or the New covenant? What difference does this make? Is it the way God communicated for a particular time in particular circumstances or is it a word from God for all time and all circumstances? We will explore this issue in more depth later in the chapter, under the heading of "a wider perspective".

What type of literature is it?

The next question concerns what type of literature it is – technically known as "genre" – that we are dealing with. We have already encountered this a little when looking at the question of inerrancy. We write in different ways. The quarterly report I write, as a College Principal, to my Board of Governors is written in a very different style from the love letters I write to my wife! The former is cool, lean and factual. I report, in a matter-of-fact way, what is going on in the college, or I raise issues for discussion, with points in favour and points against, so that the Governors can come to a decision. My letters to my wife are passionate, expansive, and full of the poetic, non-literal, language of romance (or at least, they would be if I wrote her any!). To understand what a piece of writing means, we need to know what type of writing it is. If I said to my wife that her teeth are like the ivory of elephant tusks, it would be important for the future of our marriage for her to know that I am comparing her teeth to the colour of elephant tusks rather than to their prominence.

In the Bible there is a great variety of genres. There are:

historical accounts
theological arguments
stories
laws
poetry
wisdom writings
prophecies
gospels
letters
parables
apocalyptic books

Each needs to be read according to the rules of the type of literature it is. Stories, for example, often draw a person in and arouse the imagination. They are often open-ended and leave you to sort out what was right or wrong about a situation, without explicitly telling you the answer. They mirror the untidiness of life. When Acts (1:12–26) tells us, for example, that, after the ascension, Matthias was chosen to replace Judas so that the number of disciples was made up to twelve again, were they right or wrong to take that action? Is it significant that we never hear of Matthias again? Did they act prematurely and fill the place which God had reserved for Paul, the apostle who came along later (1 Corinthians 15:8)? Is this an example of good, proactive leadership in the church or an example of presumptuous leadership which is running ahead of God? The Bible does not tell us. What is helpful at times, in trying to understand stories, is to identify with one of the characters and put yourself into the story. How would you have felt if you had been Matthias, or how would you have looked back on it if you had been Peter? That will often help to unlock its meaning from the inside.

By contrast, Paul's letters are straightforward teaching and you know very clearly what he thinks is right and wrong. Here are ideas and propositions which you either believe or reject. If you accept that they are part of inspired Scripture, you will want to believe them. That may well mean unpacking a bit of a complex argument, sorting out both the drift and details of what he is saying and then seeking to apply it to your own life.

The parables are stories, of a sort. But they function according to their own rules. In early days, people often thought they were allegories. That meant that every detail of them was symbolic of something. For example, Augustine had every detail of the parable of the good Samaritan worked out. The wounded man was Adam; Jerusalem was the heavenly city from which Adam fell; the thieves were the devil and his angels; the beast was Christ's incarnation; the inn was the church and the innkeeper was Paul. And so on. The trouble with this is that there is no control on what is right and wrong here. Anyone can make up anything they like on this basis and claim the authority of the Bible for it. The other major problem with this approach is that you can pick a story to pieces, know everything about the details and miss its overall message and direction. And, if you are not careful, you can spiritualise it out of this world: the story of the good Samaritan can be a wonderful picture of salvation while we still leave battered victims lying bleeding on the ground and fail to be good neighbours to them because they are not "one of us".

Since Augustine, people have come to understand that parables work in a different way. Many of the details are incidental. They are there to create a meaningful picture and to add interest and colour to it. But the parable is usually a story which is working towards one, sometimes two, goals. So the parable of the Good Samaritan is about being a good neighbour to those who are in need but different from us and not letting your religion, race or anything else get in the way. The parable of the Prodigal Son is about the amazing love of God who, like a waiting father, welcomes prodigals home, but it is also about older sons who never stray from home and yet do not enjoy a good and meaningful relationship with their father. The first are obvious sinners; the second are self-righteous Pharisees.

The question of genre is crucial. Is Genesis 1 – 3, for example, an historical and scientific account of the origin of the world or is it a way of teaching theological truth? If it is the first, then it may be in conflict with contemporary science and some people will feel it has been proved wrong. The Bible, they will then think, is built on a shaky foundation. But if it is theological truth, albeit with scientific implications, then we judge it altogether differently. The same is also true of the other end of the Bible. Some read Revelation as if it is prophecy and seek to use it to predict the coming events in world history. But if it is read as apocalyptic literature, not every detail will correspond exactly to some event which humans experience on earth. We need to read the documents wearing the correct spectacles or else we get them out of focus.

A great book to read if you want to think further about this area is Gordon Fee and Douglas Stuart's *How to Read the Bible for All Its Worth* (Scripture Union, 1994, 1997).

What about the author's intention?

It would seem sensible to say that another thing we should take into consideration is the author's intention and purpose in writing. What did he or she think they were doing and saying? Surely that will make the meaning more clear. On the surface, this seems a straightforward and wise question to be asking. If what I have written is open to several interpretations or lacks clarity, you only have to ask me, the author, and I can clarify the matter for you.

However, people are not so confident about giving the author's intention too much prominence these days. There are a couple of reasons for this hesitation. The authors of the Bible are no longer alive – we cannot go back to them to interrogate them about what they have written. On occasions, such as in John 20:31, the intention is clear. But most often, they have not told us explicitly what their intentions were. So to some extent our deciding what the author's intention was is guesswork. Often the decision is pretty clear but it can run the danger of being ill founded. Getting the wrong idea may lead us to read the text in the wrong way. So we should ask the questions of why the author wrote, and to whom, and what was their situation. But we need to do so cautiously.

Asking about author intent has become unfashionable these days because of the way we are understanding literature generally. It is popular to say that when an author has finished writing, he or she should fade out of the picture and let the reader make of the writing what they will. The author has no ongoing role in interpreting the text; it is how the reader responds to it which is important. In its extreme form, this is almost certainly nonsense. Of course the author remains a significant factor in understanding what was written. But, in a mild form, this position has some sense to it. Readers can sometimes see in literature things which the author did not consciously intend but which are real nonetheless, perhaps an expression of the author's subconscious mind. Sometimes, what was written long ago can be seen in a new light as events progress and circumstances and cultures change. So there are depths which can be brought out which the author may not have realised were there.

The Bible itself does this often in the way in which the New Testament handles the Old. For example, when James quotes Amos 9:11–12 in his speech in Acts 15, he almost certainly sees in it a deeper meaning than Amos would have originally intended. This fuller sense, known technically as *sensus plenior*, would have probably mystified Amos but is inspired by the Spirit and legitimate.

So the question of author intent, although significant, is to be treated with some care.

Summarising what we have written so far, we might say that it is a good rule that we must read the Bible through the eyes of those who would have originally heard it. If we fail to do this, we will miss out a lot on some of the finer details and may even occasionally get it quite wrong. "An eye for an eye", for example, as we have already written, was not commanded so that people should always extract the maximum penalty from a wrongdoer, but to limit the cycle of violence and revenge which can so easily be set in motion by a crime. What did the words mean, in their original setting? What kind of literature are we dealing with? What did the author mean?

A wider perspective

What do you do when texts appear to contradict each other? Let's take the issue of women in church leadership as an example. The command in 1 Corinthians 14:34–35 and 1 Timothy 2:12 that a woman must be silent in the church seems to contradict what Paul wrote in 1 Corinthians 11:5 where he explicitly said that women could pray and prophesy in church, providing they observed certain rules. It seems clear from elsewhere in the New Testament that women were indeed able to play a major leadership role in the church (Acts 16:40; 18:24–26; 21:9; Romans 16:3, 6, 7; Philippians 4:2–3; Colossians 4:15). So what can this mean?

Some of the tensions between the texts will be lessened as we ask the questions set out above and gain a deeper knowledge of the actual words used. For example, the context in 1 Corinthians 14 is about disorderly worship. The verses immediately before are about how speech, of any kind, should be controlled in the church service. Then Paul seems to turn to a particular example of times when it has not been controlled. Since he had earlier recognised that women prayed and prophesied in church, it is more than likely that he is not forbidding them to speak at all, but rather forbidding disruptive and uncontrolled speech. He states his case so strongly, as we all sometimes do, that he does not stop to qualify the sort of speaking he is outlawing or the sort of silence he is advocating. The context would make this plain to his readers.

1 Timothy gives us an example where a careful examination of the actual words chosen by Paul may prove significant. It seems a very personal rule he is giving – "I do not permit" – not "God does not", "the churches do not" nor "it is not permitted", but "I". His restriction seems a little inconsistent with elsewhere. Are there particular circumstances which have caused him to say this? In addition, the word he uses for "to have authority" is a particularly strong term and has overtones of acting presumptuously, even violently, to seize authority from others. Given the situation, it would seem that eager but unwise women have put themselves in the position of an authoritative teaching role before they were adequately prepared for it and may even be teaching some heresy in the church. Does that mean that his words apply to the local situation rather than for all time and everywhere?

The above discussion is not intended to sort all the issues out. Whole books have been written on these complex matters. It is intended to say that we must dig deep and, when we do, perhaps some of the problems disappear. But there is something else we must do. We must also place these texts in the wider perspective of Scripture. Here we return to the question of the theological context, which was briefly mentioned above.

Let me suggest two filters through which we must run texts, especially when we do not understand them.

Creation, fall, redemption and consummation

When we come to a passage of Scripture, we should ask if it reflects (a) God's intention in creation, (b) the state of things following the fall, (c) the position following the redemptive work of Christ, or (d) the final state as things will be when we reach full salvation.

Take the place of women, again, as an example. According to Genesis, male and female are both made in the image of God and are partners in the governing of his world. But sin upset his creation intention; consequently, male domination and pain came into the relationship (Genesis 3:16). It was not what God intended. It is a fact of life in our fallen world, but not one to be justified or complacently accepted. It is the result of sin. When Christ came, he demonstrated God's true attitude to women. They play a crucial part in the story, both at his incarnation and at his resurrection. They are members of his band and follow him. They are treated with dignity, objects of his love and mercy and recipients of his healing power. His actions scandalised the strict Jews of his day because he related to women as if they were people of significance, rather than sources of temptation or mere nonentities. Women began to be given their rightful place again in God's creation order. Then his Spirit empowered them for prophetic service alongside men (Acts 2:18) in the church, a church which came into being to display to the world what redeemed relationships were like. Of course, the situation was not perfect. There were tensions and problems to come. Social restrictions and cultural practices still had their impact. Women could not always cope well with their new-found freedom in Christ, and men still suffered from the shades of old domineering attitudes. But whether you were male and female was no longer a significant issue for salvation (Galatians 3:28). All were equal children of God, thanks to Christ Jesus. The church was on course for the day when it will finally reach the new creation and live in harmony with God, undisturbed by that which is impure and shameful (Revelation 21:27).

When we read a passage of Scripture we need to ask: Where does this passage fit in the scheme of things? It may not be advocating how we are to behave in the church following the work of Christ. It may be reporting on how people were behaving in a fallen world before the coming of Christ. The answer makes a difference.

The kingdom of God

Take a second filter, that of the reign of God which has broken into our world and is re-establishing itself through Christ. The gospels contain a good deal of teaching about the way God's kingdom operates. This kingdom is deeply subversive as far as conventional society is concerned and calls into question the values by which the wider society operates. In it the first become last, the outsiders become the insiders, and those rejected as unclean by the religious leaders of Jesus's day become clean. The kingdom is about relieving people of burdens, not tying them up in rules (Matthew 22). It is about bringing ordinary people into a direct relationship with the living God. The teaching of the Sermon on the Mount (Matthew 5 – 7) and passages such as Luke 14 have a significant part to play in shaping our understanding of God's kingdom. So when there are things we cannot quite make sense of elsewhere in the Bible, we should ask: What sense can we make of this when we relate it to the kingdom of God? Perhaps that will help us to make sense of what is written elsewhere. What impact, for example, do you think Jesus's teaching about the kingdom of God has on the place of women in the church?

This is a form of the old principle that we should interpret one passage of Scripture with the help of another. When we come to things we do not understand, we should work at them from the basis of things we do understand. When there are things which are obscure, we should come at them from the direction of things that are clear. Often then, the fog will begin to disappear.

Both of these filters would rule out the sort of oppressive and abusive interpretations of the Bible which we have mentioned previously. Reading the Bible as a whole, we can see how God feels the pain of oppressed people and moves to secure their liberty; we see how he sets himself against all injustice, wherever it comes from. We can also see that true liberty is not only about setting people free from tyranny, but also about setting people free for God. Only by being in a right and ongoing relationship with him can true freedom be enjoyed.

A closer look at the law

All this helps us when it comes to understanding the Old Testament laws which cause such confusion today. They were given to Israel when they were directly ruled by God. Do they continue to apply today?

First, we must understand something about the character of the laws in the Old Testament. They do not constitute an exhaustive statute book, like the laws of England strive to be, or the sort of judicial law which the courts deal with today. They reflect God's holiness and his concern for his people to be holy too (Leviticus 19:2). His holiness leads to our living – across the whole of our lives – according to certain principles. Sometimes these principles are expressed in great moral axioms, as in the Ten Commandments, and sometimes they get expressed in detailed, specific commands by way of illustration. They show how God's people can please him and live wholesomely in the community of his chosen people. It is not easy to translate them exactly, then, into legal dictums for a modern pluralistic and largely secular society. But the heart and intention of them, revealing as they do the character of God and his will for his people and wider creation, must be taken seriously and not dismissed as belonging simply to a bygone age.

These laws are clearly not all of the same type and today we hold on to some and we regard others as no longer in force. Why? The Old Testament laws can be classified in a number of ways. One way of doing so is to say that they were composed of moral, social and religious laws. It is not a perfect classification and not all of them fit exactly or exclusively with one group or the other. But it is a good general guide.

The moral laws, summarised in the Ten Commandments, reflect most clearly the basic unchanging character of God and are reaffirmed, one way or another, throughout the Bible and so remain obligatory for us today. They have to do with our reverence for God and our respect for others. If we revere God, we will worship him exclusively, neither making idols nor denigrating his name. If we respect others, we shall not enslave them in the workplace but create space for them to be re-created through worshipping God their maker. We will respect our parents; we will neither take life, nor prove unfaithful in marriage, nor steal, nor be dishonest, nor crave what belongs to others. But these commandments are not all there is to say on the issues. They are like windows which you can look through, onto a whole vista of revelation from God.

I would place the commandments about homosexuality in this category, and since it is a contemporary hot issue, let me explain why. We begin, not with the prohibition of homosexuality, for that is only a small part of the argument, but with the Ten Commandments. The seventh commandment instructs us not to commit adultery (Exodus 20:14). Lying behind this short command is the teaching about God's intention for marriage, which was first given in Genesis 2:24. This teaching was reaffirmed by Jesus in Matthew 19:4–6 and Mark 10:1–12, and expounded further by Paul (1 Corinthians 7:1–5; Ephesians 5:21–33). So, although the Ten Commandments were received in the wilderness, they are clearly meant to apply to God's people for all time, before and after the wilderness as well.

Now, homosexuality is in conflict with God's expressed intention regarding human sexuality. By definition, it is not about a man and a woman becoming one flesh, nor can it fulfil the command, bound up with marriage, to "be fruitful and increase" (Genesis 1:28). Homosexual practice, then, undermines God's will. That in itself should lead people to reject its practice. In case we do not reach that conclusion from the basic principles, the Bible makes God's unhappiness about it clear in a variety of places and contexts, namely, Genesis 19:1–29; Leviticus 18:22; 20:13; Romans 1:18–32; 1 Corinthians 6:9–11 and 1 Timothy 1:9–10. The cumulative teaching of Scripture, then, positive and negative, in a whole variety of contexts, suggests that here is a binding principle.

The social laws are different. These laws express the heart of God for the economic, racial, social and environmental well-being of his people. Although specific to Israel, as a God-ruled nation, they reveal God's character and have implications for all people.

Some of them still have direct application to the days in which we live. So the demand for integrity in the law courts, respect for the elderly and disabled, and not ill-treating immigrants, all laws found in Leviticus 19, stand. They are very much in line with the basic approach of the Ten Commandments. Even if the New Testament does not explicitly refer to these issues, one cannot live the sort of life advocated in the New Testament without obeying these laws still.

There are other laws, however, where the particular way in which they were expressed, when originally given, is unworkable today. What is important with such laws, then, is to get behind the particulars to discern what is the principle which lies behind them. That principle then needs to be applied to today.

So, for example, Leviticus 19:9 commands the Israelites not to reap their fields right to the very edges nor to pick up windfalls from their crops. The command is repeated in Leviticus 23:22. When you read it, you see that the point is that it was a way of ensuring that the poor, who had no means of economic support, would be able to survive and live. It would be a meaningless gesture for me to obey this literally today. Many of us do not live in the sort of small-scale communities where this command originally applied and it would not help the poor if I applied it literally. But God's concern for those who are vulnerable and marginalised in society, frequently emphasised in the law in any number of ways, continues. The work of Jesus demonstrates that, and the example of Paul (2 Corinthians 8–9) and the teaching of James (1:27) and John (1 John 3:17–18) reinforces it. So, today, I must find new ways of fulfilling the principle of caring for those who cannot support themselves.

One way I do this is through paying my taxes to support the welfare system, but I must also do it more personally by my voluntary giving to support a number of people and charities. Many of the social laws, then, have to be reinterpreted for today's world, but this does not mean they can be ignored.

Yet other social laws, such as the dietary laws, applied specifically to the Israelites and marked them out as different from the people around them. We know on the basis of the teaching of the New Testament that they no longer apply to us (Mark 7:1–23; Acts 15; Galatians 1 – 2). Even so, there are other ways in which God's people today are required to live differently from those around them.

The rituals or religious laws take us into a different area. The rules for the priests and the sacrifices were, as we have seen, just an early warning of the reality which was to come in Christ. He, the great High Priest who offered himself as the ultimate sacrifice, has fulfilled all that these laws required, and more, so we need no longer keep them in the way the Israelites had to do. They remain, nonetheless, instructive for our understanding of the work of Christ and need to be read in connection with what he has done.

Looking at the law like this shows how the theological context makes a great deal of difference to what we make of the text. We must always ask where any part of Scripture fits, in relation to God's overall work, especially as it reached its climax in Christ.

But what about "me"?

Up to now, we have been writing as if the text is "there" and, if only we ask certain questions about it, we will unlock its meaning and come up with the definitive interpretation of it. The trouble is that this leaves out one significant factor: the person doing the interpreting. We who seek to understand the Bible are not neutral people working in a vacuum. We come to the Bible with our own assumptions, personalities, social positions, cultural backgrounds and sinfulness. It is now realised that this may well bias the way we understand the text.

Let me illustrate. As a white, middle-class, relatively well-off male, living in the Western world, my culture is one of individualism. So for years, whenever I read the word "you" in the New Testament, I assumed it meant "me" – lonesome, poor, isolated, individual me. Sometimes a great weight would descend on my shoulders at the things I was supposed to do and the responsibilities committed to me. Could I really do all this on my own? Then, when I began to read the New Testament in Greek, I discovered how silly I had been. The Greek language distinguishes between "you (singular)" and "you (plural)" in a way the English language has ceased to do. I then discovered that half the things I thought applied to me individually were actually words to the church collectively. They were a shared responsibility. I did not have to carry the weight of it all myself. Someone from a different culture would never have made that mistake in the first place.

Look at how that might affect our reading of Colossians 3:15, which speaks of letting the peace of Christ rule in our hearts. As individuals who live in a touchy-feely society, we are very conscious of our inward feelings and whether we "feel at peace" about an issue. But the peace being spoken of there has nothing to do with inner, psychological tranquillity. It has to do with peaceful relationships in the church. And the heart where peace should rule simply means that our relationships with others should be genuine. People from cultures which are more relational and less individualistic would never misunderstand this verse in the way we do.

When we come to read the Bible, then, we are not free to make of it what we will, as some would argue. The text has a meaning for itself. But we must be aware that we will read it in certain ways and therefore we must do what we can to remove any barriers to hearing what that meaning might be. One way of doing this is to study the Bible with people from different cultures and backgrounds who will not share our particular assumptions. Reading it through their eyes will often open up other ways of seeing what the Bible means.

The Holy Spirit's role

It seems that interpreting the Bible is a daunting task. How can anyone possibly get it right? Shouldn't the task be left to the experts? How can "ordinary" Christians make sense of it? What confidence can we have?

First, we must reassure ourselves that the Bible was written for all Christians. Although God has given us teachers and scholars to help us in understanding what the Bible means, it was written for normal, average Christians to read and understand, not for academics. It is not their book but our book. The tools they use can be beneficial and it would be foolish to set them aside. Knowing the original languages, for example, must be a benefit, since the Bible was not originally written in English. But our understanding of it does not depend on our knowing Greek or Hebrew. God is not an inept communicator who has deliberately made his word difficult or obscure. He longs to reveal himself to us. This is what Deuteronomy 30:11–14 claims when it says, "what I am commanding you today is not too difficult for you or beyond your reach. It is not up in heaven . . . Nor is it beyond the sea . . . No, the word is very near you . . .".

Second, we can turn to the Holy Spirit, whose task it is to help us understand the Bible. His work did not end when he inspired the original documents. He has a continuing role now in illuminating their meaning for humble believers today. Jesus promised his disciples that the Holy Spirit would act in this capacity for them (John 14:26; 16:13). Paul reminds us that it is difficult for one person to know what is inside the mind of another. How much more difficult, then, is it for us as human beings to understand the mind of God. Naturally speaking, it is impossible. The situation is complicated further by our sinfulness. Not only do we struggle to understand the way God thinks because he is God and we are mere mortals (Isaiah 55:8–9), but as fallen creatures we often do not want to understand and the very way we think is corrupted and unreliable (Jeremiah 17:9). This is why God has revealed himself to us by his Holy Spirit and continues to give us the same Spirit so that we might enter into even "the deep things of God". His goal is "that we may understand what God has freely given us" (1 Corinthians 2:6–12; see also 2 Corinthians 3:12–4:6).

The Holy Spirit will never add to Scripture, or contradict it, but he may lead us to see it with fresh clarity and guide us as to how we should interpret it for the days in which we live, rather than the days in which people once lived. The Scripture which was alive with the breath of God when first written remains a living document to teach and instruct us today.

There is, then, a key to interpreting the Bible that scholars may not possess. Their research may well be helpful, as far as it goes. So too are the principles mentioned above. But ordinary believers who turn to the Holy Spirit in prayer for illumination (see Ephesians 1:17–19) and come to the Bible with humility, seeking to obey what it teaches, will get a lot further in their understanding of God's revelation than unbelieving scholars who apply only their minds and not their spirits to the task.

The chief principle of interpretation was spoken by Isaiah long ago: "This what the Lord says . . . 'These are the ones I esteem: those who are humble and contrite in spirit, and tremble at my word'" (66:2). Without that, all the study in the world will mean we still do not "get it".

14

Reading the Bible

More important than reading books about the Bible is reading the Bible itself. It remains a vast and daunting book which many fear to open. Here some guidelines are provided as to how to get started in reading it and how to get the best out of it. The ideas are not difficult and easily lie within the reach of those who are never going to be ministers or preachers. They are offered in the belief that the Bible is a book for everyone, not just for professional scholars or religious leaders. God has given it as a vital resource for Christian growth and our failure to read it will leave us enfeebled in our Christian lives. We often excuse our failure to read the Bible because of our busyness or some other reason, but, if we have an appetite for God, we will have an appetite for his book.

Reading the Bible

All that we have written will be worthless unless it encourages you to start reading the Bible, and reading it for yourself. It is good to hear it read in church and to discuss it in groups. But neither of these are substitutes for a personal engagement with the Bible and its message.

Is it reasonable to expect people to read the Bible today?

Lives are so busy and expectations and demands have risen so much that many believers, particularly of a younger age, find reading the Bible has been squeezed out. They would like to have time to do so, but they do not. The distribution of Bible reading notes is falling, while survey after survey shows that Christians are not reading the Bible as once they did. Belonging to a lively church may, unwittingly, contribute to this. We are so busy doing things, organising things, running things, that we have no time to spend alone with God.

But if the Bible really is a communication from God to the people he loves, as well as a communication to the wider world, Christians, of all people, should be eager to read it. It may seem trite, but it is true nonetheless, that none of us who received a letter from someone we were in love with would fail to read it. We would seize on it, read it as soon as we could and come back to it often. I am sure that more than one love letter has been surreptitiously read in a lecture I have been giving. How then can we be so casual about the Bible?

The truth is that we fill our lives with the things we regard as important. For all the busyness, we have a good deal of space left to fill with leisure interests. And we determine what we fill it with. So the choice is ours. The amount we spend on pursuing leisure activities is witness to the spare time and cash we have. We think nothing of shelling out money on CDs, DVDs, computer games, cinema-going, concert-attending, magazines and so on. Looking at how we spend our time and our money can tell us a lot about what our real values and priorities are in life.

If we want to know God, then reading his book will be of great importance to us, although it will not be the only thing we do, since other things will help. Reading the Bible will play a significant role in our lives, since it is one of the chief means God has given us to enable us to reach spiritual maturity.

But what if we are not readers? The Bible is a dense and daunting book. Isn't reading, of any sort, just something that a select group of people do in our society? This is a serious question for some. But the lack of a desire to read, or an inability to read, is not an insuperable obstacle to getting into the Bible. There are several versions of the whole Bible on cassette and CD, so a person can still listen to it, even if not read it. The Internet contains any number of accessible, bite-sized chunks of the Bible for those who do not want to read pages. Various publishers have produced glossy magazine-type versions, at least of books of the Bible. Those who never read a book will often pick up a magazine. Perhaps it should be said, too, that being a non-reader is a serious disadvantage in our society and it may be that churches should set up literacy clubs to help people gain not only a beneficial spiritual skill, but a useful social skill as well.

Whilst recognising the seriousness of the question for some, for others it is more an excuse than a real problem. The evidence from the wider book trade suggests that reading is still a fairly widespread activity and is not about to bite the dust as quickly as some are prophesying. Also, if older versions of the Bible are off-putting in their style and vocabulary, then there are plenty of reader-friendly versions, attractively presented, available in modern English to get people going.

The absence of Bible reading is often because we fail to see how crucial it is, or because of various excuses, rather than anything else. If we have an appetite for God we will have, or will cultivate, an appetite for the Bible. Time can be found, or made, even if only while we are travelling on the bus or the tube to work, if we want to.

How then should we set about reading it?

Read it regularly

First, we should read the Bible regularly. It is true of anything we want to familiarise ourselves with, that it is better to work at it a little and often, rather than make a huge effort at one time and then neglect it for months. Whether it be learning a musical instrument, sports, acquiring a language, or developing painting skills, it is best to engage in regular practice and gradually build our knowledge and skills. In doing so, we may feel some days that we are making no progress. But after a time we will look back and see how far we have come.

What is true elsewhere is true of discovering the Bible. It may be good occasionally to sit down and have a good long read and soak up a whole book or even several books. But most of us would not take much in that way. Reading it a little and often means we will soon familiarise ourselves with it and be much more conscious of its teaching than we might otherwise be. Incidentally, as a guide, we need to read four chapters a day to get through the whole Bible in a year. So it would take us four years to read all of it, reading a chapter at a time.

The best practice might be to set aside a time each day to

read it. There is a lot to be said for following the example of the Christians at Berea who "received the message with great eagerness and examined the Scriptures every day . . ." (Acts 17:11). If you do, it needs to be a time when you can be alert and are likely to be undisturbed. Early morning suits some people because they wake early, the rest of the house is still quiet and the phone is not likely to ring. But others would just sleep through the motions of reading their Bibles if they were to try it before mid-morning and before ingesting several cups of coffee! (We might, of course, have to examine what time we go to bed if we want to carve out time for Bible reading.) When might be a good time for you? Remember that, over the years, this time may need to change because work will make different demands on you, or the kids will be at different stages and impose their timetable on you. Be wise, not inflexible.

To read it every day, however ideal, may be impractical for some. So set yourself a realistic target, not one you are bound to miss with the result that you condemn yourself as a failure before you begin. Could you do it three times a week? Could you fit it in more easily, or less easily, at the weekends? There may be good examples to follow but there are no rigid rules to obey.

Read it systematically

Second, read it systematically. Don't just pick it up and let the Bible fall open wherever and start there. The living God, of course, is quite capable of speaking to you through the Bible if you do that. But that doesn't make it right. The Bible is not a random collection of isolated sayings, as I hope you have learned by now. The way it is put together is no accident and the way particular books are written is according to a plan. They will make more sense, therefore, if you read the Bible with some sense of working to the plan.

This does not mean you must start at Genesis and work doggedly through until you get to Revelation. But it should

mean, at the least, that you read through one book at a time
from beginning to end. If we do not do this, we will end up
with a muddled picture. We will have bits of the Bible jigsaw
all over the place and not have any idea how they fit together.
Our faith is also likely to be shambolic and confused as a
result.

If you have the time, it might well be a good idea to be reading a chapter of the Old Testament alongside a chapter of the
New, so that both are kept in view. Several people I know adopt
the practice I myself follow, which is to read a Psalm a day
alongside whatever book of the Bible I am studying at the time.
The Psalms often help me to read the Bible prayerfully and
give voice to my praise and intercession in words which are
better than any I could manage. Once I have read the Psalms, I
read and meditate on a chapter of Proverbs. This means that I
can read Psalms and Proverbs twice in the course of a year and
still have three days to spare!

Of course, there are other systematic ways of reading the
Bible which do not involve reading whole books methodically.
You could take a particular character and trace all that the Bible
has to say about him or her. You could look at the way various
leaders were "called" to their ministries – from Abraham to
Paul. You could look at the names and titles of God, or of
Jesus, or at all the passages to do with a particular theme, such
as the Holy Spirit. Each of these systems has its own strengths
and weaknesses, and perhaps should only be undertaken by
way of a change to the good, routine discipline of reading the
Bible as it was written. Although the basic diet ought perhaps
to be systematic reading of the Bible's books, there is a need to
vary the pattern to keep one's reading of the Bible fresh and
alive as time goes on.

Read it from the centre outwards

If you are new to the Bible, I recommend you start at its centre
and work outwards from there. Natural fascination may tempt

us to crack the complexities of Revelation, argue with the opening chapters of Genesis or indulge in the symbolism of Ezekiel or Hebrews (well, perhaps not the last two!), but it is better to start with what is both crucial and plain, and build from there.

The pivot of the Bible's message, as we have said, is Jesus. Start, then, by reading about him. The simplest and shortest introduction to him is found in Mark but there may be good reason for starting with another of the gospels. Chapter 7 gave you a guide to the gospels and an introduction to what is special about each one.

Having read a gospel, why not turn to one of the early letters of Paul? There you will see how he advised young Christians at the start of their life as disciples of Jesus. 1 Thessalonians or Philippians would be a good next step.

After that, fill in your knowledge of Jesus by reading another of the gospels or turning to Acts to see how the apostles preached about him. Then turn to another of the New Testament letters, perhaps Colossians, which can flesh out your understanding of him.

By now, you may well want to turn to Genesis and lay some foundations about the way God made the world and how he relates to it. Move back and forth from the simple to the complex, from the plain to the unclear, from the centre to the circumference, from the New to the Old, from what is core to what is peripheral. Over time, this will mean you have built on good foundations.

Read it questioningly

It is all too easy to read the Bible but not engage with it or remember what has been said. There is no virtue in going through a ritual, as if the act of merely reading the Bible will work its magic on us and change us. Hebrews 4:2 talks of how the Israelites received the message but how it had no value to them because they did not combine it with faith. If our reading of the Bible is to be profitable, we need to have both faith and alert minds. To avoid going through an empty ritual, it is useful to ask questions of what we are reading. These are not sceptical questions but questions designed to unlock the teaching of the passage we are reading, such as those listed below. Not all will apply to every passage, but there will always be at least one question from this list that proves useful for what we are reading.

Is there a truth about God to learn here?
Is there a revelation of Jesus to inspire here?
Is there an insight into the Holy Spirit to gain here?
Is there a spiritual principle to grasp here?
Is there a doctrine to believe here?
Is there a command to obey here?
Is there a promise to trust here?
Is there an example to follow here?
Is there a sin to avoid here?
Is there a lesson to learn here?

If all else fails, it is good to make oneself consciously stop and ask this question at the end of one's time of reading: What is the one thing this passage has said to me, the one lesson I have been taught here? It is better still if one has the chance to write it down; then it is not lost in the bustle of the day that follows.

Read it prayerfully

Since the Bible is not like any other book but is a communication from God, we need to approach it with reverence and openness to him. The best context in which to read it is the context of prayer. It helps too if we turn what we have read into prayer. This is often referred to as meditation. To meditate on Scripture is to ruminate on it, chewing it over and over in the presence of God, just as a cow chews over the grass. I know of no better definition of this than the one given by J. I. Packer in his book *Knowing God* (Hodder & Stoughton, 1973, pp. 18–19). He writes:

How can we turn our knowledge *about* God into knowledge *of* God? The rule for doing this is demanding but simple. It is that we turn each truth that we learn *about* God into a matter of meditation *before* God, leading to prayer and praise to God . . .

Meditation is the activity of calling to mind, and thinking over, and dwelling on, and applying to oneself, the various things one knows about the works and ways and purposes and promises of God. It is the activity of holy thought, consciously performed in the presence of God, under the eye of God, by the help of God, as a means of communion with God.

Read it with help

Although there is nothing wrong with reading it unaided – just you and the Bible – why not make use of some of the various aids which are available? Why struggle on your own when there are those around to lend you support? There has never been a time when there have been more Bible reading aids available than there are now. So it seems foolish, or arrogant, to ignore them.

At the simplest level, there are a number of publishers who produce daily notes. These select a passage to be read, usually on a systematic basis, then comment on it. They will often include a prompt to prayer and action as well. Scripture Union, Crusade for World Revival and the Bible Reading Fellowship are among the best-known distributors of Bible reading notes in the UK. Their addresses are in the Appendix but any Christian bookshop will be able to point you in the right direction.

The next level would involve keeping an introductory book about the Bible near to hand and referring to it as you read. There is the lavishly illustrated *Lion Handbook to the Bible* (1999), Dorling Kindersley's *The Complete Bible Handbook* (1998) and Nick Page's recent *The Bible Book* (HarperCollins, 2002). These would not be detailed commentaries but more like a *Readers' Digest* survey which helps you sort one thing out from another.

A step up from that might be a one-volume Bible commentary.

These more dense volumes will give more serious and detailed comments on the text and can prove invaluable reference books. Since all 66 books of the Bible are dealt with between the covers of one book, they are inevitably succinct in their comments. Among them are the *New Bible Commentary* (IVP, 1994) and the *Oxford Bible Commentary* (OUP, 2001).

In addition, there is a series of smaller books which cover the separate books of the Bible and are usually more readable than the one-volume works just mentioned. Some of them, like the *Crossway Bible Guides* (Crossway), not only provide a popular commentary but also include questions which are designed to be suitable for use by groups as well as individuals. In this category has been the long-established *Daily Study Bible* (St Andrew Press) in which the New Testament volumes were written by William Barclay and the Old Testament volumes by a variety of authors. Most recently, and set to replace William Barclay, is a series of volumes by Tom Wright with the title *Matthew* [that is, a particular biblical book] *for Everyone* (SPCK). Eight volumes have appeared at the time of writing, but there is an ambitious project to publish several a year and cover the whole New Testament before long. Tom Wright is a leading international Biblical scholar with a rare gift for writing at a very popular level.

Beyond these are more serious expositions aimed at church leaders or pastors, such as *The Bible Speaks Today* series, published by IVP. These are based on good scholarship but are not written technically. They are spiritually rich and contain good applications. After that, one starts to get into the more serious technical Bible commentaries. These certainly have their place but will often take a person well beyond the needs of the average Christian.

A growing number of resources are also making their appearance on the Internet but, as yet, none are well established and it is sometimes difficult to sort the chaff from the wheat.

Conclusion

At the end of the day, there is no short cut. The Christian who wants to be mature in faith must spend time in the Bible: reading it, studying it, meditating on it and obeying it. The attitude of the Psalmist in Psalm 119 when he rhapsodises on God's law (by which he meant the early books of the Old Testament) is one the church needs to recapture in respect of the whole Bible. To the Psalmist, it was not a chore to read or study the law. It was a pleasure, for it revealed the wonder of God's grace and the wisdom of his ways. God's word saves us, he says, from empty living and directs us along life-enhancing paths. It is medicine to the soul, delicious to the taste, strength for the weary, wisdom for the foolish, freedom for the oppressed, a guide to the perplexed, a defence against temptation, a refuge for the besieged, and a rock of stability in a precarious world. The Psalmist describes the law by a cascade of celebratory words. The law is a delight and contains wonderful things. It is good and an object of desire. It is the source of hope and the fount of wisdom. The words of the law are "more precious than thousands of pieces of silver". They are trustworthy and perfect. "Oh, how I love your law!," he declares.

In one section (verses 33–40), the Psalmist summarises how we should approach the Bible. Our reading of it should be marked by:

- appetite: "How I long for your precepts!"
- humility: "Teach me . . ."
- understanding: "give me understanding . . ."
- obedience: "I will . . . obey it with all my heart."
- perseverance: ". . . to the end."

A renewed confidence in Scripture would bring a new joy to living for Christ and a new vitality to a dying and declining church. It is time for the church to return to the Bible.

Bibliography

Bible Overviews

P. Alexander and D. Alexander (eds.), *The New Lion Handbook to the Bible* (Oxford: Lion, 1999)

J. Balchin et al (eds.), *An Illustrated Survey of the Bible* (Milton Keynes: Scripture Union, 2002)

J. Bowker (ed.), *The Complete Bible Handbook: An Illustrated Companion* (London: Dorling Kindersley, 1998)

D. Jackman, *I Believe in the Bible* (London: Hodder & Stoughton, 2000)

A. Motyer, *The Story of the Old Testament* (Wilmington: Candle, 2001)

N. Page, *The Bible Book* (London: HarperCollins, 2002)

J. Stott, *The Story of the New Testament* (Wilmington: Candle, 2001)

Bible Expositions and Commentaries

J. Barton (ed.), *The Oxford Bible Commentary* (Oxford: OUP, 2001)

D. A. Carson et al (eds.), *New Bible Commentary* (Leicester: IVP, 1994)

Several series are useful and have volumes on most books of the Bible:

Crossway Bible Guides (Crossway) – for personal and group study
The Bible Speaks Today (IVP) – expositions by scholarly preachers
Tyndale Bible Commentaries (IVP)   basic but more technical commentaries
Mentor Bible Commentaries (Christian Focus Publications)

Bible Helps

T. Dowley, *Bible Atlas* (Wilmington: Candle, 2002)
M. Manser, *The NIV Comprehensive Concordance* (London: Hodder & Stoughton, 2001)
I. H. Marshall et al (eds.), *New Bible Dictionary* (Leicester: IVP, 1996)

The following is an electronic resource (CD-Rom):

The Essential IVP Reference Collection, (Leicester: IVP, 2001)

Interpreting the Bible

G. Fee and D. Stuart, *How to Read the Bible for All Its Worth* (Milton Keynes: Scripture Union, 1994)
G. Fee and D. Stuart, *How to Read the Bible Book by Book* (Grand Rapids: Zondervan, 2002)
W. Klein, C. Blomberg and R. Hubbard, *Introduction to Biblical Interpretation* (Carlisle: STL, 1993)

Time Charts

Old Testament Time Line

Creation		Genesis 1–11
Patriarchs	2000–1725 BC	Genesis 12–50
Egypt	1725–1280	Exodus
Wilderness	1280–1240	Leviticus, Numbers, Deuteronomy
Conquest	1240–1050	Joshua, Ruth, 1 Samuel 1–8
United monarchy	1050–930	1 Samuel–2Chronicles, Psalms, Proverbs, Song of Songs, Ecclesiastes
Divided monarchy	930–587	1 and 2 Kings, 2 Chronicles, Prophets
Exile	587–538	Prophets
Restoration	538–	Ezra, Nehemiah, Esther, Haggai, Zechariah

(Dates are approximate.)

United Monarchy

Saul	1030–1000 BC
David	1010–970 BC
Solomon	970–30 BC

(Dates are approximate.)

Divided Monarchy 1

Judah	Israel
930–587 bc	930–722 bc
Rehoboam 930–913	Jeroboam 931–910
Abijah 913–911	
Asa 911–870	
Jehoshaphat 873–848	Nadab 910–909
	Baasha 900–877
	Elah 886–885
	Zimri 885
	Omri 885–874
	Ahab 874–853
	Elijah
	Ahaziah 853–852
Jehoram 853–841	Joram 852–841
	Elisha
Ahaziah 841	
Athaliah 841–835	Jehu 841–814
Joash 835–796	
	Jehoahaz 814–798
Amaziah 796–767	Jehoash 798–782
Uzziah 767–739	Jeroboam II 793–753
	Amos, Hosea
	Zechariah 753–752
	Rise of Assyria
	Shallum 752
Jotham 750–732	Menahem 752–742
	Pekahiah 742–740
Ahaz 735–716	Pekah 740–732
Isaiah, Micah, Joel	
	Hoshea 732–723
	Fall of Samaria 722/1

Divided Monarchy 2

Judah	Prophets	World
Hezekiah 716–687		
Manasseh 687–642		
Amon 643–641		
Josiah 641–609	*Jeremiah* ▼	
		Rise of Babylon
	Zephaniah	
		Nineveh falls 612
	Nahum	
Jehoahaz 609	*Habbakuk*	
Jehoiakim 609–598		
Jehoiachin 598–7		
Zedekiah 597–586	*Ezekiel* ▼	
Fall of Jerusalem and exile 587		

(Dates are approximate.)

The Prophets in
Historical Order

	Date (approximate)	Name
Non-writing prophets	1000 BC	Samuel
	900	Elijah
		Elisha
		Micaiah
Prophets of the monarchy	800	Joel
		Amos
		Jonah
		Hosea
		Isaiah
	700	Micah
		Zephaniah
		Nahum
	600	Jeremiah
		Habakkuk
Prophets of the exile and after	500	Daniel
		Ezekiel
		Obadiah
		Haggai
		Zechariah
		Malachi

Exile and
Restoration

Judah	Prophets	World
Deportations		
597 BC		
587 (Jerusalem falls)		
582		
		Rise of Persia
		Babylon falls 539
		Cyrus edict 538
Temple is rebuilt	*Haggai and*	
525–520	*Zechariah*	
Ezra 458?		
Nehemiah		
	Malachi 440	
		Rise of Greeks
		Rise of Romans

(Dates are approximate.)

New Testament: Time Chart

Date (approximate)	Event
5 BC	Birth of Christ
30 AD	Crucifixion
35	Conversion of Paul
46–48	First missionary trip
49/50	Council of Jerusalem
50–52	Second missionary trip
51/52	Earliest NT letters
53–57	Third missionary trip
57	Romans written
59–62	Paul in prison
62	James executed
67/68	Death of Paul
70	Fall of Jerusalem
90–95	John exiled
95	Revelation written

Appendix

Useful addresses for
Bible Reading Notes

Bible Reading Fellowship
Elsfield Hall,
First Floor,
15 Elsfield Way
Oxford
OX2 8FG
www.brf.org.uk

Crusade for World Revival
Waverley Abbey House
Waverley Lane
Farnham
GU9 8EP
www.cwr.org.uk

Scripture Union
207, Queensway,
Bletchley,
Milton Keynes
MK2 2EB
www.scriptureunion.org.uk